T0194911

THE

GREAT
TRANSITION
The Personalization
of Finance is Here

————— THE —————

GREAT
TRANSITION

The Personalization
of Finance is Here

Emmanuel Daniel

With forewords by
Barney Frank, Dodd-Frank Act
Richard L. Sandor, founder, AFX

World Scientific

NEW JERSEY · LONDON · SINGAPORE · BEIJING · SHANGHAI · HONG KONG · TAIPEI · CHENNAI · TOKYO

Published by

World Scientific Publishing Co. Pte. Ltd.

5 Toh Tuck Link, Singapore 596224

USA office: 27 Warren Street, Suite 401-402, Hackensack, NJ 07601

UK office: 57 Shelton Street, Covent Garden, London WC2H 9HE

National Library Board, Singapore Cataloguing in Publication Data

Name(s): Daniel, Emmanuel. | Frank, Barney, 1940–   author of foreword. |
  Sandor, Richard L., author of foreword.

Title: The great transition : the personalization of finance is here / Emmanuel Daniel ;
  with forewords by Barney Frank, Richard L. Sandor.

Description: Singapore : World Scientific Publishing Co. Pte. Ltd., 2023.

Identifier(s): ISBN 978-981-12-6530-3 (hardcover) | ISBN 978-981-12-6562-4 (paperback) |
  ISBN 978-981-12-6531-0 (ebook for institutions) |
  ISBN 978-981-12-6532-7 (ebook for individuals)

Subject(s): LCSH: Finance. | Economics.

Classification: DDC 332--dc23

British Library Cataloguing-in-Publication Data

A catalogue record for this book is available from the British Library.

For any available supplementary material, please visit
https://www.worldscientific.com/worldscibooks/10.1142/13113#t=suppl

Desk Editor: Geysilla Jean

Printed in Singapore

Dedicated to my father

Ponniah Daniel

probably the meekest man who walked the face of the earth

Contents

Foreword by Barney Frank ix

Foreword by Richard Sandor xiii

Preface xvii

CHAPTER 1
From platforms to personalization **1**
The industrialization of finance 3
Even mobile will end 7
Mapping the transitions 12

CHAPTER 2
The personalization of finance **19**
In search of the 'CFC' of finance 20
Whoever controls identity, controls finance 21
If energy is the currency of the universe 26
The game changers 31

CHAPTER 3
The financialization of everything **37**
The financialized corporation 39
Almost anything can be financialized 43
Say goodbye to the real economy 47
When perception becomes reality 48

CHAPTER 4
Rise of the rebels **53**
The mass amateurization of finance 55
The hyper-personalization of APIs 61
Crypto's WiFi moment 65

CHAPTER 5
The agents of change **69**
People shape people 71
The power of the 'dysfunctional' state 75
The 'fifth estate' 80
The geek army 87
The venture capitalists 91

CHAPTER 6

The anatomy of innovation **99**

The post-Bretton Woods creations 100

The triumph of capital over labor 105

The ravages of zero marginal cost 108

Blockchains, killed in the back office 112

The symmetry of deception 116

CHAPTER 7

The institution crumbles **119**

The balance sheet never lies 121

The ring-fencing riddle 125

The liquidity sitting outside 128

But we want to be banks too 133

CHAPTER 8

Reimagining the product **137**

Mapping the birth of new products 138

Dump the deposit account 143

Credit in a capsule 148

Rewriting the P2P playbook 152

CHAPTER 9

The great transitions **159**

From tribes to networks 162

LIBOR, again and again 169

The next financial crisis… 174

Glossary for the General Reader **183**

Notes **191**

Acknowledgments **203**

Index **205**

Foreword by Barney Frank

This is a tough book in the very best sense of that word. Readers should be prepared to pay serious attention to complex issues of fundamental social and economic importance.

Unlike many whose familiarity with a particular status quo induces a sense of comfort in their thinking about the subject, Emmanuel Daniel builds on his lifelong study of the financial system not to just confront the hardest questions that have been raised about it since the crisis of 2008, but to formulate newer and more profound ones.

He has for decades been a trusted source of expertise about banking in its most expansive definition. I met him, in fact, through his global response to requests for information about American regulatory policy after that upheaval. Shortly after my retirement from Congress, he included me as a speaker in conferences of regulators and banking officials in Asia, Africa, and the Middle East.

But even as he organized these expositions about the past and the present, I observed that he always stressed to his audiences the importance of thinking ahead about how the financing of economic activity would – and even more importantly, should – evolve. This book is an elaboration of that challenge.

I use the word "challenge" deliberately. This is a tough book for those who are complacent about the stability we have seen in the banking system over the past decade. Having fixed many of the problems that caused the crash of 2008, what we have put in place should be a foundation for a focus on preventing future shocks, rather than an occasion for self-reassurance.

One of the most profound lessons of 2008 is that failure to adapt the economic, legal, and regulatory frameworks that govern the financial system to fundamental shifts as they are occurring – and well before they have taken root – is the only prudent strategy.

He is appropriately tough on those seeking a shortcut to understanding the role that digital currency should play. Too much current public discussion is on the near-term speculative aspects of monetary digitization and the assets that are created from them. He points out that digital currency will shape and be shaped by the changes coming to the financial system, and that will have grave consequences at a broader level in society.

Having chaired the Committee of the US House of Representatives that had a leading role in dealing with the crisis of 2008, I commend Emmanuel's analysis to my successors as they discharge their responsibility to minimize future turmoil and cope with it when it inevitably comes.

I have one potential dissent. I agree with Emmanuel about the forces that will enhance the financial system by reducing the need for intermediation. I know he does not predict the withering away of conventional banking, but I think that the willingness – and ability – of significant numbers of people to dispense with the current level of services banks now provide may be overestimated.

Harnessing the potential of digitization to improve the ease of transactions between and among large economic actors has already begun to show its worth. But for the foreseeable future, the majority of individual and small organizations that rely on financial institutions to help manage their dealing with others will continue to need that help.

Emmanuel has provided some ideas of how the traditional bank might evolve over time, but the challenge for banks is to serve both sets of needs. (In the interest of transparency, I note that Signature Bank of New York, of which I am a director, is a pioneering example of how to do this.)

Emmanuel has performed an important service in describing the imperatives that are reshaping the financial architecture that undergirds our economy. As policymakers undertake the difficult job of ensuring that the rules keep pace with this evolution – ending the pattern of severe regulatory lags that has been so demanding – this book has a very important role.

Barney Frank

US House of Representatives 1981-2013
Chairman, House Financial Services Committee 2007-2011
Co-author, The Dodd-Frank Wall Street Reform and Consumer Protection Act 2010

Foreword by Richard Sandor

The Great Transition: The Personalization of Finance is Here is an engaging and thoughtful book on how the trend in the "personalization" in an increasingly interconnected and online world will potentially shape the infrastructure of finance in years to come, creating efficiencies and empowering individual choices. Simply put, it is not only a vision of the future but an encyclopedia of what is currently happening in the digital world. Like all encyclopedias, it inspires the reader to learn more. In doing so we also are motivated to question some of the author's prognostications. That is a sign of the quality of this book.

Emmanuel Daniel has been very perceptive in his analysis that market disruptions can be catalysts for positive change. The electronic and virtual worlds, coupled with the information economy, may generate new goods and services which none of us can yet imagine. All these unborn products may ultimately become online markets. His admonition that the genius will "not be in the sophistication but in extreme simplicity" is typical of the wisdom that he periodically shares with the readers.

With the evolution from Web 1.0 to Web 3.0 (the move to a "permissionless" and decentralized web run on the blockchain), as greater communication between machines (the "Internet of Things") becomes more prevalent, they could be used for a variety of applications and new products. The pace of innovation in the space continues at a staggering rate. What insights do we have from other markets which at one time were permissionless environments? The personalization of finance will certainly include new goods and services based on externalities and new digital goods and services. Environmental goods and services are one obvious example. Art is another. Even now, the need for a standard designated clearing organization (DCO) is being debated.

When Emmanuel gives examples of existing goods and services, he avoids being dense. His description of community currencies is clearly written, as is the assertion that the DeFi model is "going down the path where anyone can share a ledger and simultaneously create, add, contribute, issue, or trade in financial products." He has great clarity, and his thoughts are easily accessible to the reader. I also particularly enjoyed his incorporation of academic research, such as David Ronfeldt in the section, "From Tribes to Networks". Some might argue that this is distracting but this reader liked it.

I felt a connection to this book because as a young academic at Berkeley in the 1960s, I designed an all-electronic, for-profit commodities exchange. The technology and the concept were too early. It took another three decades for both electronic trading and demutualization to become ubiquitous in financial markets. The paradigm has now changed due to new technologies that can speed up this process and take us into new and exciting realms. Although he uses the example of Lloyd's exchange (while one could argue that the trading of risk was already embedded in stock index futures in Amsterdam in 1605), and there is some reference that the Stockholm Stock Exchange was the first exchange to be demutualized with no mention of for-profit futures exchanges, this should not distract from the point he is making.

I fully enjoyed the history and the way forward he provides as both an academic, a practitioner and inventor of new markets, and from the perspective of an author of a recent book on electronic trading and the blockchain. His last section, "The Next Financial Crisis", leads us to wonder about the regulatory regimes that will be required in the age of the personalization of finance.

Emmanuel's book can help guide readers through the history, development, and exciting prospects in this new electronic world where the individual is front and center. From its use of the ice trade near the beginning as a teaching tool to the policy challenges of ring-fencing banks near the end of the book, it helps inform and guide us to think about problems in a new way. It is a highly readable and encyclopedic narrative on the current and future digital world where these new disruptive technologies, processes, and inventions can help 'leapfrog' entire societies and individuals in the years to come.

Richard L. Sandor, Ph.D, Dr. sc.h.c.
Founder and CEO, American Financial Exchange and Chicago Climate Exchange
Aaron Director Lecturer in Law and Economics, University of Chicago Law School

Preface

"No, no! The adventures first, explanations take such a dreadful time."
Lewis Carroll, *Alice's Adventures in Wonderland*
& Through the Looking-Glass

As the story goes, the ice trade was pioneered by one notable individual, Frederick Tudor, who managed to run a rather profitable business through most of the second half of the 1800s. The business involved transporting ice over thousands of miles, from the frozen lakes of Massachusetts to the cocktail circuits in New York and way down south to tropical Havana, in the days before refrigeration.

Tudor came to define this nebulous industry, despite ridicule and the absence of any technology to store and transport something as perishable as ice. He was a 'Bostonian Brahmin', an acerbic reference to aristocratic Anglo-Saxon high society with the wealth to pursue whatever causes they so wished. In his case, this happened to be transporting ice from frozen lakes into cocktail glasses.

When the trade peaked in the US in the 1890s, around four million tons of 'harvested ice' were routinely stored in the Hudson River and Maine areas alone, with more than 135 major ice warehouses employing 20,000 people. A similar industry flourished in Europe. At around the same time, the raw ice trade peaked at about one million tons in Norway alone.[1]

As the transportation of harvested ice became increasingly commercialized, incentives for investment in the technology to manufacture ice gained pace. Ice was becoming an increasing necessity, used not just

---

[1] R. O. Cummings, *The American Ice Harvests: A Historical Study in Technology, 1800–1918* (Berkeley: California University Press, 1949).

for drinking but for refrigerating food, adding value and urgency to the innovations that were needed to support it.

But the transition came slowly. 'Plant ice', or artificially manufactured ice, required an industrial process that still needed the ice to be stored in warehouses and transported to homes. This trend reached a halfway point by 1914, when there was about 26 million tons of plant ice compared to 24 million tons of harvested ice in the US. The industry was very clearly changing, but not enough for the incumbents to be phased out just yet.

At the top of the ice transportation industry were the 'ice merchants', with huge warehouses for storing and distributing ice to the local community and the end consumer, the vestiges of which we see to this day. They captured much of the profitability of the industry and were visually and conceptually central to the trade.

This story is so easily transposable to the story of the future of finance. The ice merchants are the financial institutions of our day, sawing, parcelling, and distributing capital around the world at great cost and wastage. Their majestic buildings hover over the industry just like the warehouses of the ice merchants of old, unaware of the revolution under way.

The great transition today is that from 'platforms' to 'personalization'. It is a huge and fundamental transition that involves all of society, all of economics, and finance is just the catalyst. One day, when the huge exchanges and foreign exchange processors in New York, London, and Hong Kong are replaced by tokens in everybody's hands, and managed from a holiday resort in Cancun, Côte d'Azur, or Bali, we will be astonished at how inefficient our monetary transactions used to be.

At the moment, bankers use phrases such as 'inclusive finance' to reach the 'unbanked'; to try and harness the platform industry to onboard millions of borrowers at the lowest possible cost and turn them into subscription-based addicts. They add, not reduce, costs to users. They make finance an end in itself and prolong the longevity of the current regime. There is nothing transformational about them.

In the platform era, finance was a beneficiary of the technologies that defined it. In the personalization age, it will be embedded in everyday life. Finance will no longer be an activity for its own sake. As it makes this transition, it is bizarre that societies that are politically more dysfunctional are embracing the benefits of personalization more naturally than those that are more organized.

The personalization of finance is not an abstract phenomenon unique to the industry. Just like how the refrigerator grew in popularity in parallel with conveniences like the automobile, air travel, and suburban owner-occupied homes in its day, all industries are going through their own versions of personalization today.

The financial centers will not necessarily go away. They will evolve to do different things, just like the entire ice trade gave way to a whole new industry of consumer durables such as refrigerators, freezers, better food and transportation, and logistics.

All this is part of the march of civilization itself towards greater levels of personal choice and freedom. Although I am writing this book from the perspective of a practitioner in finance today, the shift in favor of personalization has profound repercussions for how societies and governments are organized, the philosophies that we choose to define us, and the ways in which we exchange value with each other.

I would go even further to suggest that the 'inevitability' of humanity that political commentator Francis Fukuyama had in mind might not be liberalism, but personalization. "All human history will end in the victory of liberalism," he wrote, couching the inevitability of humanity in political terms.[2]

Well, that was not what happened. While we now know that liberalism — as well as its antithesis, conservatism — are equally flawed, they are also being transformed in an age of increased personalization. New levels of personalization are also pushing the boundaries of the influence that the individual wields over the rest of society.

---

[2] See F. Fukuyama, *The End of History and The Last Man*. (New York: Free Press, 2006).

The Covid-19 pandemic of 2020 and the Russian invasion of Ukraine threw up many more issues of seismic consequence. In this regard, a great drama in humanity is under way, and it starts with the ways in which we transact with each other at all levels.

At the onset of the platform era in the early 2000s, the finance industry was preoccupied with the introduction of Basel III, the fallout from the 2008 US banking crisis, and so on. As I write this, the industry is only just wrapping its head around digital banking, cloud computing, and cryptocurrencies.

Much of the conversation on the transformational changes taking place today is focused on containing their effects and guarding the existing order of the world as we know it. The personalization era will evolve much more swiftly and powerfully. The advent of quantum computing will neither respect institutions nor give regulators time to curate the process as deliberately as they have been able to thus far.

The millions of blockchain, crypto, and non-fungible token (NFT) programmers, traders, and users today are defined not by the technology they transact with, but by the profound sense that every individual is potentially an 'institution' in their own right.

It is the thesis of this book that finance will become the 'operating system' of the personalization of society as a whole. Individuals building functionalities and interoperability on tokens in their bedrooms today are also creating new values and social norms that will define society in the future.

Long after cryptocurrencies become passé, the march of humanity towards greater empowerment of the individual over society will continue unabated, and even newer technologies will facilitate that process. All this will come at a great price to society.

This book focuses on the great transition, an enigma whose anticipated arrival will confound us. Many of the tensions in societies and the ways in which we are governed today have to do with curating the process of getting there. A society that embraces personalization will face so many ramifications that we cannot begin to understand today.

Our conversations today should focus on recalibrating all our existing assumptions to help us embrace this future as it unfolds. Some of the assumptions I have outlined in this book are counter-intuitive, such as the financialization of entire economies and the role of dysfunctional rather than controlled states. Whatever it is, the march towards personalization is inevitable, and finance will be at the center of everything we do in a way it has never been before.

Emmanuel Daniel
Seattle, Washington, May 2022

Readers are invited to access Powerpoint slide decks, video resources related to this book, or to interact with the author on www.emmanueldaniel.com

CHAPTER 1

From platforms to personalization

"Dr. Dillamond, if something bad is happening to the animals, someone has got to tell the wizard, that's why we have a wizard."
Elphaba, in the Broadway musical *Wicked*

Personalization is not a financial concept. It is not even a business one. Nor is it about technology, although that's what makes personalization possible. The personalization of technology, businesses, the economy, finance, and society itself are all expressions of the continued march of civilization towards a realization of the full potential of the individual.

Humanity may have been very communal in the early years of civilization in order to survive. But over time, for better or worse, countries, businesses, and institutions have been trending towards greater empowerment of the individual, with tools and ways of life never imagined before.

Having said that, personalization is not to be mistaken for mass individualism. Since World War Two, corporations have perfected the art of achieving industrial levels of individualism by promoting greed, consumption, and self-gratification. This is typified by being able to push a whole range of consumer products from bottled milk of a hundred different flavors to credit cards. The individual imagines that he or she is being given choices, based on a sense that they are unique in their tastes and preferences, when they are really just a digit in a corporation's industrial levels of production.

Digital platforms and the finance industry, in the way they are commercialized today, are merely the internet era's manifestation of mass individualism. It was worst during the platform era, because we could only participate by handing over our identities in a helpless manner to be monetized by all kinds of digital applications.

As this book will repeatedly emphasize, the platform economy that promotes mass individualism still has a long way to run. The technologies that sit on Web 3.0 increasingly mimic personalization, but the rules will change as the transition unfolds.

More eminent writers have already described how this new industrial revolution will continue to evolve well into the future. Klaus Schwab's seminal book, *The Fourth Industrial Revolution*, and Erik Brynjolfsson and Andrew McAfee's *The Second Machine Age* both describe the work already in progress astutely.

When Professor Klaus posits that a day will come when one trillion sensors will be connected to the internet, it is precisely such a level of industrial technology that will eventually facilitate greater personalization. Personalization will then become not only a derivative of industrialization, but will also take on a life of its own.

Meanwhile, McAfee proposes that in the second machine age, technology will augment cognitive as opposed to manual and more industrial tasks. This idea is closer to the industrialization of the individual. I would add that much of what has been hitherto achieved in digital finance in the platform era falls into this description.

We are now entering a new phase where personalization will itself be the phenomenon, with finance as its 'operating system'. Personalization, as an idea, was never thought possible in human civilization before because individuals never had control over their interactions to the extent that is becoming increasingly possible today.

Personalization is based on the innate human desire to be in control of our identities, relationships, and interactions. The advent of new technologies, including cryptocurrencies, AI, blockchain, the Internet of Things, and the better bandwidth that 5G brings, will disintermediate the current 'ice merchants' of finance and lead to a greater degree of personalization. Many of these are already here.

In the future, every individual is potentially a platform owner, interacting with all other individuals as fellow platform owners, but this does not mean that personalization will not have its own set of issues. All societies are dealing with the same insidious forces arising from individualism which have been creeping into everyday life, and will shape how the world will look well into the future.

The industrialization of finance

Many technologies today boast of being revolutionary or transformational when they are simply incremental improvements in the industrialization phase of finance.

The industrialization of finance began in the 1950s, when the first clumsy mainframe computers were introduced in US banks. As cost destruction became the focus, there was a time in the 1990s when the most prominent US financial companies were 'mono-liners' like GE Capital and First USA. These operated like factories where each processed about 60-80 million credit card customers, the highest numbers in their time.

This was the pre-digital era, and the biggest players became industrial mono-liners to scale their businesses as profit margins dropped. The law of large numbers dictated that the more transactions you pushed through the system, cost per transaction fell and profit per customer rose. Commercial banks ate, walked, slept, and talked this industrial language (and still do today). Even now, we still carry some of this language into the platform era.

The legendary chairman of Wells Fargo, Dick Kovacevich, used industrial language such as "cross-sell-ratios" and "products-per-customer", for which he and his bank became the global gold standard. He chipped away at the Glass-Steagall Act, which limited banks from cross-selling products until it was repealed in 1999.

But it was China's entry into the industrialization of finance that unleashed the forces at play, at a time when the combination of mobile devices, no-code application development, venture capital funding for fintech (financial technology) as an asset class of its own, and the scale and energy of its own economy were growing at a rate unparalleled in history.

The philosophical underpinnings of how China rose to become a force to be reckoned with in technology and finance are worth understanding in greater detail. As a country, China has five times the population of the US. Its provincial governments manage GDPs and populations the size of entire nations.

A window of opportunity arose when several positive factors in China's development all came together. It was admitted into the World Trade Organization (WTO) in 2001. Its well-run educational institutions had been churning out massive numbers of engineers. It had a generation of young people who were unburdened by the historical baggage of their elders, including the Cultural Revolution and the Great Leap Forward.

Meanwhile, global investors had coined the acronym BRIC, referring to Brazil, Russia, India, and China – the countries with the largest populations, and thus the largest markets to be tapped, in the world. China made the most of every one of these opportunities.

Even in pre-digital times, China's 'big four' national banks were each already behemoths in their own right. On average, each had about 400,000 employees and 300 million customers, larger than entire banking systems in many other countries. The surprise was in how fast they moved when the country reopened to the rest of the world.

When the big four banks revamped their core banking structures in 2004, every one of the four consolidated around 1,000 data centers down to two in just under a year. They shed staff, reduced costs, and off-loaded non-performing loans in preparation for their IPOs from 2004 onwards, raising between US$20-$30 billion in the international capital markets. This was unprecedented by the standards and speed of banks in any country at that time.

At the same time, the Chinese embraced new payment platforms wholeheartedly, initially outdoing the US players on the now-ancient industrial age platforms. By early 2015, China UnionPay, the Chinese equivalent of Visa and MasterCard, reported US$1.9 trillion in transaction value against Visa's US$1.75 trillion.[3]

As a result of not being allowed to operate in China initially, despite the terms of WTO membership, Visa and MasterCard both lost the ability to play in the new Chinese marketplace to significant effect. China UnionPay even cheekily offered its platform to process the transactions of Visa's member banks in other countries by routing them on their own network at a much lower cost per transaction.[4]

By 2016, China UnionPay had issued over 5 billion cards in over 40 countries and was accepted by over 26 million merchants in 150 countries globally. But the real story lies in how it transitioned to 'lighter' technology by using distributed servers instead of huge mainframes, coded in a new open programming language. In the meantime, Visa and MasterCard were falling behind on the weight of their expensive legacy technology.

In the rest of the world, much of the finance industry was still busy with just digitizing manual processes for the very first time, putting them on digital platforms, and working with new programming languages.

In the insurance industry, hugely successful digital platforms like Lemonade and Trov simplified the selling of insurance on mobile devices on a pay-per-use basis. Just by streamlining areas such as claims processing, they were able to report greater customer satisfaction and lower costs.

Buy-now-pay-later (BNPL) is an ancient financial tool that once sat in tiny notebooks, one for each family in the neighborhood, kept by the owner of the local store. It then got carried onto the credit card companies extending credit at the point of sale.

---

[3] "UnionPay network processed transactions worth 53.9 trillion Yuan in 2015", Unionpay International news center, 22 January 2016. Available at https://www.unionpayintl.com/en/mediaCenter/newsCenter/companyNews/3009190.shtml.

[4] "Visa, China UnionPay in Dispute on International Transactions", *Bloomberg News*, 4 June 2010. Available at https://www.bloomberg.com/news/articles/2010-06-04/visa-hong-kong-says-there-is-no-change-to-how-it-s-handling-transactions?sref=7pLQsG4I.

The BNPL industry got a facelift when Klarna Bank AB in Sweden perfected the digital version of what many credit card companies were already doing. Although these developments were in no way an overhaul of the status quo, Klarna had 18 million customers and a respectable US$1.2 billion in revenue in 2020.

Likewise, the mobile trading company Robinhood, self-styled as 'brokerage made easy', was incorporated in 2013 and launched its app in 2015. By 2022, it had up to 22.8 million users.[5]

Although these platforms were described as transformational, they were merely a digitization of the existing world order. As huge as their numbers appeared, they had not reached the point of dislodging the larger incumbents.

Robinhood was just the new-age mobile equivalent of Charles Schwab, the largest traditional broker in the US. To put things in perspective, its assets under management (AUM) reached an estimated US$80 billion, compared to US$300 billion for E-trade. Charles Schwab has US$3.8 trillion with only 31.9 million customer accounts.[6] While the personalization era is still in its early stages, for the time being, the mechanics of the stock trading industry have yet to be truly shaken up.

In the insurance industry, it was companies like Quantemplate that were fast digitizing the industry, albeit not quite transforming it. At the back-end, the industry's troubles remained the same, with opaque agencies and tie-ups with pharmaceuticals and hospital systems that continued to work against customers.

These platforms increasingly applied artificial learning and gamification designed to track habits and promote addiction, now an old social media platform trick. However, the products they sold remained the same as in the physical realm: good old consumer loans and insurance coverage that were still sensitive to rate changes, liquidity, and funding costs.

There is still plenty of ground to cover. Simply digitizing the existing

---

[5]   Number of users of Robinhood from 2014 to 2022, via Statista.com.

[6]   D. Curry, "Robinhood Revenue and Usage Statistics (2022)", via BusinessofApps, 9 May 2022. Available at https://www.businessofapps.com/data/robinhood-statistics/.

industry will keep new players busy for many more years. But as recent as these developments are, they are just incremental tweaks to the old industrial model still propping up an aging financial system that is, itself, ready for a change.

Even mobile will end

2011 can be described as a great transition point in the history of browser technology. It was the year when browsers that previously worked on desktops had to go mobile. As such, it was also the year when the pioneers of browser technology – such as Netscape, which started in 1994 – reached the end of their era.

The mobile era arrived surreptitiously. Although the iPhone iOS and Android operating systems were launched in 2007 and 2008 respectively, there was a lag of about three years for smartphones to become commonplace in many countries, and for the applications on them to reach critical mass.

Many forget just how difficult it was for Amazon and Facebook, created between 1991 to 2007, to shift from their native desktop formats to being mobile-driven. They did not navigate the transition very well and eventually came under constant threat from newer, mobile-native players like TikTok.

The Chinese copies of these platforms, while hopeless as desktop platforms, took to mobile like fish to water just as the technology matured. The technology investor, Lee Kai Fu, has described in great detail how the first Chinese social media platforms were direct imitations of the original US players.[7]

WeChat was launched only in January 2011 as a brand new, mobile-native social media application after a decade of incremental evolution from its predecessors, the QQ instant messaging and Q-Zone social network. Both had spent the previous decade going nowhere. Baidu was an equivalent of Google; Alibaba was a combination of Amazon and eBay; Sina was akin to

---

[7] K. F. Lee, *AI Superpowers: China, Silicon Valley and the New World Order* (New York: Houghton Mifflin Harcourt, 2018).

AOL, and so on. But when their mobile versions were launched, they broke away from their US cousins.

As mobile natives, the Chinese players were able to make great strides in the 2010s, making the most of social media applications, building incredible microsite ecosystems, and closing the last mile in transactions by integrating financial products with other services such as bicycle ride-hailing. Tencent's WeChat was Facebook, WhatsApp, and PayPal all rolled into one. JD was Shopify with actual delivery. By contrast, their US peers steered clear of payments and finance, and instead focused only on social media, content, and advertising.

New players in the US without the burden of a desktop legacy also scaled very quickly. Stripe, the US payments platform, was launched in 2011 as a mobile-native payment platform and scaled significantly faster than its payment processing predecessor, PayPal, which was established more than a decade earlier. Stripe provided greater integration into the ecosystem of its small business users.

The Chinese regulators licensed non-bank third-party payment players in 2010, which saw the launch of Alipay and WeChat Pay in 2011. These practically threw out the China UnionPay and US credit card processing models, and replaced them with the digital wallet format as an all-encompassing platform on mobile devices.

Eventually, the Koreans and Southeast Asians also developed the same all-encompassing ecosystems on the back of chat and ride-sharing platforms. In Southeast Asia, Grab and Go-Jek (now GoTo) became the regional version of the super-apps, with a fuller suite of financial products for their drivers and customers – credit cards, automobile, small business loans, and digital wallets[8] – that superseded the banks in these countries.

Application development tool sets became available to support this phase for players around the globe. The lower cost of telecommunication

---

[8]   E. Huet, "Uber Continues To Finance Its Drivers With New Gas Credit Card", *Forbes*, 9 June 2015. Available at https://www.forbes.com/sites/ellenhuet/2015/06/09/uber-driver-gas-credit-card-fuel-mastercard/#2c3e9b36ca2c.

infrastructure, made possible in no small part by players like Huawei, empowered the rapid rise of mobile devices in many developing countries.

All these developments stood the US monoline model from the 1990s on its head by showing that digital could handle far more customers and create new ecosystems. By June 2020, Alipay alone had 1.3 billion users worldwide, and was processing US$17 trillion worth of transactions in China for more than 80 million merchants and 2,000 financial institutions.[9]

As of 2017, WeChat Pay had 1 billion digital users and 40 million merchants, amassing US$5.5 trillion (RMB 37,183 billion) on their QR code-based payment wallets.[10]

Alipay users alone conduct 180 million transactions per day, or 85,000 transactions per second, against Visa and MasterCard's 20,000 transactions per second. PayPal, which had a much longer global history, had only 192 million active users worldwide and saw a mere 5 million transactions a day.

Nothing captures the extent of the impact financial platforms have had on society as well as the marketing phenomenon known as 'Singles' Day', a digital shopping day held by Alibaba every year on 11 November, akin to the Black Friday or post-Christmas sales in the US.

Alibaba's gross merchandise volume surged past US$1.8 trillion for the fiscal year 2021, on the back of 1.2 billion users worldwide.[11] In 2019, its ability to exceed US$1 billion worth of sales in the first 68 seconds and $12 billion in the first hour of Singles' Day was an indication of the computing power of its infrastructure.[12] Not surprisingly, 90% of Alibaba's sales come from smartphones.

The introduction of Singles' Day reorganized e-commerce. Figures from 2021 suggest that more than 290,000 brands participated in it that

---

[9] Alipay, via Chinainternetwatch.com (accessed 12 February 2022).

[10] "China Third Party Payment Report 2017 Q4", AnalysysMason report.

[11] Alibaba Group Announces March Quarter and Full Fiscal Year 2021 Results", *Businesswire*, 13 May 2022. Available at https://www.businesswire.com/news/home/20210513005533/en/Alibaba-Group-Announces-March-Quarter-and-Full-Fiscal-Year-2021-Results

[12] J. Horwitz, "Alibaba Singles Day sales hit $13 billion in the first hour - up 32% from 2018", *Business Insider*, 11 November 2019. Available at https://www.businessinsider.com/alibaba-says-singles-day-sales-hit-912-billion-yuan-in-first-hour-2019-11

year, including more than 22,000 foreign brands from 78 countries. One million new products were launched on that day alone. All in all, 299 brands surpassed US$14.3 million each in gross merchandise volume, many closing their year's total sales in a single day.[13]

It also became increasingly international. The top five countries selling to Chinese consumers via cross-border platforms on Singles' Day are Japan, Korea, Australia, Germany and – yes – the US.

To put the comparisons in context, in the US, the combined Black Friday and Cyber Monday sales for all merchants in 2020 totaled US$19.8 billion.[14] This figure declined in 2021 because of the pandemic – Amazon's Prime Day revenue in 2021 was just US$11.19 billion[15] – while Alibaba's continued to grow. In terms of user numbers, Amazon had 300 million active buyers on its site in 2021, while eBay had 159 million and slowing.[16] By contrast, Alibaba had 863 million active buyers on its site.[17]

Even more impressive are the logistics required for Singles' Day, a demonstration of the massive impact of the Chinese propensity for speed and scale on global supply chains. More than 1.7 million employees, 400,000 vehicles, 5,000 warehouses, and 200 aircraft are mobilized to handle deliveries made on the day alone.

The ten short years of the 2010s will be remembered as the period of China's digitalization of finance, driven by mobile, just like the 1990s are now remembered for the industrialization of finance in the US. In the same way, the mobile era will also fade away as personalization technologies mature.

---

[13] "Alibaba Group Announces March Quarter and Full Fiscal Year 2021 Results", above, at 11.

[14] F. Holmes, "No, Really, It's Good That Black Friday And Cyber Monday Sales Declined This Year", *Forbes*, 2 December 2021. Available at https://www.forbes.com/sites/greatspeculations/2021/12/02/no-really-its-good-that-black-friday-and-cyber-monday-sales-declined-this-year/?sh=17267ef9726e.

[15] F. Ali, "Amazon's Prime Day 2021 sales total $11.19 billion", *Digital Commerce 360*, 23 June 2021. Available at https://www.digitalcommerce360.com/2021/06/23/amazons-prime-day-2021-sales-total-11-19-billion/

[16] eBay: total active buyers worldwide 2010-2021, via Statista.com (accessed 19 August 2021).

[17] Alibaba recorded 863 million annual buyers in China retail marketplace in Q3 2021, via Chinainternetwatch.com (accessed 20 November 2021).

That process has already started. Facebook and WeChat are already tired versions of their former selves. A data monitor that tracks application downloads revealed that Byte Dance's Tiktok exceeded 3 billion installations in July 2021.[18] (This figure includes its numbers in China, where Facebook is banned, but excludes those on Android.)

Facebook and Microsoft have started the arduous process of including virtual and augmented reality in their platforms, but they are not native to these. These original players will attempt to make the transition, but will fall short in areas that subsequent generation of players – first those native to the mobile era, followed by those native to the personalization era – will supersede them as they come of age.

The rise of platforms like Parlour and Ramble are merely reactions to the current platforms' increasingly untenable misuse of personal data for advertising and censorship. These are preliminary and tentative attempts to give control back to platform users, which will themselves give way to the true prototypes of personalization.

In fact, the successors of TikTok are already in sight, even as it is still on the rise. Blockchain-based applications like Chingari in India enable creators to post their videos on their own site; whoever chooses to visit them generates tokens from which the creators get paid.

Although cryptocurrency tokens are important in the personalization phase, their use has been severely curtailed in China. With tokens and new chip technology, transactions will be device-independent – and the technology to make this transition already exists.

Currently, the Chinese players are continuing a push for more use-cases in areas like smart health projects and smart cities to populate the mobile platform era. But at the dawn of the personalization era, platforms which saw tremendous growth over the last decade – whether Asian, European, or American – will also see their progress set back. Bursts of innovation

---

[18] S. Chan, "Tiktok becomes the first non-Facebook Mobile App to reach 3 billion downloads globally", *SensorTower* blog, July 2021. Available at https://sensortower.com/blog/tiktok-downloads-3-billion.

are always followed by a long tail of compliance and consolidation before another evolutionary wave can take the industry to the next level.

The 'metaverse' is designed to destroy the very platform model that Facebook sits on today. The stage is set for a player, born and bred of the personalization era, to take the industry into its next leap forward. Also, Mark Zuckerberg, the founder of Facebook (now Meta) is himself a millennial in generational terms, while the metaverse is native to Gen Z.

What the new era will involve is not clear as yet, but it will clearly be device-independent. The Internet of Things, where a wide variety of daily activities will have different levels of autonomous technology built in, will start to play an important role in how we organize ourselves around technology and finance.

Mapping the transitions

Having said all this, the platform era is far from over. As I write this, attention is focused on a future based on Web 3.0: a third iteration of the World Wide Web, as its name might suggest (Web technology is popularly described as having evolved from Web 1.0 to Web 3.0). The blogging site, *Flat World Business*, called Web 3.0 the 'emotional web'.[19]

The onslaught of artificial intelligence, machine learning, neural networks, chip technology, quantum computing, and even battery technology is putting much more power into digital platforms – which are beginning to look highly personalized, even if they are technically still platforms. By bringing features like machine-human symbiosis, autonomous vehicles, smart buildings, robotics, and social media integration to maps and other platforms, these developments create vibrant, multi-dimensional data visualization.

In a 2014 TED talk, Nicholas Negroponte, the founder of MIT Labs,

---

[19] "Web 1.0 vs Web 2.0 vs Web 3.0 vs Web 4.0 vs Web 5.0 – A bird's eye on the evolution and definition", *FlatWorldBusiness* blog, 2011. Available at https://flatworldbusiness.wordpress.com/flat-education/previously/web-1-0-vs-web-2-0-vs-web-3-0-a-bird-eye-on-the-definition/

suggested that under Web 3.0, the goal should not be for an oven to 'talk' to a mobile phone – which would still involve receiving instructions from the end user – but for the oven to independently detect that it is roasting chicken (and not, say, a duck or beef), and then decide how best to cook the meat. In other words, it is not the outcome that has been transformed but the process, made possible by the amount of AI and machine learning that has been thrown at it.

In the advanced platform age, as devices interact and connect with each other, they will evolve to form the 'symbiotic web', a term coined in 2009 by the legal scholar Paul Bernal to denote an internet version of the human brain.[20]

Despite all these advancements, the platform era is stuck in a Gordian knot of its own making. The most powerful platforms today operate in silos, working independently and unable to connect with each other, with each determined to retain its monopolistic features. Tim Berners-Lee, the creator of the World Wide Web, has made it his personal crusade to break down these silos on the premise that user-defined data is the property of users themselves, who should be allowed to transfer their data between platforms.[21]

Another factor driving the rise of personalization and the pushback against platforms is the pushback against technology companies becoming 'governments' in their own right. Platform owners regulate who has access to their platforms and what they can say or do on them – and, to some extent, wield powers that even governments do not have. As a result, users are migrating to models which favor direct, peer-to-peer action over centralized control.

This conundrum is being solved right now – but not on the World Wide Web. A new world is arising where interoperability is *de rigueur*. Protocols like Chainlink, Cosmos, Hybrix, Polkadot, Wanchain, Aion Ark,

---

[20] P. A. Bernal, "Web 2.5: the symbiotic web", *International Review of Law, Computers & Technology* 24 (1) pp. 25-37 (2018). DOI: 10.1080/13600860903570145.

[21] D. Weinberger, "How the father of the World Wide Web plans to reclaim it from Facebook and Google" *Digital Trends*, 8 October 2016. Available at https://www.digitaltrends.com/web/ways-to-decentralize-the-web/.

Table 1: From platforms to personalization

	Before 1991 (Emergence of the internet/ Finance 1.0)	1991-late 1990s (Web 1.0/ Finance 2.0)	1999-late 2000s (Web 2.0/ Finance 3.0)	2010-late 2020s (Web 3.0 / Finance 4.0)	2020 onwards (Finance 5.0)
The internet	Computerization	Early web browsers like Netscape	'Social web' User-generated social media Emergence of large technology platforms like Google, Facebook, and Amazon	'Semantic web' Dominance of mobile Advanced platforms using AI, machine learning, and open-source software	'Emotional web'/ personalization Device independence, Internet of Things Increases in blockchain and token use
Financial platforms	Electronic Finance	Funds Supermarket websites, e.g., OCBC Singapore which simply listed funds	The advent of secure online and mobile payments – PayPal, WeChat Pay, Alipay Loan comparison aggregator websites	AI and machine learning platforms e.g., Nutmeg in the UK Frictionless interaction (e.g., Robinhood, Klarna)	Device independence Mutually validating devices Token-based exchanges User-defined protocols

Technology	Passive core banking system General ledger batch-processed in the backend, not linked to transaction systems	Straight-through processing (backend connected to the frontend) Ability to process transactional data (but still batch-processed)	Standalone banking applications linked to Customer Relationship Management (CRM) and other analytics Real-time processing The advent of big data	Cloud-based digital communities APIs Algorithms, machine learning, and artificial intelligence Multiple data points	Data is external to institution User-defined protocols Peer-to-peer data exchange Self-learning applications Personalization of big data
Distribution channels	Automated teller machines (ATMs) and call centers	Websites	Platform wars – focus on scale and market share	Mobile, 'always on' finance Blockchain linkages to supply chains	Internet of Things Interactive, interoperable tokens User-defined Protocols
Cybersecurity	No or limited online security	Secure Sockets Layer (SSL) Digital Certificates Encryption	Transport Layer Security (TLS) Manual, multi-factor authentication	Biometrics, usage-based identities Enterprise TLS	Open participation network effect, mutually validating identity

ICON, Transledger, and Overledger are competing to become the 'internet of blockchains'.

I have set out these all-encompassing transitions in finance in Table 1, spanning the age of simple computerization to the invention of the World Wide Web, and into the eras of platforms and personalization. The phases are not neat; they overlap with each other. As can be seen in the table, the personalization era will first co-exist with the platform era before becoming a pronounced era in its own right.

In Table 1, I have introduced the terms Finance 1.0 to Finance 5.0 as shorthand to help label and map the transitions through Web 1.0 to 3.0 described earlier. As I write this, the world is currently in the Finance 3.0 phase and going on to Finance 4.0; moving from platforms to advanced platforms, but not quite into personalization.

The personalization phase of finance will be characterized by three essential features, all of which already exist but have not yet become commonplace.

First, finance will be externalized. In other words, data which is collected and interactions which take place outside formal institutions will become far more valuable than those contained within any single entity. When this happens, it will not only undermine institutional power, but emphasize the interactions between many different individual actors across broader networks. I discuss this in greater detail in Chapter Five.

Second, finance will become device-independent. That is, as the Internet of Things connects all kinds of devices to each other and makes them mutually validating, we will move away from the current mobile-dependent world that we have become overly comfortable with. This transition alone will make cryptocurrencies eminently useful in a way we cannot currently imagine in the mobile-driven world.

Peer-to-peer data exchange is currently very slow and cumbersome. But with greater bandwidth, lower latency on 5G and 6G networks, and the advent of quantum technology, the peer-to-peer business models that did not quite succeed the first time will be given a second chance.

Detractors also point out the 'Oracle problem', where external data cannot be incorporated to be processed in a peer-to-peer platform unless it is scrubbed, entered, and processed manually by an intermediary. These are some of the problems that will be overcome over time.

Third, the defining super-structures of financial transactions namely identity, security, and the integrity of transactions, will be controlled by the transacting parties themselves in a network, rather than placed in the hands of an intermediary. The network ecosystem will look very different from what we understand it to be today.

The early evidence suggests that the role of the intermediary is not to facilitate the transaction but to provide the ecosystem, such as in a metaverse, inside which the parties interact with each other. I discuss this in more detail in Chapter Two.

These three features will result in finance becoming the 'operating system' of the personalization phase. In the platform era, finance was merely an afterthought, often just consigned to an application which tended to be nested inside another application. In the personalization age, it will be central to the architecture of how we interact with each other.

CHAPTER 2

The personalization of finance

"Energy is the currency of the universe."
Emily Maroutian

"Some things have to be believed to be seen."
Ralph Hodgson

To apply the ice trade analogy that I outlined in the introduction to this book to finance, just as the pricing and delivery of ice across huge distances were subject to many vagaries of the elements, the pricing and delivery of financial services today are at the mercy of a whole range of variables. The global economy, trade, foreign exchange rates, inflation, capital flows, local interest rates, and loss through fraud and non-performing loans are only some of them.

Today's financial institutions are like the ice merchants of the ice trade, visually and conceptually central to the industry. Economists and investment analysts encourage the impression that the 'ice merchants' of finance have control over the cost of manufacturing, delivering, and valuing financial assets.

We reward economists and analysts for predicting the movements of the global economy in language that sounds intelligent. But as no less than the learned central banker, Alan Greenspan himself, openly admitted, "What I've learned at the Federal Reserve is a new language which is called 'Fed-speak'. You soon learn to mumble with great incoherence."[22]

---

[22] J. M Bessette and J. J Pitney Jr., *American Government and Politics: Deliberation, Democracy and Citizenship* (Boston: Cengage Learning, 2010).

Just as the ice merchants transported ice across thousands of miles in their day, the financial intermediaries of today are at the mercy of the elements, beneath their veneer of control and order. In truth, an entire industry profits from the churn, fluctuations, inefficiencies, and uncertainties of trading financial assets. It is as raw as sending cut ice from Maine to Havana in the days before refrigeration.

In this chapter, I build on the elements of the ice analogy to find the parallels that will catalyze the personalization of finance. These include identity, the assets or tokens on which value is transmitted, and the new industries that arise from the process .

In search of the 'CFC' of finance

The game-changer for the ice-making industry was the development of chlorofluorocarbons (CFCs, also known by the trade name Freon), a synthetic chemical compound which produces a cooling effect by absorbing heat from its surroundings.

Although CFCs were eventually phased out due to their environmental impact and replaced by safer alternatives, it was their discovery that finally industrialized home refrigeration, making it safe enough for ordinary consumers, and thus finally presided over the end of the ice merchants. In the same way, we need to search for the 'CFC of finance': a breakthrough that will make the industry increasingly personalized and render its chains of intermediaries obsolete.

This is not the same as the claim that the finance industry has become better managed due to automation, robotics, and better data flow in recent years. These are merely intermediate developments which neither unseat the incumbent players nor bring about the rise of new financial platforms.

In the same way that CFCs did not set out to mimic the production of ice per se, but the conditions required to manufacture it in a controlled setting, the CFC of finance will not preserve the institutions of finance as they currently stand. Rather, it will democratize finance, making it available in a manner that individuals can control and personalize.

This will be achieved in three important ways. First, it will help parties validate each other's identity without the need for an intermediary. Second, it will make transactions immutable between all parties – again, without the need for intermediaries.

Thirdly, it will enable exchanges to take place directly between parties, albeit in a digital form, so that the value of a transaction will be held by its owner and not sit as information in the balance sheet or general ledger of a bank, fund manager, or third party of any kind.

Let's look at each of these in turn, but not in the language and metaphors of finance today. Over-reliance on the concepts that drive finance as we currently know it will trap us and make the intermediaries we know appear invincible.

Whoever controls identity, controls finance

The core of finance is not money, wealth, transactions, or customer data. It is irrefutable proof that the participants in the ecosystem – of the customers, institutions, counterparties, and beneficiaries of an exchange – are non-fungible or non-refutable.

With proof of identity, unique to and carried by the owner, a customer who is native to the digital world can traverse it almost without limits. Conversely, without an identity that can be digitally validated, such a person barely exists in the digital realm. (This said, there is a need to distinguish between 'identity' and 'personal data', where much activity is still evolving.)

At present, the process of authenticating an individual's identities is managed by institutions. To give an example, in banking transactions, it is currently the bank that validates the parties' identities and the transaction. However, what the bank technically has is passive information on the customer in its own databases. All it holds is a statement of account and a general ledger of the person's transactions that passes as 'identity' – but it does not matter if the customer actually exists. Any user can pretend to be the customer by a validation process initiated by the bank.

In this way, banks today do not actually validate parties' identities per se, but *information* on the parties and their transactions. Even where a customer carries a card or a token given to them by the bank, that token is just a facsimile of the information that the bank has on that customer. These are, strictly speaking, ledger data and not proof of identity – but it is here that our understanding of what could constitute identity in the personalized world starts.

Biometrics were an early iteration of authentication in the digital world. It will become more fully developed when devices can authenticate each other, but it is still not the same as identity itself. It is a representation of identity, or to borrow the words of the old banking legend, Walter Wriston, it is "information on identity".

Once deployed, this information is not 'cancelable'. In other words, once it is released, the owner loses control over how and where this information is used. In other words, if biometric authentication is obtained fraudulently, it can be misused by thieves and malicious actors. Cases of fake fingerprints and the use of a real person's biometric data to gain access to their bank account fraudulently are commonplace today.

However, 'cancelable' biometrics could be made possible if the recording of biometric data required tagging at the point it is read for that specific use only, such that without the tag, that data becomes unusable for any transaction other than the one the user intended.

In the platform phase, the finance industry tried to make identities irrefutable by drawing from the tons of data generated on the open web. Every second, hundreds of thousands of photographs, comments, status updates, and 'likes' are posted online,[23] providing tons of data points that can be used to create facsimiles of identity.

The more data there is, the clearer the facsimile of the identity, much like

---

[23] A. Monnappa, "How Facebook is Using Big Data - The Good, the Bad, and the Ugly", *Simplilearn*, 16 March 2022. Available at https://www.simplilearn.com/how-facebook-is-using-big-data-article

how a high-resolution image is sharper and more detailed – but information on identity is still not identity itself. In 2012, Google made a breakthrough when it trained its artificial intelligence (AI) to recognize cats by feeding it with thousands of cat images.

But it is also true that the less data there is, the less accurately the facsimile represents the identity. The Google application mentioned above was then only 70% accurate, and it had problems identifying variations of related animals that were not cats.

As Muneeb Ali, the founder of the start-up Blockstack, puts it, platforms like Google and Facebook will cease to dominate the internet in the way they do now, as users gain more control over their own digital identities and select the communities they want to participate in.[24]

There are several different breakthrough digital identity projects already under way, mostly based on cryptocurrencies and blockchains. The cryptocurrency news site, Cryptomorrow, identified Pangea Arbitration Token, Block Verify, XID, Keytokens, Civic, Shocard, UniquID, Netkey, Uport, and BlockAuth as contenders.[25]

If the blockchain model prevails, no user of finance will be able to perform transactions unless their identity can be cross-validated by several other (already authenticated) identities. In the blockchain, where users cross-validate individuals they have previously interacted with, one exists 'because one has existed before'. This is generally called a centralized identity framework.

The Self-Sovereign Identity (SSI) approach gives the owner control over his or her own digital identity, where the other party can trust the credentials provided. The European Union (EU), which has its own SSI framework, is a major supporter of this approach to privacy management. In Korea, the city

---

[24] M. Ali, R. Shea, J. Nelson, and M. J. Freedman, Blockstack Technical Whitepaper version 1.1, 12 October 2017. Available at https://pdos.csail.mit.edu/6.824/papers/blockstack-2017.pdf

[25] D. Kariuki, "10 Projects in Blockchain-based Identity Management", *Cryptomorrow*, 28 August 2019. Available at http://www.cryptomorrow.com/2018/01/17/10-projects-in-blockchain-based-identity-management/.

of Busan is using blockchain to provide decentralized identity, developed by a company called Coinplug.[26]

Some of these identities are based on the emerging ERC-20 standard, which is used for application development on the Ethereum protocol.[27] Consequently, identity transactions and tokens could all conceivably be captured on the same token, making identities potentially tradeable and bringing a whole new dimension to interactions.

Blockchain companies like Civic, Evernym, and Uport are developing irrefutable identities that use everyday names, although the cryptography underpinning their systems is invisible to their users.[28] However, to the extent that these are commercial ventures, it becomes more challenging to build a genuinely ubiquitous identity system that is not a for-profit intermediary.

Technically, as identity authentication technologies develop, individuals could have multiple identities for different types of transactions. Any individual can then have multiple identities for use in different situations and with different communities.

The function of identity today in the so-called 'dark web' is also instructive. Ironically, trust and verification are far more important on the dark web than on regular sites. Browsers like Tor, Freenet, and 12P protect their users by encrypting their data and distributing their movements across several servers to conceal their activities.

Consequently, users have devised several ways to validate each other's identities and facilitate trust while remaining anonymous. Buyers make a prepayment to a custodian third party, which holds the payment in escrow for the distributor. The custodian then pays the distributor, who sends the buyer the goods.

---

[26] "South Korea's Busan city launches decentralized identity platform for public services", *Ledger Insights*, 9 June 2019. Available at https://www.ledgerinsights.com/south-korea-busan-city-decentralized-identity-public-services/.

[27] N. Reiff, "What is ERC-20 and What Does it Mean for Ethereum?", *Investopedia* blog, 20 June 2017. Available at https://www.investopedia.com/news/what-erc20-and-what-does-it-mean-ethereum/.

[28] R. Hackett, "Why Blockchain and Identity Go Together", *Fortune*, 20 January 2018. Available at http://fortune.com/2018/01/20/blockchain-identity-civic-silicon-slopes/.

All this is complicated by the extent to which identity can be manipulated. Individuals increasingly ask for the 'right to be forgotten', which, while understandable, also gives rise to the right to edit identities. This raises many new permutations of what can be done with identities, including creating fake composites from real identities. The EU General Data Protection Regulation (GDPR) introduced the right to have data erased from specific transactions, but current platform technology is not designed to enable this. The HTTP protocol on which the internet is run is constructed to enable connectivity between computers, not moderate the data that flows between them.

Advancing the right to be forgotten will require considerable technological genius. The goal is to achieve the digital equivalent of someone entering and leaving a room, with no trace that they had ever been there.

In the meantime, legislation in the EU and the UK has begun trying to redirect control of personal data from the platforms to the user. Some of this is being achieved in finance. The PSD2 (Payments Services Directive 2) in the EU and the Open Banking Guidelines in the UK became enforceable in early 2018. Both try to give the owner of the identity or data some control over who they are free to share it with. Similar GDPR-type rules in other countries are all moving the needle in favor of the individual at the expense of the institution.

The finance industry, however, creates other issues in moderating identity – for example, the immutability of transactions where parties cannot renege on an agreement. Decentralized finance introduces another dimension: where transactions are carried out on tokens leads us in turn to the question of where identities would be located.

The legendary television and movie series, *Star Trek*, alludes to some of the potential complications that can arise from overlap in the digitization of the *person* and the digitization of their *identity*.

Most importantly, the genius of the personalization of identity will not lie in the sophistication of the technology but the extreme simplicity of its process, design, and use. It is first and foremost a philosophical, social, and physical problem – and only then a technological one.

If energy is the currency of the universe

The poet Emily Maroutian romanticized the phrase "energy is the currency of the universe," in applying a biological concept to life. In her words, when you "pay" attention to something, you "buy" that experience.[29] A payment of money, in this respect, thus has no value in itself except when it captures something of value.

I am told that players of Stellaris, the video game, already practice the notion of using energy credits as currency. The Kardashev scale measures civilizations' technological advancement based on their use and production of energy. The only problem is that any advances in energy technology would necessarily make its value to the economy deflationary. The cheaper the cost of energy, the cheaper everything produced from it will be, but that is a discussion for another book.

Just as the sun's energy finds its value as it synthesizes everything on Earth, the value of money is found in the value of the assets it synthesizes. We do not appreciate how this concept applies to money until we see how, when society itself is left broken and lame after a war or a natural disaster, it needs to be rehabilitated not with money but with the value of assets and activities.

During the Bronze age, the Lydians were amongst the first civilizations to introduce the practice of using gold coins as a medium of exchange. A precious metal, like gold or silver, facilitated transactions by providing a separate, socially accepted standard for pricing and valuing the goods and services being exchanged. Money thus became a store of value in and of itself, accumulated for its own sake.

In the same way, although businesses and social activities of all kinds today are measured in monetary terms, they do not capture the actual value created by a transaction. Unbridled capitalism has, over time, valued only the token or currency, and not the value actually created in the process. The

---

[29] E. Maroutian, *Thirty: A collection of personal quotes, advice, and lessons* (Los Angeles: Maroutian Entertainment, 2018).

result was the creation of our highly financialized economy, where money itself is the be all and end all.

This was not always the case. Archaeological discoveries from ancient Mesopotamia (now modern-day Iraq) suggest that the Sumerians devised early writing systems in order to develop logs of inventories and debt, which could be passed from hand to hand as a record of the value created. In this way, a contract document passed on from one person to another actually passes on the value described in the document, which is then traded and realized. As such, the written contract was the first token as we know it today, but it carried a record of the value being created or transferred, recognizing all the parties involved in the process.

Vitalik Buterin, the founder of the Ethereum cryptocurrency, introduced the modern-day digital equivalent of such a document, known as the 'smart contract'. These run as a program on the Ethereum blockchain, which details the operations of a transaction and when and how value is transmitted and satisfied between parties.

Decentralized applications (dApps) are built on smart contracts. The first dApp on Ethereum, the original smart contract protocol, was only published on 22 April 2016 and is still in its formative years, although new dApps are being developed every single day.

The crypto world today now contains thousands of dApps to support very specific functions, most of which are based on Ethereum. Filecoin, for example, was designed to be used for storing files, while Tezos is emerging as storage for bond transactions. Uniswap is an automatic market-maker to swap crypto without an order book – almost like an exchange in its own right. (If all of this sounds very technical, it is; for now, it still mostly attracts only computer geeks who are able to navigate the technology.)

Decentralized exchanges make up more than 60% of dApps, followed by finance (26%), gambling, and gaming.[30] But the real breakthroughs occur

---

[30] K. Wu, Y. Ma. G. Huang, and X. Liu, A first look at blockchain-based decentralized applications. *Journal of Software: Practice and Experience* 51(10) pp. 2033-2050 (2019). DOI:10.1002/spe.2751.

when an interesting use case comes around. In December 2017, one of the earliest blockchain-based games, CryptoKitties, was so popular that it nearly crashed the Ethereum network.[31]

In addition, smart contracts also function as a decentralized autonomous organization (DAO) which helps facilitate transacting parties' interactions. At all levels, they need a token that can be created, bought, and sold to validate their identities.

As we seek to recreate sustainable societies, it is worth emulating the concept of tokens as they exist in nature. In his seminal blog essay, *Resisting Reduction: A Manifesto*, Ito Joichi, the serial entrepreneur, activist, venture capitalist, and director of MIT Labs, explains how the role of currency in nature differs from its role in finance. Although Joichi was later censured for his relationship with the convicted pedophile, Jeffrey Epstein,[32] some of his seminal work in the area of tokens is still frontier science.

In nature, energy facilitates value creation as 'currency', but does not possess value in and of itself. Sunlight is therefore used in photosynthesis to create new organisms, which then unleash their energy to create other more complex organisms than themselves.

Energy is thus described as the currency that enables organisms to create life as we know it. In the same way, if money was always intended as 'currency', in the realm of finance, its purpose in payments was to enable us to create something that otherwise would not exist. Joichi believes that this enables sustainable complex systems to be built and developed, beyond the remit of what capitalism as we know it today would otherwise permit.

In nature, there is no master currency, no 'comptroller', and no need to trade or exchange value because each unit of energy is only valid for a particular transaction. It is validated when the products from those initial transactions go on to create new organisms – which is where value

---

[31] "CryptoKitties craze slows down transactions on Ethereum", *BBC News*, 5 December 2017. Available at https://www.bbc.com/news/technology-42237162.

[32] L. Beckett, "MIT to investigate research lab's ties to Epstein as director resigns", *The Guardian*, 7 September 2019. Available at https://www.theguardian.com/education/2019/sep/07/jeffrey-epstein-mit-media-lab-joi-ito-resigns-reports

is ultimately to be found. As one transaction gives rise to another in turn, this chain creates complex, interdependent, and sustainable systems. It is this function that 'community currencies' are trying desperately to recreate.

Joichi argues that as humanity moves into a networked digital phase, these concepts help us move away from the desire to accumulate money for its own sake and towards building a 'shared' economy. In my view, community currencies – currencies which are unique to and can be used in a specific locale, though they may not be recognized as legal tender – arguably lend themselves as rudimentary iterations of these concepts.

Surprisingly, there have been hundreds of community currency initiatives worldwide, many from long before the pandemic. From the Ithaca Hour in 1991[33] to Wayne Fournier's Tenino Dollar in Washington state,[34] there are easily 30 community currency experiments in the US alone and hundreds more around the world, including the UK,[35] Austria, and Thailand. Many community currencies were created in bootstrapped communities, which became even more prominent in the wake of the Covid-19 pandemic.

One very well-constructed community currency today exists in Kenya. Caroline Dama and Will Ruddick, the founders of an NGO called Grassroots Economics, launched a community currency called Sarafu Credit in 2018, which circulates within the closed communities where they operate and generates the token's value directly within those groups.[36]

At the moment, its value is protected by its own reserves and collateral pools in Sarafu Credit itself. There is also a secondary market in the form of a 'bonding pool'. Dama and Ruddick made it interchangeable with the national

---

[33] H. Sheffield, "Do community currencies really work?", *Milken Institute Review* blog, 23 September 2019. Available at https://www.milkenreview.org/articles/do-community-currencies-really-work.

[34] M. Waters, "Why a small town in Washington is printing its own currency during the pandemic", *The Hustle*, 12 June 2020. Available at https://thehustle.co/covid19-local-currency-tenino-washington/.

[35] S. Hargrave, "From Brixton to Totnes, the UK's dream of local currencies is over", *Wired*, 2 March 2020. Available at https://www.wired.co.uk/article/local-currencies-dead.

[36] See Sarafu.Network, via Grassroots Economics. Available at https://www.grassrootseconomics.org/pages/sarafu-network.html

fiat currency, the Kenyan shilling. Although Dama and Ruddick were initially arrested and imprisoned for undermining the national fiat currency, the Kenyan central bank eventually came around to supporting their initiative, which now runs in multiple villages in Kenya and other countries.

Sarafu Credit worked brilliantly during the Covid-19 crisis, when the Red Cross was able to distribute aid money into the community currency as a reserve pool but enhanced its value by circulating it within closed communities, thus adding value from self-supporting communal activities which would otherwise go unrecognized. Dama and Ruddick are now trying to put it onto a blockchain platform to digitize and enhance its uses.

Such tokens can potentially work in the developed world too as more digital assets are created. In countries like Germany, an early iteration can be seen in how renewable energy grids are shared across hundreds of buildings, bringing the cost of electricity and, therefore, the cost of production, down towards zero.

These concepts tie in neatly with the economist Jeremy Rifkin's idea of a "collaborative common", where the value of an asset lies in the fact that it is shared, because the marginal utility cost of the underlying asset or activity itself (such as renewable energy) actually tends to zero on its own.[37] In other words, the activity itself has no commercial value except that which it creates for society. Such a notion, if picked up on by more advanced economics, stands to revolutionize our concept of wealth management as well.

In healthcare, the pioneering work of George Church in genome engineering is way ahead of its time. He is setting out to associate individual's DNA with non-fungible tokens (NFT),[38] which would enable every human to have control over their personal DNA and to share or commercialize it.

At a more prosaic level, Luna DNA is a block-chained genomic and medical research knowledge database with an inbuilt cryptocurrency

---

[37] J. Rifkin, *The Zero Marginal Cost Society: The Internet of Things, The Collaborative Commons and the Eclipse of Capitalism* (New York: St Martin's Press, 2014).

[38] N. Jones, "How scientists are embracing NFTs", *Nature*, 18 June 2021. Available at https://www.nature.com/articles/d41586-021-01642-3

capability (not to be confused with Luna, the beleaguered cryptocurrency). Another example, Robomed, uses blockchain technology to manage health contracts and payments, which could in turn be used to finance ideas like universal health coverage. Meanwhile, MintHealth is a blockchain-powered personal health records management system, where users are incentivized to engage in healthy behaviours with VIDA tokens which can be traded for value.[39]

This line of thinking could arguably be extended to capture value generated within a multi-dimensional ecosystem, such as the Eurozone, and overcome the limitations of a shared currency in accommodating conflicting institutions.[40] However, this approach to value creation is diametrically opposed from those which promote the singularity principle – in other words, seeking to endlessly connect different entities into one huge monolithic whole – though this argument would require a book all on its own.

The only limitation of these monetary and financial concepts is that they work well within closed communities, like the Sarafu Network, but start to fray when they have to venture outside this ecosystem. This brings us back to why the Lydians introduced coinage.

The game changers

The gaming and esports industry is a living, breathing workshop of all the ideas discussed in this chapter. It is creating a prototype of the personalization universe to come.

Newzoo's 2021 Global Games Market Report estimates that the global digital games market was worth US$180.38 billion in 2021 – one of the most profitable years for the gaming industry to date. About half of that value

---

[39] See Digihealth Informer, Digital Health Maven. Available at http://digitalhealthmaven.com/digihealth_informer/

[40] M. Brunnermeier, H. James, J. Landau, The Euro and the Battle of Ideas, Princeton University Press , 2017.

came from the Asia Pacific, giving us a sense of the shape of things to come.[41]

These are still small numbers, if we compare them to, say, Walmart's total annual sales for 2020, which amounted to US$559 billion.[42] But they are still real transactions, driven not by anyone but *everyone*, with as many females as male players and still growing dramatically.

The esports industry is made up of 3.5 billion fans, with 2.5 billion in digital gaming alone[43] – clearly, more than just a prototype and not a figment of anyone's imagination. The esports industry is projected to generate US$500 billion in market value worldwide over the next few years. The mobile segment of the gaming industry alone is now worth US$68.5 billion – almost half of the entire gaming market – and is growing fast, and advancements in the Internet of Things will expand the industry further.

Many developments already under way in gaming are token-related, mostly sports rights and assets from the sporting industry, and tokens from gaming have found their way into real-life transactions. Some companies have tokenized ticketing for global events, such as the 2018 World Cup. (The effects of tokenization in the gambling industry, which is increasingly digital, would take these numbers to a whole new level.)

But it was the advent of NFTs, first created in 2014, which turbo-charged the gaming industry's potential for value creation. CryptoKitties, discussed above, were so successful that some kitties were said to have changed hands for more than US$100,000. Today, game tokens such as these routinely change hands for thousands of dollars.

In 2019, Dapper Labs went one up and released a tokenized collection of highlights from National Basketball Association (NBA) games, including

---

[41] T. Wijman, "The Games Market and Beyond in 2021: The Year in Numbers" *Newzoo Insights* blog, 12 December 2021. Available at https://newzoo.com/insights/articles/the-games-market-in-2021-the-year-in-numbers-esports-cloud-gaming#:~:text=The%20games%20market%20in%202021,%2B1.4%25%20over%20last%202020.

[42] S. E. Kohan, "Walmart revenue hits $559b for fiscal year 2020", *Forbes*, 18 February 2021. Available at https://www.forbes.com/sites/shelleykohan/2021/02/18/walmart-revenue-hits-559-billion-for-fiscal-year-2020/?sh=797882c13358

[43] J. Harty, "Newzoo's Games Trends to Watch in 2022", *Newzoo Insights* blog, 13 January 2022. Available at https://newzoo.com/insights/articles/newzoos-games-trends-to-watch-in-2022-metaverse-game-ip-vr

video clips of LeBron James. The project purportedly raised around US$230 million, although its success may have been helped along by the closure of sports stadiums during the Covid-19 pandemic.

In July 2019, the blockchain voting platform, Socios, tokenized the famous Dota 2 esports team OG, with fan tokens that allowed players to earn OG rewards. It set the stage for eventually enabling esports to tokenize not only players, but entire teams, contracts, merchandise, memberships, and sponsorship deals as assets for a wide range of investors.

That same year, Nike launched its own collectible NFT, Cryptokicks, creating a new asset class in sports collectibles. Adidas, Stock X, and others soon followed suit. Stock X, already a successful platform for communities that bid for alternative assets like limited-edition sneakers, announced its own NFT business model called VaultNFT, which stores the actual physical product in its own warehouse against a blockchain token.[44]

In gaming, new digital tokens are already being created and used in transactions for physical goods and services. 'Play-to-earn' elements are now not only a worldwide phenomenon, but a source of real income that puts food on the tables of thousands of professional players in countries as diverse as Indonesia and Venezuela.

In 2020, during the shutdowns induced by the Covid-19 pandemic, more than 100 families in Cabanatuan City in the Philippines were documented to be earning around US$200 a week by playing Axie Infinity, a dApp created by Sky Mavis, a Vietnamese start-up, on the Ethereum blockchain non-stop.[45] In the game, players "breed, raise, battle and trade" adorable digital critters called Axies.

Two entrepreneurs, Gabby Dizon and Colin Goltra, took things one step further by creating guilds that brought players together to bid and share in the proceeds of gaming, especially when the tokens became increasingly

---

[44] K. T. Smith, "StockX's Move Into NFTS has major implications for the retail industry", *Highsnobiety*, 10 February 2022. Available at https://www.highsnobiety.com/p/stockx-nft/.

[45] L. Callon-Butler, "The NFT Game That Makes Cents for Filipinos During Covid", *CoinDesk*, 26 August 2020. Available at https://www.coindesk.com/markets/2020/08/26/the-nft-game-that-makes-cents-for-filipinos-during-covid/.

expensive. This had the effect of making the individual players as important as the gaming companies in influencing the shape and preferences of the industry. The number of players is now said to be in the tens of thousands.

In this way, blockchain technology has launched new commercial initiatives, such as community-backed sponsorships, tokenized-merchandise sales, and even tokenized contracts, which allow fans, participants, and a whole range of investors to partially co-own the teams or assets created. Such a development carries us right into the potential for the digitalization of investment banking, where esports teams could also tokenize their potential winnings in return for an upfront payment, creating equity in the business, assets, or intellectual property.

Fractionalized contracts, teams, and brands could exist on immutable blockchain ledgers that enable frictionless peer-to-peer transfers, without the need for lawyers, intermediaries, funding rounds, or any public offerings. This also introduces liquidity into esports assets while boosting transparency and community within its ecosystem, developing a parallel universe even as traditional banks protect their own turf with archaic practices.

The proliferation of new technology almost never originates from incumbent, mainstream players. Also, the successful adoption of new technology tends to depend on taking the path of least resistance common to the widest possible audience, in the shortest possible time, on the hottest possible topic.

The fact that all these protocols are being developed in the esports, gambling, and collectibles universe is entirely consistent with how technological advancements generally proliferate before they become mainstream. The metaverse, as a combination of virtual and augmented realities, creates new venues for these interactions to take place – as well as new communities unhindered by borders or geography.

Meanwhile, gamers are quietly transforming finance itself by 'staking' stablecoins such as USD Coin (USDC) and Tether (USDT) and lending miniscule amounts of money on highly technical platforms like ALGO, Yearn, and AGFI. Curiously, in the post-pandemic, intermediary-free world, stakers earn anything between 8-20% annual percentage yields (APY) on their daily trades.

For these reasons, the real-world impact of these games makes all the pilots and 'proof of concepts' (POC) experiments that traditional banks are carrying out in the areas of blockchain and application programming interfaces (APIs) look like too little, too late. Technological applications never proliferate in the rational, organized way that finance professionals imagine they are able to curate.

When the Gutenberg press was invented in 1440, the first subjects to reach widespread circulation were inflammatory religious and revolutionary pamphlets and pornography. The first version of the Gutenberg Bible, which kickstarted the rise of mass-produced printed books, is recorded to have been printed only in 1455, a good 15 years later. More respectable uses of the printing press, such as printing the first scientific journals, the *Journal des sçavans* and the *Philosophical Transactions of the Royal Society*, would only follow in 1665.

These give us an idea of the long gestation process that lies ahead for the gaming industry, personalizing platforms and building networks in ways that will one day become mainstream. More importantly, however, these phenomena all contain aspects of finance. Each token created is worth something in and of itself while also representing something of value to the owner, be it a game collectible, a meme, or a work of art. These transactions set the stage for the personalization of finance in a way that those looking at current financial infrastructures will not be able to understand.

Eventually, everyone and anyone will be able to issue their own tokens for mass consideration, adoption, and commercialization. Just which token, generated from which game and for what value in a networked world is entirely frontier territory, for which we will develop a body of knowledge over many years to come.

CHAPTER 3

The financialization of everything

"Rising prices or wages do not cause inflation; they only report it. They represent an essential form of economic speech, since money is just another form of information."
Walter Wriston

"I can't go back to yesterday, because I was a different person then."
Lewis Carroll, *Alice in Wonderland*

The most dramatic financial trend of our time has been how entire economies have gone from being valued against something as physical and tangible as the price of gold to a mere perception of the value ascribed to an ephemeral asset on any given day.

Financialization refers to the process by which the value of a real asset, such as property, a share, or even physical gold, is increasingly based on a piece of information, data, digital token, an index, or information of any kind, and no longer the asset itself. Financialization is the precursor to personalization because it reduces all kinds of financial assets to mere information that can be transmitted digitally.

In ancient times, financialization was contrived to mitigate risk, where the value of an underlying asset could be either hedged or preserved to create certainty of income for its owners by trading, hedging, or distributing that risk.

At the time, the industry monitored information pertaining to ships and the cargo they carried out on the high seas. This was used to ascertain whether they were coming back with commercial cargo, the profits of which would then be shared between investors. Trading on a Lloyds List in the 1700s was as much about the financialization of information on ships as the online trading of foreign exchange (FX) derivatives is today.

The industrialization of information in the 1980s abetted the financialization of anything that could be reduced to a piece of data. Michael Bloomberg launched the terminals business that still bears his name in 1981, riding on the advent of desktop computers in banks.[46] Within one short decade, thousands of Reuters and Bloomberg terminals were installed in banks and corporate dealing rooms worldwide and connected to each other, effectively allowing users to buying and sell information.

Over time, the financial information industry delved deeper and broader into markets. Reuters launched an equities system in 1987, followed by a commodities system in 1988, in a joint venture with the Chicago Mercantile Exchange. Today, financial information players publish a plethora of indices and benchmarks for financial markets to productize and industrialize their data.

The securities industry moved away from trading in the actual underlying securities of any asset a long time ago, and now trades mostly in derivatives. According to Bloomberg, the number of actual tradable stocks in the US marketplace peaked in 1995. Today there are three times more indexed and mutual funds than there are actual shares to support them.[47]

Today, there are many financialized assets, of which cryptocurrencies, non-fungible tokens (NFTs) and virtual real-estates are only some of many. There are also new virtual marketplaces, where initial coin offerings (ICOs) and other transactions that support the trading of new digital assets will take place.

Understanding why and how information and perception, and not real

---

[46] H. McCracken, "How the Bloomberg Terminal made history – and stays ever relevant", *Fast Company*, 6 October 2015. Available at https://www.fastcompany.com/3051883/the-bloomberg-terminal.

[47] J. Fox, "Mutual Funds Ate the Stock Market. Now ETFs Are Doing It", *Bloomberg View*, 16 May 2017. Available at https://www.bloomberg.com/opinion/articles/2017-05-16/mutual-funds-ate-the-stock-market-now-etfs-are-doing-it

money, property, or even gold, became the real assets in finance today gives us a glimpse into the path of no return that financialization is taking us on.

The financialized corporation

In 2021, the world's gross domestic product (GDP) was US$94 trillion, just shy of US$100 trillion, a milestone in itself that I will discuss later in this book. But according to the International Monetary Fund (IMF), the total value of bonds, stocks, and trading assets was more than US$300 trillion. In addition, the notional amounts of derivatives traded over-the-counter (OTC) and not on any formal exchange rose to US$640 trillion at the end of June 2019.[48] In other words, the size of financialized assets already far exceeds that of the real economy.

The mother of all financialization endeavors is, of course, the massive quantitative easing (QE) and economic stimulus packages that have been pumped into the global economy by almost every major economy since the 2008 US financial crisis.

The US pumped about US$3.7 trillion of QE into its economy between 2008 and 2016. Between 2015 and 2016, the Eurozone pumped in US$1 trillion (€1.1 trillion) in one year alone. China first injected US$100 billion in 2016, since adding more, and under Abenomics, Japan has been pumping US$660 billion (¥60 to ¥70 trillion) into its economy yearly since 2013.

All the same players raked it up further in the wake of the Covid-19 pandemic. In the fiscal year 2021, the US budget deficit hit US$1.7 trillion because of spending on various pandemic-related programs.[49] Other economies are pumping in similarly unfathomable amounts of money, funded through QE.

Mostly, these liquidities pumped into the economy stay as financial

---

[48] "Statistical Release: OTC derivatives statistics at end June 2019", Bank for International Settlement report (2019).

[49] A. Rappeport, "The U.S. budget deficit hit a record $1.7 trillion in the first half of the fiscal year.", *The New York Times*, 12 April 2021. Available at https://www.nytimes.com/2021/04/12/business/united-states-budget-deficit.html.

instruments. They do not go into repairing roads or building bridges or schools or high-speed railways, but are captured by financialized securities with little to no inherent value.

The story of how the US economy became incredibly financialized as an end in itself was captured by Rana Foroohar in her book, *Makers and Takers*.[50] Her key point, echoed by other writers in the UK and Europe, is that only about 15% of all the money in the US financial markets is invested in the real economy. The rest is traded within the closed financial community, generating profit for its own sake.

Eventually, the finance sector accounted for a quarter of all corporate profits in the US, although it created only 4% of American jobs. The part of corporate America that actually manufactures real goods could not match the top-line profitability generated by the finance sector. The US outsourced its manufacturing jobs to other countries, exacerbating the conundrum.

A low interest rate regime made the cost of money cheaper. The largest global corporations bought back their own stock and invested in like financial companies because it gave much better returns than spending on infrastructure or research and development to build their real business.

Corporations like AIG and GE Capital had been just as highly financialized as banks during the 2008 banking crisis. But by the end of 2014, GE Capital had amassed a net investment of over US$360 billion and controlled assets worth about US$500 billion.[51] This made GE Capital the seventh-largest bank in the US, far outstripping its core engineering businesses.

Apple alone had an excess of US$200 billion in cash in January 2020.[52] A lot of that was invested in esoteric investments which had nothing to do with its core business or the real economy. That is how unreal the largest

---

[50] R. Foroohar, *Makers and Takers: The rise of finance and the fall of American business* (New York: Penguin Random House, 2016).

[51] B. Noverini, "Plan to Shrink GE Capital a Needed Shot in Arm for GE", *Morning Star*, 10 April 2015. Available at https://www.morningstar.com/articles/692310/plan-to-shrink-ge-capital-a-needed-shot-in-the-arm-for-ge.

[52] W. Feuer, "Apple now has $207.06 billion in cash on hand, up slightly from last quarter", *CNBC Tech*, 20 Jan 2020. Available at https://www.cnbc.com/2020/01/28/apple-q1-2019-cash-hoard-heres-how-much-cash-apple-has-on-hand.html

corporations have become, with more capital lodged in one company than in 70% of the countries in the world.

Even universities have become huge asset management companies. At US$53.2 billion as of June 2021, Harvard University's endowment fund was larger than the annual GDPs of at least 100 countries.[53] This is on top of the fact that student loans are being securitized and traded, just like mortgages were in the years before the 2008 crisis.

The addition of crypto-assets put corporate America on a no-turning-back journey of becoming increasingly valued on their ephemeral assets instead of their original businesses. US corporations now plough into Bitcoin and other cryptocurrencies as investments that show up on their balance sheets – and shareholders reward them for it. A company called Microstrategy, whose core business had been declining in profitability in recent years, invested fully in Bitcoin and saw its share price rise in a very short time.

The share prices of online payment companies like PayPal and MasterCard went up when they announced that they would process cryptocurrency transactions. When *bona fide* crypto trading corporations like Coinbase became publicly listed, they added a sense of respectability to this new financialized asset class.

Importantly, the process of financialization has been aided and abetted by legislation. To financialize an asset also involves technically removing the underlying asset from its investors. Not many Americans know this, but in the 2013 privatization of Dole Food by its controlling shareholder, it was shown that thanks to the role of the Depository Trust Corporation, shareholders in the US had a beneficial interest in the proceeds, though not necessarily ownership of the actual shares themselves.[54] Technically,

---

[53] S. Goldman, "Harvard's endowment gains are not something to be celebrated", *The Harvard Crimson*, 25 October 2021. Available at https://www.thecrimson.com/article/2021/10/25/goldman-harvard-endowment/.

[54] S. D Solomon, "Dole case illustrates problems in shareholder system", *The New York Times*, 21 March 2017. Available at https://www.nytimes.com/2017/03/21/business/dealbook/dole-case-illustrates-problems-in-shareholder-system.html

the actual shares are held in trust by fund managers, so that shareholders don't even realize they have no recourse from the institution they thought they owned.

In the UK, the application of capital gains tax on shares created the Contract for Difference (CFD) industry, which allows investors to trade in the same shares on the exchange without actually owning them. Today's CFD industry is entirely digital and nearly twice as large as all the stock exchanges of the world combined, but investors don't really care that the underlying asset is just a piece of information – and that they have no recourse against the actual business itself.

This distinction between ownership and beneficiaries turns capital into a living, breathing beast, capable of inflicting real consequences on the real economy without accountability. Huge corporations from China are openly listed in US stock markets through variable interest entities (VIEs) which exclude foreigners from ever having recourse to their business in China, but this hasn't turned investors off.

The volumes of FX, indexed futures, open interests, and plain indices of all kinds – each even more financialized than their predecessors – increased dramatically after 2015, encouraged by the very regulators who thought they were clamping down on unregulated assets.

Outside of stocks, the largest derivatives market in the world today is still interest rate derivatives, because most of the cash flows banks receive (such as loan repayments) or pay out (such as deposits and interbank borrowings) have interest rates which are not matched by their maturities. They tend to 'borrow short' and 'lend long'.

Being able to balance their books is a real-world problem for banking. But as more of the contracts held by banks were slapped with regulation and expensive capital charges, the banking industry looked for easier and cheaper assets, leading to the rise of futures of all kinds.

Putting derivatives on exchanges also transformed the very exchanges that carried them. Exchanges that were pure equity plays lost their attractiveness to those dealing in derivatives. At both the London Stock

Exchange Group (LSEG) and Intercontinental Exchange (ICE), equity now accounts for less than 10% of revenues; they don't represent the real economy any more.

SwapClear, owned by the LSEG, traded US$665 trillion in notional trades – or nearly US$2 trillion a day – in 2016 alone, driven by banks wanting to take counterparty risk off their books. In the same way, ICE bought NYSE Euronext, which owned Liffe, the European derivatives exchange, and introduced data and indices to support exchange-traded funds.

Financialization also transformed the asset management industry. Today, more than 20,000 funds track 18,000 stocks, commoditizing the industry in the UK and the US. According to the data provider Morningstar, exchange-traded passive funds that are not actively managed or invested against any underlying corporate earnings grew 230% globally since the last crisis in 2007, hitting US$6 trillion. Over the same period, actively managed funds still doubled, albeit more slowly, to US$24 trillion.

The impact of all these developments on society is both profound and very simple: the worth of entire economies is now increasingly found in their financialized assets, rather than actual economic activity that generates work and value for society. This phenomenon is not only continuing unabated as the financial industry becomes even more financialized, but is irreversible.

Almost anything can be financialized

After General Electric (GE), a complex conglomerate, perfected the manufacturing of sophisticated machinery, the business of manufacturing itself became highly commoditized. Today, any number of lower-cost manufacturers elsewhere in the world can take on highly sophisticated corporations like GE and produce the same goods faster and more cheaply. Even GE, as a result, moved its manufacturing to these low-cost locations overseas and out of the US.

In the 2010s, GE modified its manufacturing model to focus on data captured from machinery and processes. At the 2013 Fortune Global Forum, its then-CEO, Jeff Immelt, claimed that the company managed 50 million data points generated by US$10 million sensors on US$1 trillion worth of internet-connected industrial equipment.[55] It now aspires to become the largest producer of manufacturing data in the world.

Similarly, Tesla, the electric vehicle company, claimed that as of November 2018, it had amassed 1 billion miles of autopilot data, and that each of its cars processed four terabytes of data every day.[56] Its closest competitor, Waymo, had at that point collected only about 15 million miles. Tesla was in the position to sell, trade, leverage, or produce new products on its data.

More recently, Elon Musk, the CEO of Tesla, declared that the software created to run the vehicle will one day be worth more than the vehicle itself and could be used for a variety of other functions, including robo-taxis that plan and execute routes.[57]

With the onset of 5G technology, quantum computing and the Internet of Things, tons of data will flow out of activities from sports to entertainment to virtual reality, alongside a sea of devices that can be leveraged and monetized en masse. The data created from the networking of primary data generates another layer of information, which could potentially give rise to further industries in themselves.

Theoretically, this proliferation of data increases the ability of economies to absorb even more risk and volatility than they do today. The activities these data underpin can be precisely measured and analyzed. This prepares society to absorb and manage more significant disruptions, and even value and monetize its response to different types of risks. Consequently, risks can be taken off the balance sheets of traditional banks, distributed, and traded

---

[55] H. Clancy, "How GE generates $1b from data", *Fortune*, 10 October 2014. Available at https://fortune.com/2014/10/10/ge-data-robotics-sensors/

[56] G. Paolini, "Tesla, the data company", *CIO*, 28 August 2019. Available at https://www.cio.com/article/3433931/tesla-the-data-company.html.

[57] H. Jin and N. Balu, "Musk's bets on Tesla: human-like robots and self-driving cars", *Reuters*, 27 January 2022. Available at https://www.reuters.com/article/tesla-robots-idCAKBN2K1110.

as assets with far more granularity than at present.

This trend will keep evolving over many years. One day, villagers and farmers could conceivably financialize their next year's harvest estimates based on indices they create, corroborated with open-source information downloaded on their handheld devices over morning coffee. This would in turn reduce the need for traditional credit, which requires actual money.

Technically, just about anything we value can be financialized: a property, a commodity, securities, derivatives, money, energy, time, loyalty points, a bet on a future outcome. The Nasdaq platform, for example, already sells or trades in container space, ticket sales, and loyalty points.

However, it does not necessarily follow that all data will be tradeable. As data becomes prevalent, many industries will go through the process of trying to financialize anything and everything. The list is potentially endless, until over time it becomes easier to distinguish data that is tradable from that which is useless.

An analogy can be drawn to historian Jared Diamond's observation that humans have been able to tame just 14 species of large animals over 100 lbs (45 kg) out of a list of 148.[58] Tigers and lions consume too much energy, and zebras are too nervous compared to horses. Through trial and error, we have tried taming all kinds of animals throughout history, compounded by factors like ease of socialization and their ability to learn from habit – but managed to bring only some to heel. In the same way, out of data's many uses, that which is good to be traded will be distinguished from data that are better suited for other purposes, such as identity verification.

There is no shortage of other examples. Thanks to their long ripening period, a futures market exists for kiwi fruits today. For a brief period in 1636 - 1637, even tulips were reported to have been financialized until they went back to being just the pure, ordinary tulips that the Dutch love. Conversely, mangoes might never be financialized because they are seasonal (liquidity issues) and ripen too quickly.

---

[58] J. Diamond, *Guns, Germs and Steel, The Fate of Human Societies* (New York: W. W. Norton, 1997).

With the advent of 5G and greater bandwidth on telecommunication networks, the information generated by millions of devices interacting with each other will create many opportunities for financialization. Entire economies will start to look different as they shift from trading in goods and services to trading data and analytics on those same goods and services.

As the world becomes increasingly networked, many asset classes can be assembled and disassembled between interested parties. The trades themselves can be conducted personally between individuals or communities of individuals, without requiring wholesale intermediaries.

Industries that were previously put on the backburner, especially peer-to-peer lending, will get a new lease of life because the parties will not be exchanging just loans but a whole range of data, strengthening trust and interactions in the process.

At one level, fads like buy-now-pay-later (BNPL) and stock trading platforms like Robinhood are merely digitizing businesses that already exist in analog forms. But when the element of community data is added, they can potentially begin to look like whole new businesses that did not exist before. However, the short-term mindedness of the new players in these areas makes it unlikely that these new business models will come to life any time soon.

Mobile devices have helped facilitate these new platforms, but device independence will take them to a whole new level. Today, about 45% of the gaming industry revenue described in Chapter 2 is already generated on mobile devices.[59] A game like mixed martial arts (MMA) can bring together theater, sports, gymnasiums, video games, personal equipment, social media, and merchandising entire lifestyle and entertainment ecosystems.

If such an industry was loaded on a multi-device platform, the element of community created, with individuals interacting with each other in real time, would turbo-charge augmented reality and make it a practical and economically useful activity beyond the games it is used for today. Finance

---

[59] O. Kaplan, "Mobile gaming is a $65 billion global business, and investors are buying in", *Techcrunch*, 22 August 2019. Available at https://techcrunch.com/2019/08/22/mobile-gaming-mints-money/.

can no longer function successfully as independent products that exist outside these and other new ecosystems to come.

Say goodbye to the real economy

As I write this, the world is still nursing its wounds from the Covid-19 pandemic. Even so, Morgan Stanley has estimated that the combined global GDP will surpass US$100 trillion in 2022 or shortly thereafter, subject to the vagaries of the global economy.[60]

Much of the GDP growth in the past two years has been on the back of sovereign debt generated by leading countries. The US alone currently has a national debt of US$27 trillion against an annual GDP of US$20 trillion. Globally, government debt runs to about US$60 trillion today and comprises about 70% of the world's GDP. Debt has now become the economy.

At the same time, the application of digital technologies is imposing dramatic deflationary pressures on the global economy. The vast majority of industries are being defined by their propensity to make things cheaper, faster, and closer to their users. Both these forces are transforming how wealth will be created and distributed in the future.

When some analysts believe that the US economy alone could be worth a staggering US$45 trillion by 2045, they are almost talking about a new country, defined by a debt-fueled, technology-powered economy, and driven by the value created by a network of both digital and intangible assets.

In 2013, the US Bureau of Economic Analysis (BEA) redefined the way the US calculated its GDP. It added intangibles from the digital economy, such as royalties from the entertainment industry, software, and research and development assets, amongst others, to its new definition of assets.[61]

---

[60] "2022 Global Macro Outlook: Growth Despite Inflation", report by Morgan Stanley (accessed December 2021). Available at https://www.morganstanley.com/ideas/global-macro-economy-outlook-2022.

[61] D. J. Fixler, R. Greenaway-McGrevy, and B. Grimm, "The Revisions to GDP, GDI, and Their Major Components", US Bureau of Economic Analysis report, 20 August 2014. Available at https://apps.bea.gov/scb/pdf/2014/08%20August/0814_revisions_to_gdp_gdi_and_their_major_components.pdf

On top of this, highly financialized exports such as financial markets and breakthrough technologies also now feature prominently in the US' GDP. The largest companies on its stock markets are futuristic technologies that don't yet generate the revenue required to support their stock prices – although, again, foreigners continue to plough into them.

Economists Jonathan Haskel and Stian Westlake have argued that the definition of capital itself has to be restated.[62] Similarly, in a piece in the *New York Times*, the economist Martin Feldstein was quoted as suggesting that with the shift towards an information-based economy, traditional measures of output needed to be updated.[63] The crashing prices of traditional goods and services reflected that the economy was not actually shrinking, but taking on a new form.

When perception becomes reality

The first impact of financialization lies in how the value of assets are determined. There was a time when the value of a country's financial resources was measured against the amount of gold it carried. As financialization gathers momentum, the value of sovereign assets is also becoming more ephemeral, determined by nothing more than mere perception.

The UK, as an economy, carries more debt as a percentage of its GDP than Greece, Italy, Portugal, or Spain. But it is the *perception* of its creditworthiness, its ability to meet the financial commitments, that keeps it going as an investable economy, while the Mediterranean states are easily embroiled in financial crises. If that perception is lost, it will not matter what the actual balance sheet of the UK looks like.

In 2011, when the US' own rating agencies downgraded its creditworthiness, the world's investor community responded hurriedly by

---

[62] J. Haskel and S. Westlake, *Capitalism without capital: The rise of the intangible economy* (Princeton, New Jersey: Princeton University Press, 2018).

[63] P. Cohen, "The Economic Growth That Experts Can't Count", *The New York Times*, 6 February 2017. Available at https://www.nytimes.com/2017/02/06/business/economy/what-is-gdp-economy-alternative-measure.html.

moving their investments into – what else – US Treasury bonds. It was a bizarre episode that underscored just how the perception of the US economy as a bastion of financial stability continues to endure, despite all evidence to the contrary.

The price-earnings (P/E) ratio of Tesla, the top-performing stock on the financial market in August 2020, was 1,030 times the actual book value of the business.[64] Technology disruptor companies like Tesla can boldly proclaim that they will not be profitable for a long time, and still be valued over and above those that are. Once the perception of value is established, the actual balance sheet ceases to matter.

Even as I complete this book, US corporations are being rewarded by their shareholders for falling, herd-like, into buying cryptocurrencies as an investment, purporting to support cryptocurrency payments, or playing the crypto-field in one way or another.

Companies like Microstrategy are shamelessly transformed into investor darlings the moment holding crypto-assets became part of its core business. Payment companies like PayPal, Visa, and MasterCard have already boosted their share prices by demonstrating their acceptance of cryptocurrency payments.

It is only a matter of time before banks copy their corporate cousins. At the time of writing, several US banks, such as Signature Bank and Silvergate Bank, provide payment services for cryptocurrency trading. They maintain that they are not themselves invested in cryptocurrencies, at least for now, but this perception gets translated into their share prices nonetheless.

Perception has a price, and it is not cheap. Cristiano Ronaldo, the Portuguese football player, once removed two Coca-Cola bottles sitting in front of him at a press conference table and replaced them with a bottle of water. He did not say a word. The incident reportedly caused Coca-Cola's share price to crash US$4 billion overnight, going from US$56.1 billion

---

[64] M. Fox, "Tesla just surpassed Walmart in market value. Here are the 8 remaining S&P 500 companies worth more than Tesla", *Business Insider*, 21 August 2020. Available at https://markets.businessinsider.com/news/stocks/tesla-surpasses-walmart-market-value-most-valued-sp500-us-companies-2020-8-1029524035#.

before stabilizing at US$55.2 billion the next day.[65]

Today, shareholder value is increasingly based on investors' impressions of companies' commitment to a whole series of values, including taking action on climate change, the environment, and corporate social responsibility. And yet, even those kinds of tangible commitment collapse when we consider the rise of meme stocks, driven by nothing more than a mere puff.

The power of perception in the networked world today cannot be underestimated. It can even create entirely new territories out of thin air, as was the case with the Islamic State of Iraq and the Levant/Syria (ISIS). In the early 2010s, Islamic militants recruited thousands of gullible young people from around the world to travel and become combatants themselves, conquering territories in the regions between Syria, Jordan, and the Kurdish Republic to form a rogue quasi-state. In doing so, ISIS worked the internet as any regular marketing team would to global effect..

In the same way, the valuation of cryptocurrencies was driven by the power of mere belief in a networked world, taking the industry to a whole new level and displacing the price of physical gold in the process. Bear in mind that this was between participants in a network who didn't belong to any regulated marketplace, dealing with assets with no underlying value except that which the participants gave it.

The main driver of perception in the digital world is the network effect. It is also the result of more data points. Both technologies enable us to construct a perception of realities that did not exist before.

We have arrived at a point where lenders, in general, are able and willing to take lifestyles, behavior, personal preferences, supply chains, and a whole range of nebulous insights into account when making their assessments. Behavioral and scenario scoring is already making traditional credit scoring models look – well – industrial-age.

The combination of so much more real information available on the

---

[65] P. Villegas, "Cristiano Ronaldo snubbed Coca-Cola. The company's market value fell $4 billion.", *The Washington Post*, 16 June 2021. Available at https://www.washingtonpost.com/sports/2021/06/16/cristiano-ronaldo-coca-cola/.

individual – from where they shopped this morning on the way to work or how many hours they spend on leisure – coupled with all sorts of public and private data gives the bank patterns from which it can determine their creditworthiness. Such data may give the impression of much more nuanced insights into a person, but it is still, fundamentally, an impression.

Managing perception is a wild ride. We now live in a world where the Spanish hit song *Macarena* or the infectious Korean *Gangnam Style* can spread like wildfire and capture the shared imagination of many, regardless of culture, nationality, or age, for a short time and then disappear as mysteriously as they surfaced. What pop culture fads like these demonstrate is that perception is based on the lowest common denominator that can be shared across cultures and communities that have nothing to do with each other.

The same phenomenon can be seen today in how some cryptocurrencies surge in value and then crash on the strength of a mere tweet by celebrities like Kim Kardashian or Elon Musk. Endorsements from such personalities can capture the popular imagination and ride out periods of extreme volatility, until a stable community forms around the subject matter over time.

In a world where value is relative, perception is a strange friend. The more intangible an asset, the more its value is driven by nothing more than perception. We are still in the early days of the networked economy. Every single episode adds to our understanding of the elements that define it. Regulators can only sit watching helplessly from the sidelines until a core body of knowledge is distilled over time, such that they can step in.

This phenomenon has profound implications for civilization as a whole and not just finance. The world will certainly settle into new patterns of behavior as it evolves. We have a long way ahead of us in learning the patterns that will arise and the full impact of the network effect on humanity – the topic to which we shall turn to next.

CHAPTER 4

Rise of the rebels

"We are at that very point in time where a 400-year-old age is dying and another is struggling to be born."
Dee Hock, founder, Visa International

"Never bet against dedicated people."
Nuseir Yassin, vlogger, Nas Daily

When ordinary people do what institutions used to, on account of enjoying better access to information and data and becoming organized enough to match those institutions themselves, we have the setting for a long-drawn revolution.

It's not that this hasn't happened before. The invention of the printing press in 1450, for example, set in motion a whole series of overhauls in the Church, the sciences, and eventually European civilization as a whole.

Fast forward to early January 2021, when retail investors furiously networking with each other on messaging platforms appeared to have brought down several Wall Street institutional investors who were habitually shorting the market. Users on the Reddit discussion board r/wallstreetbets believed they were able to dismantle the plans of institutional investors setting out to short-sell the stocks of companies like Gamestoppers, AMC Entertainment, Express, and Koss listed on Wall Street.

A subsequent report by the Securities Exchange Commission (SEC) later that same year revealed that the institutional investors had mostly exited their short positions. The stock prices had indeed been dramatically pushed up by the retail investors themselves, who eventually got their profits burned.[66]

This episode is just one of many in the early days of an increasingly networked world, inundated by a deluge of data, information, and knowledge. But without new institutions to moderate the process of originating, verifying, and delivering information, the effect is wild fluctuations in prices and sentiments.

Similar fluctuations are evident in the price of cryptocurrencies. As I have said in earlier chapters, the network effect is still in its formative days. As it builds, we will start to see patterns, like we do in stock markets, but they will be fundamentally different. We must avoid the temptation of seeing traditional markets and the network effect through the same lens.

In the case of the 'Reddit revolution', the network effect showed us how it renders the distinction between valid influencers and unverified conjecture. For now, the principal institutional players still dominate the market, but this will evolve as the power of individual participants increases.

However, while individual participants in a networked world have the potential to contribute data and knowledge, the network still lacks the infrastructure to process these coherently – for now. It is only a matter of time before retail participation is captured in the ecosystem and contributes to the overall liquidity in the network.

Market infrastructure is still overwhelmingly built for institutional investors, which is why the initial assumption that the 'Reddit revolution' upended the institutional players was subsequently found to be mistaken. The irony was that retail investors were shown to be just as capable of the collusion, manipulation, and other acts they were accusing institutional investors of (although their organizational prowess still had quite some way to go).

The power of the individual to participate in and affect markets has been growing for some time now. Just over a decade ago, Navinder Singh Sarao,

---

[66] "Staff Report on Equity and Options Market Structure Conditions in Early 2021", US Securities and Exchange Commission report, 14 October 2021. Available at https://www.sec.gov/files/staff-report-equity-options-market-struction-conditions-early-2021.pdf.

trading from his father's humble home outside London, was taking bets on the other side of the trade from institutional fund managers.[67]

He generated about US$50 million in income using a readily available online high-frequency trading system, but was able to short an entire market across the pond in the US. In doing so, he allegedly caused the 'flash crash' of 6 May 2010.

The US and UK regulators were caught flat-footed in the Navinder episode. They were found wanting again when lay investors banded together on Reddit in 2021. The US regulator only had wire fraud legislation dating back to 1872 and the Dodd-Frank Act with which to go after the home-based traders, leading one analyst to proclaim that "ETFs are a digital-age technology governed by Depression-era legislation".[68]

The US Commodity Futures Modernization Act of 2000 and the Futures Trading Practices Act of 1992 started this journey towards a networked economy by liberating trading from the constraints of regulation.[69] They allowed individuals to participate in the market, but controls were not in place to manage the new forms of malfeasance these liberalizations also made possible.

The disciplines required to tame the networked age are being formulated not just with technology, but in the ways that individuals, societies, and institutions will organize themselves in the future.

The mass amateurization of finance

On 25 August 1991, Linus Torvalds, a Finnish programmer working in his bedroom in Portland, Oregon, shared the full source code of an

---

[67] S. Brush and L. Fortado, "How a Mystery Trader With an Algorithm May Have Caused the Flash Crash", *Bloomberg*, 22 April 2015. Available at https://www.bloomberg.com/news/articles/2015-04-22/mystery-trader-armed-with-algorithms-rewrites-flash-crash-story.

[68] A. I Weinberg, "Should You Fear the ETF?", *The Wall Street Journal*, 6 April 2015. Available at https://www.wsj.com/articles/should-you-fear-the-etf-1449457201..

[69] R. Cooper, "US has itself to blame for flash crash trading", letter published in *The Guardian*, 24 April 2015. Available at https://www.theguardian.com/business/2015/apr/24/us-has-itself-to-blame-for-flash-crash-trading.

operating system with his developer friends, all of whom were connected to each other online. The operating system – Linux – eventually came to be named after him.

This set off a movement where application development began to move out of the large technology companies. The best programmers were free to work independently on multiple projects according to their preferences, improving the quality of work and bringing the cost of development crashing down.

By 1998, the open-source movement was immortalized in the iconic essay, *The Cathedral and the Bazaar,* by computer programmer Eric Raymond. The article and subsequent online book outlined a world where the 'cathedral model' of the past involved the source code of a computer program being developed as part of a large software company's assets. The 'bazaar', by contrast, was where a program's code could be developed collaboratively, in full view of the entire community, who could cut, copy, paste, and modify it at will.

This open-platform approach stood in contrast to the proprietary approaches of software giants like IBM, Unisys, and Microsoft. The freelancers and independent coders who used Torvald's Linux eventually grew in numbers and ganged up against the established names. The free-for-all was open to anyone, including the established institutions that tried to push back against this decadence.

In the hands of Steve Ballmer's Microsoft, an operating system like Linux would have produced one application at a time, but with thousands of users pitching in, working collaboratively resulted in the development of thousands of applications for all kinds of different user needs around the world.

Much later, several academics, including Yochai Benkler, Charles Leadbeater, Clay Shirky, and a whole string of business writers, predicted that the economy would increasingly become a participatory one. In particular, Clay Shirky introduced the concept of 'mass amateurization', or technology that turns consumers into producers, who then inadvertently contribute to an enterprise's manufacturing process. In *Here Comes Everybody: The Power of Organizing without Organization*, he points out that institutions do not need as many full-time employees to manufacture their so-called content in the digital age.[70]

Using the example of the now ancient photo-sharing platform, Flickr, Shirky showed how information that used to be generated at high costs by one institution in a hierarchical structure was now being produced by countless volunteers and tagged automatically, so that a much larger repository needed little managing.

It also inspired other areas where new content could be generated collaboratively. Wikipedia, the world's largest text-based encyclopedia, is run by thousands of volunteers who feed, edit, and protect the integrity of its content. The entire blogosphere itself is an example of mass amateur participation in its own right.

Similarly, otherwise old-fashioned companies like Havens Hallmark, the Oxford English Dictionary and the fast-moving consumer goods conglomerate Procter & Gamble (P&G) have been pivoting towards this model.

The upshot of this is that products are now designed in conjunction with their users. The mountain bike is often held up as a product that was designed collaboratively, with users volunteering what they would like to see in a bike.[71] As the academic Yochai Benkler writes, all businesses will eventually have to embrace the economics of shared knowledge and community.[72]

The way cutting-edge companies build and innovate is changing as well. The writer Don Tapscott has pointed out that P&G already had 7,500 very expensive scientists on its payroll. The only way to build its research and development capability without adding any more costs was to start a P&G Innocentive network.

---

[70] C. Shirky, *Here Comes Everybody: The Power of Organizing Without Organizations* (New York: Penguin Press, 2008).

[71] G. Bhalla, *Collaboration and Co-Creation: New Platforms for Marketing and Innovation* (New York: Springer, 2011).

[72] Y. Benkler, *The Wealth of Networks: How Social Production Transforms Markets and Freedom* (New Haven, Connecticut: Yale University Press, 2006).

The network eventually sourced 50% of the pool of scientists it required in a purely voluntary and collaborative ecosystem.[73] This approach enabled access to the long tail of outstanding outlier researchers who were either too expensive to hire or did not want to work for any one organization, but whose expertise companies like P&G desperately needed.

In 2005, Torvalds initiated another genius to continue dismantling the institutionalized approach to software development. He made Git, the code-hosting website, into a completely open-source 'version control system' available for free, not aligned to any vendor. Git and its peers, such as Redhat, enabled changes to a source code by multiple programmers working simultaneously to be attributed, tracked, and kept clean. The result transformed coding and collaboration in software development.[74]

The concept also set the stage for the attribution, tracking, and housekeeping of all kinds of software-like shared coding platforms, such as algorithms, application programmable interfaces (APIs), and blockchains.

Blockchain technology is also moving down a similar path of hosting applications that can be simultaneously edited and personalized, just like Linux-based applications can with Git. The experience with Torrent, the forerunner of blockchain, suggests that ordinary people want the right to edit blockchains to produce their own variations of products. On the blockchain, every user is an API developer.

When we speak of 'users' in the networked world, we no longer mean just customers or buyers, but an entire ecosystem of users, developers, partners, and collaborators who collectively contribute to the development and use of digital information and create value out of it together. Shared platforms are where communities of user-coders develop content collaboratively.

Mantra DAO, one of the 3000 Ethereum-based community-governed decentralized autonomous organization (DAO) tokens, has a suite of multi-

---

[73] A. Tapscott and D. Tapscott, *The Blockchain Revolution: How the Technology Behind Bitcoin is Changing Money, Business, and the World* (Toronto: Penguin, 2016).

[74] S. Chacon and B. Straub, *Pro Git, 2nd Edition* (Apress, under Creative Commons license, 2014). Available at https://git-scm.com/book/en/v2.

asset lending products called ZenInterest, with features that include swapping and fundraising with staking. The community wants the ability to define what finance means to them at every step of the way – what its products are, how they should be packaged and delivered, and when and where they are used.

The decentralized finance (DeFi) model is clearly trending towards allowing anyone to share a ledger and simultaneously create, edit, contribute, issue, or trade in a financial product, just like how Git enables Linux coders to build on each others' work. It is decentralized because no intermediary is required to broker the transaction. Buyer and seller meet each other directly on the platform, which has serious repercussions for the future roles of intermediary banks, agents, and other brokers.

Thirteen years after the launch of Linux, in 2004, Andy Jassy launched Elastic Compute Cloud, which was later rebranded as Amazon Web Services (AWS) in 2006. The development brought collaboration to a new level, creating an ecosystem where computing activities could be organized, shared, and personalized over the cloud.

The migration of technology companies towards an open-source work model is now threatening to transform the finance industry. In the bad old days of banking technology, just before open platforms and the cloud came into being, companies like FIS, one of the world's largest and earliest proprietary core banking system vendors, were quietly making more money charging banks just to maintain their existing systems than they spent on improving them.

The advent of cloud-based systems delivering complex core banking solutions, such as Avaloq, Mambu, and Thought Machine, started eroding the hold that the established vendors have held on the industry. The traditional so-called 'enterprise software' in finance from vendors like Sungard, Temenos and Oracle Financial have started being built on collaborative open-source platforms, some in the cloud.

Today, banks and insurance companies work by populating platforms with their own products, obliterating any user-generated content. The next frontier is to create platforms on which customers, even if non-professionals, can voluntarily participate and design applications themselves that are specific to their personal needs.

To be clear, mass amateurization is not the same as creating content platforms for marketing purposes. In Spain, Santander Bank's "Prosperity" campaign, which curated user-generated videos ,was actually a heavily edited marketing campaign to sell products that the bank had already designed.

BCG, the consulting firm, estimates that the standalone retail media industry, characterized by extensive customer interaction and deep first-party data, is already generating US$100 billion in income.[75] Retailers create loyalty through the 'personalization of retail'.

Some of the challenger banks in the UK, such as Atom, Mondo, and Starling Bank, have gone half the way in asking customers to talk to them about their needs and wants. Their problem is that despite all the data they have on customers, they still push the same old products. To paraphrase the immortal words of the late Douglas Adams, author of *The Hitchhiker's Guide to the Galaxy,* to these banks, no matter the question, the answer will always be 42.

Mass amateurization must always be distinguished from institution-driven endeavors. It may be helpful to consider a few more examples. Building products around Fitbit data, for example, is also not mass amateurization because these do not (as yet) result in shared products or networked games that customers can use collectively in a shared ecosystem.

By contrast, Italy's Neo and the US-based Shift collect data from multiple points that become the source of new, albeit more defensive, products, such as insuring homes and tracking claim fraud. In China, insuretech companies like Zhong An, Tencent's WeSure, Alipay's Xiang Hubao, and PingAn's HealthConnect potentially turn customers' transaction data into instant, tailored products at the point of need.

We will eventually reach a stage where digital banks' new products will

---

[75] L. Wiener, L. Kelman, S. Fisher, and M. Abraham, "The $100 Billion Media Opportunity for Retailers", *Boston Consulting Group* blog, 19 May 2021. Available at https://www.bcg.com/publications/2021/how-to-compete-in-retail-media.

be akin to Waze, the crowdsourced mapping platform that reports on traffic conditions through user-generated contributions. In terms of platforms for 'rebels' to collaborate, there is no place where this is more possible than in APIs, the topic to which we now must turn.

The hyper-personalization of APIs

The advent of application programmable interfaces (APIs) should have democratized finance and put power in users' hands, but it did not. It should have empowered end-users to develop and use their own APIs, but this did not happen. When the current era of APIs in finance is finally over, history will show just how much time the finance industry squandered by simply using APIs to produce interfaces to push their own products, instead of steering the industry towards its user-driven phase.

The API platform business model transformed other industries entirely. Companies like Salesforce, which started in the good old days of standalone software, reportedly generates 50% of its revenue through APIs. eBay allegedly clocks in at nearly 60%, and Expedia a whopping 90%.[76] These companies are now leaders in allowing their users to produce their own interfaces for their applications. The finance industry, by contrast, treated APIs as mere cost-management technology.

APIs were meant to be so open, simple, and magical that anyone would be able to use them to build any function they fancied. Even kids today already develop their own APIs on gaming platforms on a whim – but no such thing happens in finance. The industry's excuse? APIs have to be very secure, which effectively excluded partners who could have helped them grow access to their core applications. The finance industry largely missed out the meaning and promise of APIs.

The writer Yochai Benkler introduced the concept of 'hyper-personalization', where the end-user is so intimately involved in the

---

[76] B. Iyer and M. Subramaniam, "The Strategic Value of APIs", *Harvard Business Review*, 7 January 2015. Available at https://hbr.org/2015/01/the-strategic-value-of-apis.

production process that they are able to edit the final deliverable to meet their needs exactly. Today, we talk about individuals being able to do their own coding, but even that will be made much easier when individuals are not even required to do any actual coding. Customers want access to the source code to be able to personalize the service they want very quickly.

The line between API developers and users is already blurred. Already, Microsoft Windows, SAP, Salesforce, Facebook, and Google are but some of the many players that offer API kits to build a developer dependency on their respective platforms. Contentful, a third-party API platform, makes its software development kits (SDKs) available on GitHub so that developers can experiment as they please. The real benefits of this are speed, creativity, and personalization of the benefits of the network effect.

It is in the virtual reality gaming industry where APIs have been taken into a whole new level. Platforms like Unity provide toolsets for developers and users alike to create their own augmented realities in games like Minecraft. According to one account, the company provides toolsets (read APIs) that powers millions of games, including 71% of the top 1000 mobile games and half of all console and PC games.

There are literally billions of players and 4.5 billion devices with Unity powered software, where users, including children, can create their own realities and play in them.[77] The big deal is that the games on Unity platforms, such as Minecraft, can now be created using blockchain technology via a partner software development toolkit called Enjin.

The open-ended culture in which games are built from these APIs is diametrically different from the way APIs are developed in business today. Many cloud platforms, like Amazon Partner Network and AliCloud, are powerful communities that build on themselves, sharing content and coding tied intimately to their end-users' needs.

This phenomenon is supported by free, collaborative source codes

---

[77] J. Koetsier, "With Billions of People and Millions of Apps, Can Unity Create The Metaverse?", *Forbes*, 7 December 2021. Available at https://www.forbes.com/sites/johnkoetsier/2021/12/07/with-billions-of-people-and-millions-of-apps-can-unity-create-the-metaverse/?sh=4459fdbc6b8c.

that have already transformed the software industry from the inside out. Power in application development has been moving from the institutions to developers and now, to the end-users.

In finance, Venmo, the US payments platform, started life as an API in 2009 until PayPal acquired it in 2013. It then became the *de facto* debit account payment platform in the US. Venmo tried to build its own communities of texting and social media users outside the realm of finance to attract APIs to plug into its networks. Unfortunately, its hand forced by both regulation and its new owners, Venmo appears to have given up the idea of being an API after its acquisition.

Today, independent API developers can plug into companies such as Stripe and Plaid for volume discounts on pooled payment connectivity, Twilio for volume discounts on telephony, Factual for location-based data, and Algolia for developing creative applications.

The network effect of individual APIs interacting with and feeding off each other is still unexplored. Today, each API player interacts with their host banks as a standalone technology company commissioned to solve a very specific technology problem. Many regulators hold back their incumbent banks from the sheer synergies that might be reaped from allowing API developers to collaborate.

Underlying this behavior is the belief that data held by traditional financial institutions is more valuable than the data that sits outside these institutions, and as such must be protected at all costs. Bank technology heads understand the SaaS model (software as a service) mindset, but are held ransom by legacy technology architectures.

For the most part, banks treated their API partners very poorly, more as patch solution vendors to help them resolve legacy issues on their existing mainframe computers rather than partners to build new ecosystems external to the bank. Many financial institutions cite cost savings as the key motivation for their API projects but still develop everything in-house.

In 2017, the Monetary Authority of Singapore (MAS) published 150 projects in its original API Playbook List. It read like a list of repair works for local banks' legacy problems that employees had been unable to solve.

The MAS project obviously started on the myopic assumption that APIs' purpose in financial services was to support banks and all their wrinkles, instead of inventing the future. The developers who responded to MAS' original list did not stand a chance of being profitable in any meaningful way. It was a defensive strategy that history will judge as a monumental waste of time.

In countries with more enlightened regulators, APIs were meant to be independent service providers for end-users, drawing financial data from banks on customers' behalf. The UK's Open Banking Working Group's guidelines on the use of APIs in finance and the EU's Payment Services Directive (PSD) mandating that the data belongs to the customer were enlightened approaches.

When Open Banking legislation was introduced in the UK, preliminary survey results showed that bank customers still trusted traditional banks more than APIs. The APIs were projecting themselves as aggregators of bank information, instead of putting finance firmly in the user's hands. These legislative innovations turned out to be slightly ahead of their time. They will make absolute sense when data belongs to users.

In most other markets, the finance industry reduced their API vendors to mere technology companies selling software back to the powerful incumbents. Today, bank APIs spend unnecessary time retagging historical data, reconstructing siloed systems, and creating obsolete links before they are even commissioned. The relentless effort of platforms like Google to make the locations of their data files virtual, rather than picked up from specific servers located in any one physical location, runs counter to attempts to contextualize data.

The monolithic enterprise infrastructure and applications that have powered big businesses will eventually give way to distributed and modular alternatives. Small, independent, and reusable microservices can be easily assembled into more complex applications at will by users. All these developments inch us towards greater personalization of finance, where users will be at the wheel.

Outside of finance, there are many examples of companies which have benefited from opening up their APIs to third-party vendors, something financial institutions still find unthinkable. Houzz, an interior design and decoration company, predicates its API infrastructure on the premise that one cannot buy all of the creativity in the design world.

The path to success in this new collaborative model lies in externalizing business entirely and putting the power of APIs, blockchains, and any collaborative technologies firmly in users' hands, without trying to dictate outcomes for institutions.

Crypto's WiFi moment

The wonder of cryptocurrencies is not that their values can suddenly spike by thousands of dollars, but that anyone can build and launch one for any whimsical purpose. The world will have millions of cryptocurrencies. The next step for blockchain technology, which is based on cryptocurrencies, is to be able to connect cryptocurrencies with each other.

When that happens, this will, in effect, be akin to re-creating the shared platforms we see on the internet today, such as Wikipedia and social media, except that these will be controlled by participants and not by software sitting on a platform. It will cause a rethink of all the business models that have been built on the internet in the past 50 years.

Charles Hoskinson, a co-founder of Ethereum, the world's largest decentralized blockchain platform (who went on to found its competitor Cardano, the so-called "Ethereum killer"), has said there will be an "internet of blockchains". Similarly, the technology entrepreneur and venture capitalist Roger Lee has spoken of a "Netscape moment," where it will be possible to search for just about anything on blockchain networks just like we did in the early days of the internet.

In a recent interview, Hoskinson commented that all cryptocurrencies are infrastructure.[78] In his view, Polkadot was a 'layer zero' protocol, Ethereum a 'layer one' protocol and so on; in other words, they all build on each other to create a blockchain universe that is secure, scalable, and remains decentralized, out of the reach of big business. This enables cryptocurrencies to operate like a WiFi network between themselves.

Such a trend will usher in a new era in the way areas such as APIs will function when they are openly interoperable with each other. As discussed in the previous section, while some of the largest technology businesses incorporated APIs as partners to extend the use of their own applications, financial institutions reduced APIs to point solutions to solve legacy problems in their respective organizations.

The universe of APIs in the blockchain-era today already makes them interoperable, but in a cumbersome way. 'API mashup' protocols enable interoperability between blockchains outside the purview of large businesses. Today we already see cryptocurrencies such as Cardano, Solana, Polkadot, and Avalanche creating features that enable them to draw from each other.

Wanchain, which houses all sorts of digital assets on one blockchain, claims to be the world's first wide-area network for blockchains to be interoperable. The Cosmos blockchain, described as "one network many chains", is yet another interoperability project.

Online casinos that use digital tokens, including converting cryptocurrencies into tokenized chips, are routinely interoperable today. Some cryptocurrency casinos have taken things a step further and tokenized their profits, allowing investors to purchase tokens representing a fraction of the revenue generated by the platform. A fully player-owned casino is already very possible, from which we might one day see a player-owned stock-market and so on.

Crypto-based assets are also being 'forked' to support a wide range

---

[78] C. Shumba, "Cardano founder Charles Hoskinson says crypto world needs 'that wifi moment' - where users can work with any blockchain seamlessly - more than it needs a dominant network", *Business Insider*, 14 September 2021. Available at https://news.yahoo.com/cardano-founder-charles-hoskinson-says-070725626.html?fr=sycsrp_catchall.

of different ecosystems in trade, supply chains, inventory management, medicine, airline ticketing, government-issued identity programs, and a whole range of industries where the identities and integrity of transactions are immutable, but interoperability remains important.

All these developments are critical to the personalization of global finance, where literally anyone can issue a currency of their own but make it available to be transacted ubiquitously on any other platform in the world. The discipline, mores, culture, and patterns that will determine which crypto asset will survive and which will fail is frontier science. The collapse of the algorithm-defined cryptocurrency, Luna, in 2022 is just one early lesson of many more to come that will add to this knowledge.

To try and reign in the evolution of cryptocurrencies as a media-fed phenomenon is to miss the point of how they are evolving as a basic infrastructure of the networked age. The ways in which crypto-based platforms are creating interoperability while retaining the ability to respond to unique opportunities is not just a technology phenomenon, but a social and knowledge one as well. It is reminiscent of the ways in which the world's religions proliferated in their early days.

The proliferation of religions involved the sharing, disseminating, and forking of ideas. In fact, it is possible to identify the specific individuals who drove specific initiatives, which were subsequently interpreted differently by others. In Christianity, the message of Jesus Christ was 'amplified' first by the apostle Paul and later by Martin Luther, John Wesley, and leaders of more modern denominations like the Pentecostals and the Mormons. Islam has the Sunni and Shiite branches, driven by different personalities.

Without belaboring the point, all major religions eventually give rise to sects and denominations that appear to be in conflict with each other, but are often just different ways of responding to different realities. Underlying all religions is a layer of 'interoperability' that enables us to retain our personal choices and yet be able to live alongside each other. It is symptomatic of the way in which ideas and knowledge have evolved throughout human civilization.

Bewildered global banks have been playing both sides of the fence in the hope of staying in the game. J.P. Morgan, for example, has its own blockchain-based exchange called Onyx in the US which trades using its own JPM digital coin, while it collaborates with banks in the Far East on another cross-border payment platform called Partior. Its own Baton System competes with similar players like Ripple, which has its own token called digital XRP. In both cases, their overlapping users are financial institutions throwing darts in the dark, but they miss the point that cryptocurrencies are neither designed around them nor with them in control.

These legacy institutions need to realize that we now live in a world where the network of individuals will replace institutions as we know them: without the form, but with all the substance we see in the latter today. The rise of the rebels will result in a fundamental shift in the way that society is organized. The rebels will eventually gentrify, and as this happens, finance will become a personalized infrastructure.

Still, the biggest detractors of the wifi effect of the crypto model of the world are those who are still building the platform version where all the social media and online transaction applications are run. The platform players argue that cryptos and blockchain-based models are not able to incorporate external data without there being an intermediary involved in scrubbing, entering, and validating data before it is fed into the application's protocols. They call this the Oracle problem.

The detractors claim that the Oracle problem invalidates the very reason that cryptos exist, to remove the role of intermediaries. It can be argued that it is precisely in finance, where all information and assets are digital, that this problem would not exist. In fact, in the derivatives world, it sets the stage for the creation of new asset classes.

As we will discuss in the next chapter, the institutions that we know today are undergoing a very different metamorphosis, devoid of the revolutions already under way, but we need to understand their course to be able to construct the overall tale.

CHAPTER 5

The agents of change

"Our crisis was largely a failure of imagination. Every crisis is."
Tim Geithner

"Not all who wander are lost."
Gandalf, *The Lord of the Rings*

It is a basic tenet of innovation that the most significant transformations in human civilization have never taken place in normal times, let alone those of abundance, but in periods of extreme distress.

Entities, be they individuals, corporations, or countries, do not change unless they have to. Every person, company, industry, or country does what it does best until someone else manages to do it better. Kodak film, the cable TV industry, and even the US as a country actually moved from one sputnik moment to the next forcibly, often out of dire circumstances or perceived threats.

Contrary to popular belief, the US – which is often seen as a champion of innovation – is often one of the very last countries to fully embrace the very technologies invented on its shores. The nature of its viciously capitalistic society is such that it extracts all value out of existing capital investments before it is ready to move on to the next.

Often, the US sits on a lot of legacy technologies and infrastructure until they are fully amortized financially, structurally, and even socially. This is the country where fads can become movements that resist change. Every surge in innovation tends to have the same effect of creating devotees who actively resist the next wave for its own sake.

China was seen as moving faster on advanced 5G technology when US telecommunication companies were still struggling to write down their investments in 4G and other previous infrastructure. As a closed market, Chinese state-owned telecommunication companies did not face the same capital cost constraints and the layer of legacy that fierce competition in the US creates.

Developing countries often appear nimble and more receptive to new technologies because they start with less existing, or legacy, infrastructure. New technologies are also often cheaper and faster to implement than the original ones in the so-called 'advanced' countries that have them.

Developing countries often catch up pretty fast and soon look better than the countries they aspire to become. This said, as soon as they have their own infrastructure, they too often sink into the same inertia and the pattern is repeated.

Political and economic change is even harder to bring about. Many countries arrive at a level of comfort in their social structures and systems such that changes become nearly impossible, even when it is sorely needed.

The countries which eventually made the transition liberalized their economies, opened up to foreign investors, and floated their currencies, but all did so only when they were absolutely in deep trouble and there were no alternatives. This is true of Japan, Indonesia, Ghana, Mexico, Iceland, and even China today.

Similarly, a good proportion of more enlightened legislation and policies in the US were crafted during times of crisis. These include the Dodd-Frank Act that regulates the financial sector broadly today, born, as it were, out of the 2008 financial crisis.

So, who will bring about this change? Today, institutions and even nation-states race to be viewed as leaders in the digitization of finance. Nonetheless, nation-states make the transition only when they have to, no matter what their intention. As I outline in the sections below, the real agents of change that we need to be mindful of are neither the obvious technologies nor well-curated processes, but some things a little more counter-intuitive than they appear at first sight.

People shape people

Innovation starts with people, not technology. It is first and foremost about the men and women who pioneered the breakthroughs that helped these innovations gain acceptance in the first place. They were mostly brave individuals of character, some even larger than life, with a strong sense of purpose.

Walter Wriston, the originator of many innovations in finance that are still in use today, had many run-ins with his regulator, Paul Volcker, the then-Chair of the US Federal Reserve. Both men were very tall, imposing but congenial, sparring to bring out the good each recognized in the other.

Dick Kovacevich, the founder of Wells Fargo, consistently pushed the Glass-Steagall Act to its limits, pioneering the cross-selling of investment products to his customers way before the law was actually dismantled.

John Bogle invented indexed funds because he wanted to reduce fees, and he was willing to destroy his own business and rebuild it from the ground up in order to achieve this. He was even proud that he never became the billionaire many so-called entrepreneurs today aspire to become.[79]

Richard Sandor, known as the 'father of financial futures', pioneered the markets for interest rate futures. In addition to coining the term 'derivatives' in the 1970s,[80] he later pioneered the first carbon trading market to offset greenhouse gases in the US, which remains the model copied worldwide today.

I have had the privilege of meeting some of these giants and calling them friends. These were incredible men with great personalities who never pulled their punches – but they were always gentlemanly about it, even with their regulators. (They never took no for an answer either, not even from regulators.)

---

[79] J. Sommer, "Vanguard's Jack Bogle Wasn't a Billionaire. He Was Proud of That", *The New York Times*, 16 January 2019. Available at https://www.nytimes.com/2019/01/16/business/vanguard-jack-bogle-death.html?.

[80] W. B. Crawford Jr, "Pioneer Still Trying to Change the World With Futures", *Chicago Tribune*, 2 October 1993. Available at https://www.chicagotribune.com/news/ct-xpm-1993-10-03-9310030118-story.html.

The golden age of innovation was also a time when regulation itself was still in its formative years. The system provided structure, but left many areas open to entrepreneurs in finance to influence things in a consultative manner. This culture defined innovation in finance in the US from after the end of the Bretton-Woods era in 1971, but went into decline over time. By around the time of the banking crisis of 2008, regulators had become more proscriptive and protective of the incumbents they had grown familiar with.

This pattern was repeated in China when it took over the baton of introducing the more recent innovations in finance in the 2010s. China was especially fortunate to have Zhou Xiaochuan as the governor of the People's Bank of China (the Chinese central bank) from 2002 to 2018. He put in place as much financial infrastructure as he could to absorb the country's export-led growth, given the enormous constraints he was working under.

China was also very fortunate to have had Liu Ming Kang as its first banking regulator, a very enlightened man who kept his focus on regulating banks but still allowing innovation to continue throughout the industry. The rise of Chinese technology players mostly took place under his watch, although regulatory agencies tightened the process in subsequent years.

Personalities like Jack Ma, who once said that he was willing to go to jail if he was not allowed to build Alipay, complete the picture of a period when China's financial system was made up of personalities who built the system as well as those who challenged it. Both are equally important.

I would also add names like Tang Ning, the founder of CreditEase who was one of the pioneers of peer-to-peer (P2P) lending in China, although he had to change course to wealth management later when the Chinese government clamped down on this industry. Within Chinese circles, he is treated more like a maverick, but to me, he represents exactly the kind of entrepreneurs we need in finance, capable of reinventing themselves as regulation evolves.

Most governments have their own concerns about oligarchs being allowed to do their own thing, but neither were personalities like Ma wrong in trying to push the envelope a little bit further. It is this tension between the regulator and regulated that shapes the innovation that eventually results.

One person who profoundly innovated financial services *without* the use of technology was Muhammad Yunus, the founder of Grameen Bank in Bangladesh, for which he became a Nobel Laureate.

He made it possible to lend to even the destitute, who often lacked proof of identity and needed to borrow very small sums of money, by using the concept of mutual help. Many technology innovations today attempt to tackle exactly these issues – verifying customers' identities and providing low-cost credit – not realizing that the solution was already right there in the community.

Neither commercial credit scoring nor existing technology could have made credit available to the destitute. The tons of venture money being thrown at these problems are just an excuse to onboard even more people, especially the unbanked, onto platform technologies – and make them commercially viable at the expense of local communities, sometimes even obliterating them.

In the original model of the microfinance industry, Muhammad Yunus lent money to poor women in villages in groups of six or so for an enterprise of their choice, and then ploughed back the profits on the loan to fund further lending. Over time, the liabilities side also grew off the back of the network until the business model became self-funding.

The Grameen Bank model inspired similar microfinance banks all around the world. The self-funding aspect not only kept the business model honest, but enabled the desperately poor to actually enjoy better credit than the middle class.

The private equity industry in India, funded mostly by Indians residing abroad in the US and other countries, got wind of the business model. They reasoned that if it managed to be so profitable, using organically sourced money from the assets created, it could be scaled just by pouring private equity money in to fund it. This turned out to be the equivalent of flooding a mangrove swamp.

By 2007, the migrant poor in India were finding that they owed two or three such funds a grand total of US$2,500, more money than they had ever seen in their lives. The private equity-driven funds, realising that they were crowding the market with too many loans, even scheduled their collections on different days so that they could stagger collections. As more and more people began drowning under loans they barely understood, the situation grew grossly out of control. After a spike in suicides, triggered by mounting debt and financial distress, the state of Andhra Pradesh eventually banned micro-finance.[81]

The secret sauce to succeeding in this business lay in the credit quality modeling. Grameen kept to the simplest model of lending only to groups of women for very specific purchases, such as buying a bicycle to take fresh produce to the market in the neighboring village.

However, the private equity-driven funds lent instead to village migrants living on the fringes of major cities, who were not part of any established communities. These borrowers used the money for conspicuous consumption which resulted in considerable social ills, including the aforementioned high incidence of suicides.[82]

The worst that can be said about the current generation of entrepreneurs in finance is that they are clueless at steering their platforms around regulators to successfully innovate. The main reason appears to be that while personalities like Mark Zuckerberg succeed in their platform business, they are not finance natives. As such, they are unsure how to deal with the plethora of regulations and government policies.

But the industry is now giving rise to a new generation of personalities who are shaping the token economy. It will become harder to pick out future leaders when many have their minds wrapped around the issues far better than the regulators trying to circumscribe them. Many are young, even in their 20s, and already skilled at circumventing the establishment because of the very nature of decentralized finance.

---

[81] N. Acharya, "Why microfinance crisis is still not over even 10 years after the clampdown" *Business Standard*, 14 March 2020. Available at https://www.business-standard. com/article/finance/why-microfinance-crisis-is-still-not-over-even-10-years-after-the-clampdown-120031401057_1.html.

[82] I. Guerin, M. Labie, and J. M. Servet (eds.), *The Crises of Microcredit* (London: Zed Books, 2015).

The power of the 'dysfunctional' state

The mighty US dollar did not become the global trading currency that it is today as a result of any conscious policy. In fact, US policy in 1959 was to restrict the use of the dollar beyond its shores. There were never any operating manuals or statements of intent by the Federal Reserve to externalize the dollar.

The Eurodollar, the dollar in circulation outside the US, took on a life of its own in the 1950s despite – or precisely because of – legislation proscribing its return to the US. The sponsors of the first euro-bond issuance in 1957 were surprised by just how amiable the European market was to the dollar when they offered an interest rate that was higher than in the US, but still lower than that for all the other currencies in Europe at the time.[83] It has been pretty much the same deal ever since, which has made the US dollar the preferred currency even for domestic transactions in many markets.

When the US' gold peg was unilaterally withdrawn in 1971, most countries kept the dollars they had acquired through trade, the Marshall Plan, or simply by converting their gold holdings in Fort Knox without floating their own currencies.

Most countries still transferred parts of their respective currencies from gold to the dollar, or a basket of currencies with the dollar as the anchor. You can almost see how all these could be easily repeated when countries transfer parity from dollars to crypto or other digital assets in the future, should the US itself do so.

Likewise, US Treasury bonds became the most widely held sovereign debt globally because of the perception that the US was the largest, most liquid, credit-worthy nation in the world. The trading house Cantor Fitzgerald started a global electronic marketplace for US Treasuries as early as 1972, which supercharged the spread of the trend.

These developments took place despite the perennial discussion over the state of the US economy. In 1960, US government debt stood at US$320

---

[83] G. Goodman, *Paper Money* (London: MacDonald and Company, 1983).

billion, and even then it was already perceived to be unsustainable. By 2016, US public debt had risen to US$17 trillion – almost the GDP of the entire economy. In 2020, it was set to explode past US$27 trillion against a GDP of US$19 trillion, or 130% of GDP.[84] Worrying about the US' national debt has always been a conversational staple – until we realize that the US has always been in debt since its inception as a nation-state.[85]

We need to start seeing debt in a different perspective. As the US generates more debt than the size of its GDP, its ability to repay its debts is now moot. US debt *is* the new global economy. The only way left to ameliorate this level of debt is to continue securitizing and externalizing – which only the US has always been able to do with abandon.

The total assets created by the Federal Reserve, mainly to fund liquidity in the securities markets, ballooned from US$2 trillion during the 2008 banking crisis to US$7 trillion during the Covid-19 pandemic. Incidentally, these assets have been a very profitable venture and a source of income for the central bank.

As of 2020, approximately 39% of US national debt was held by foreigners.[86] It is ironically the largest debtor nation in the world, a role that enables the US to provide the rest of the world with the liquidity to keep the dollar as the currency of choice. It is also this externalization which has enabled the US to exert influence on both the global payment infrastructure and financial assets.

Just like the Eurodollar eventually became the global currency for trading a whole range of commodities, pegged to several other currencies, new types of digital payments will keep the externalized version of the US dollar an essential part of the global economy.

---

[84] Duffin, E. (2022, January 7). *United States - public debt by month, 2020/2021*. From Statista: www.statista.com

[85] M. Phillips, "The Long Story of US Debt, from 1790 to 2011, in 1 Little Chart", *The Atlantic*, 13 November 2012. Available at https://www.theatlantic.com/business/archive/2012/11/the-long-story-of-us-debt-from-1790-to-2011-in-1-little-chart/265185/.

[86] "Major Foreign Holders of Treasury Securities", US Department of the Treasury. Available at https://ticdata.treasury.gov/Publish/mfh.txt.

An estimated 70% of the US dollar in circulation is held outside the US. Corporations in many countries borrow in US dollars because it continues to be cheaper than their own currencies. The inherent bias to support the dollar persists in almost every country, but the US Treasury has fewer options than it did in 1933 and 1971 to ensure that the liabilities it owes to foreigners do not come home to roost all at once.

Because of the sheer volume of dollars circulating globally, the US is able to control global dollar payment flows through the Society for Worldwide Interbank Financial Telecommunications (SWIFT). Although SWIFT is not a US institution, almost all its dollar payments are cleared in the US and subject to its laws. This power to police all dollar payments worldwide was amply weaponized during the Russian invasion of Ukraine in 2022, when the US ordered several Russian banks to be banned from processing dollar payments on the SWIFT network.

There are countries that wish this was not the case because the US is also a bully on the global stage: increasing scrutiny of all dollar flows worldwide, and punishing individuals and corporations for violating its will.

Nonetheless, attempts to dampen the influence of the dollar have not succeeded for now, mainly because there is a level of hazard that no other country wants to risk by exposing their currency to the possible consequences of global circulation. These include being attacked by global traders whenever interest or exchange rates are manipulated to support national interests. The US has no such fear because of the sheer quantity of dollars in circulation worldwide.

These factors set the stage for the US to continue wanting to dominate global finance in the digital age. The advent of digital currencies, whether in the form of cryptocurrencies, stablecoins or central bank digital currencies (CBDCs), are all factors that the US Congress and central bank have been considering deeply. Ultimately, however, their choices will follow the path of least resistance because it is simply too hard to get any bill passed by the legislature.

It was ill-conceived of Facebook to ask the US Congress for guidance on how the Libra cryptocurrency (now called Diem) should be designed, because the US legislature is not the forum to ask for collective guidance on almost any such issue (except when it involves a foreign enemy.) Equally, the fact that Janet Yellen, the current Treasury secretary, may be conceptually opposed to cryptocurrencies out of a belief that they are used for illegal activities is immaterial to the trends shaping this country for exactly the same reason.

The US political process looks distinctly dysfunctional today relative to other, seemingly more organized major countries experiencing the same troubles as the US. Take Japan, where public debt is 230% of GDP. The big difference is that Japan's debt is not externalized; the investors in Japan's public debt are its own people. Very little of its debt even trades outside Japan. This makes Japan appear relatively stable, but it also limits Japan's influence on the future of global financial infrastructure.

China's state debt-to-GDP ratio was reported to be 70% in 2020, up from 50% the year before: steeply rising, but still apparently sustainable. But China's total debt-to-GDP ratio is reported to be about 310%, driven in most part by non-financial corporations. However, because many of these corporates are still state-owned enterprises,[87] the state still carries the overall burden.

China has been able to keep its debt mostly domestic by creating huge asset management companies to carry it. For the moment, its own GDP growth is able to fund its liabilities, even as it has been working to externalize its debt. Still, like any country in its situation, it is unlikely to liberalize its economy until it absolutely has to.

In a piece for the *Financial Times*, Ruchir Sharma, the Morgan Stanley Investment Management global strategist, pointed out that the number of countries with national debt-to-GDP ratios of more than 300% has doubled

---

[87] "China's debt ratio is growing as its economy loses steam", *Bloomberg News*, 16 July 2019. Available at https://www.bloomberg.com/news/articles/2019-07-16/china-s-debt-growth-keeps-marching-on-as-economy-loses-pace.

to about 24 in the past 20 years.[88] In response, a reader recalled Adam Smith's saying that nations never ever pay off their debts; they always only pretend to.[89] Debt becomes the real economy.

Given this trajectory, it is now entirely possible for the US to slide into embracing Bitcoin, Ethereum, or any one of the 37 dollar-denominated stablecoins currently in circulation worldwide as an asset class on which to continue externalizing its liabilities. These are digital versions of the US dollar already in circulation today. They are global. They build on the existing story of how the US has been externalizing its economy.

Whatever policy discussions stand to be made in the future are almost immaterial given the unstoppable march of the trend. Cryptocurrencies enable the US to externalize its debt without losing its libertarian values.

For these reasons, stablecoins issued and circulating in US dollars appear to be the most likely candidates. The US is most capable of promoting a global digital payments infrastructure on the back of the digital assets circulating in its economy. It 'leapfrogs' its own antiquated domestic payments infrastructure not by building on it, but by succumbing to a whole new trend when the time is right.

Unlike much more highly organized countries, which can coherently create and issue their own digital currency as a state infrastructure, the US, as a state, always defers to the private sector to construct any new digital infrastructure. Despite the interest in central bank digital currencies (CBDCs) in many countries, there is no political will to drive a state-owned digital currency infrastructure in the US.

There are also conversations at the Bank for International Settlements (BIS) to make CBDCs interconnective. It is clear that such an initiative will be unilaterally rejected by the US, which despises any initiatives that limit its ability to control a dystopian world.

---

[88] R. Sharma, "There is no easy escape from the global debt trap", *Financial Times*, 21 November 2021. Available at https://www.ft.com/content/c9e0c2c1-55af-4258-9c92-92faa111f41e.

[89] S. Legge, "What Adam Smith said on inflation and the debt trap", letter published in the *Financial Times*, 17 January 2022. Available at https://www.ft.com/content/27c76498-937f-41b4-a552-338b105235b4.

As I write this, El Salvador just announced that it would accept Bitcoin as legal tender. The move – unsurprisingly – was not supported by the IMF or the World Bank, but it is yet another example of how innovations in digital currency can emerge out of dire straits.

Bitcoin is already the preferred mode of payment in distressed economies like Honduras, Venezuela, and Zimbabwe (not that these countries are similar to the US; they are all dystopian in different ways). They are also just a few of many more. The IMF says that in 18% of countries worldwide, more than 50% of total deposits are held in foreign currencies. Each of these are prime candidates for a digital dollar in a stablecoin of some kind.

When the US finally makes the transition to digitizing its currency, this will be abrupt, driven by extenuating circumstances. The development of CBDCs in all other countries will have to be sent back to the drawing board.

The 'fifth estate'

The most curious institution we need to understand in mapping the evolution of finance is the central bank. The global finance architecture we have today is predicated on a dire history of public debt. In 1694, the idea of the Bank of England as an early modern-day central bank arose from funding losses incurred in very messy wars, as well as spending to expand the British navy.

Similarly, the history of finance in the US involved lurching from one episode of financial strain to the next, starting with the need to fund the wars of attrition from the UK in the late 1700s, the American Civil War in the 1860s, and every financial crisis since.

Both the Anglo-Saxon countries went down the slippery slope towards financialization and abruptly leaving the gold standard, beginning with the UK in 1931 and then the US in 1971. Both also applied Keynesian economics that contributed to even more financialization.

The establishment of the Bretton Woods agreement in 1944 proved to be formative to the role of the central bank in their present form. However, it was only after Bretton Woods was dismantled in 1971 that central banks moved to the front and center of national politics, as we continue to see today.

Central banks have acquired a position that is best described as the *de facto* 'fifth estate'. After the executive, legislature, and judiciary, the media (often called the fourth estate), the central bank is an institution whose independence is not to be questioned.

In most countries, this 'fifth estate' is charged with ensuring price stability in the economy via the primary means at its disposal. These include implementing macroeconomic policies and monitoring jobs, as well as managing financial intermediation. This, in turn, involves managing the banking industry and the flow of money through the issuance of currency notes and payment systems.

One of the curious characteristics of central banks is the way in which they write their own job descriptions and establish their own key performance indicators (KPIs). For example, in 1990, the New Zealand central bank gave itself the job of 'inflation targeting', which meant keeping inflation within a 2% range.

The idea proved so good that it was copied by the Canadian central bank in 1991 and the Bank of England in 1992, followed by most of the rest of the world after that. Global 'central bank culture' now clearly tends towards learning from and copying each other. Even central bankers tend to be erudite personalities: usually reserved, but amiable and fully cognizant of the power they wield.

All of these factors appear to have played a role in the rise of CBDCs. Several countries experimented with them, including Uruguay (which quietly shelved theirs after a pilot). But when the People's Bank of China (PBOC) announced its pilots, all the other major central banks, including the Federal Reserve, started taking the technology seriously.

At that point, the payments industry was already becoming very digital. More than 60 countries had already launched some form of bank-centric instant digital payments infrastructure. Banks in the UK introduced FasterPay, which was subsequently copied in Singapore as PayNow. Europe had the TARGET Instant Payment Settlement (TIPS), the US had Venmo, and so on. The Federal Reserve is currently preparing to launch FedNow in 2023.

This trend has gone even further in China, where technology companies were early adopters of digital wallets, allowing digital money to exist entirely inside an electronic ecosystem outside of the banking system. The largest of these were Tencent and Alipay, which by 2017 accounted for 88.54% of the US$5 trillion mobile payments market.[90]

It was in response to these developments that the PBOC started a process in 2014 to bring the intermediation function back into the country's banking system. Their CBDC also helped the country's leadership pursue its struggle to stamp out corruption.

At the same time, tiny nation-states with physically dispersed populations and a weak banking industry have found CBDCs very useful in building a state-sponsored payments system without having to worry about traditional banks.

CBDCs are already proving their worth in the constellation of tiny eastern Caribbean islands such as Antigua and Barbuda, Grenada, Saint Kitts and Nevis, and Saint Lucia.[91] These are countries too small for a banking system to manage an inter-island payments network; as such, it is run by the state.

Countries with strong banking systems found that they had to deliberately ensure that their CBDCs are distributed through existing licensed institutions and not directly to the public, so as not to disintermediate them. They also found it difficult to assure that CBDC transactions would be anonymous when the technology clearly makes them auditable in the central bank's database.

Overall, the more developed countries indicated that their CBDCs would be just one of several payment options in the existing payment

---

[90] "China Third Party Payment Report 2017 Q4", AnalysysMason report.

[91] "Eastern Caribbean launches central bank digital currency pilot DCash", *Ledger Insights*, 1 April 2021. Available at https://ledgerinsights.com/eastern-caribbean-launches-central-bank-digital-currency-cbdc-pilot-dcash/.

infrastructure (including cash), an approach which fragments rather than consolidates the trend.

On the other hand, India's Aadhar launched in 2014, which operates as an identity verification system for basic banking accounts, is turning out to be halfway between a digital bank account and a CBDC. Its approach involves registering the identities of all Indians, and then leaving it to individual users to choose the bank accounts they want to use.

According to the Unique Identification Authority of India, its system has already registered 1.3 billion individuals. It is reported to support more than 420 million new bank accounts, especially amongst the previously unbanked, and has seen a formidable 1 billion transactions, all conducted through the existing banking industry.

Aadhar was developed collaboratively between the Indian central bank, technology companies, and the banks, as opposed to unilaterally by the central bank. Its existence was established by legislative charter and interpreted by the courts. All of these ensured that the central bank alone did not control it.

At the same time, the Indian central bank announced that it will be pursuing its own CBDC. This 'fear of missing out', or FOMO, is very real in central bank circles. The announcement, however, was coy: it appeared to reserve the option of launching a CBDC, while leaving it open-ended as to exactly how it would do so.

Countries and regions with established bank-owned payment consortiums for retail payments from the 1980s appeared content not to consider a CBDC for retail use. Several countries with highly developed banking systems, like Canada, France, Hong Kong, and Singapore, focused on 'experimenting' with CBDCs for wholesale payments.

There is a lot of disingenuous rationalization going on by central banks for justifying cross-border payments using CBDCs. They claim to want to reduce netting parties, increase liquidity, and process cross-border payments in real time at lower cost by using CBDCs, as well as reducing payment fraud and money laundering.

Netting and liquidity arrangements are already present in inter-bank payments built and run by organizations like SWIFT, the global payments association, and CLS, the banking industry's currency exchange. Banks with SWIFT codes can already deal directly with each other. For the most part, the experiments with wholesale and retail CBDCs being conducted by central banks today are just transposing the entire existing industrial nature of fiat money into the digital world.

SWIFT's much vaulted ISO 20022 payments infrastructure uses a relational database management system (RDBMS), which requires instant payment platforms to invest in a lot of physical infrastructure just to achieve 10,000 transactions per second. There are blockchain transactions today that are packed into small bits and pre-authorized to run across multiple cloud environments without having to invest in any servers.

The many new CBDCs multiplying around the world are trying to recreate features that are already in development in the blockchain ecosystem. But CBDCs will take many years – by which stage the technology itself would have evolved several times over.

Moreover, superimposing digital currency onto an existing framework is clearly a waste of time when the real competitor to CBDCs is the network effect of cryptocurrencies, which are fast gaining pace based on an entirely different set of priorities.

The best thing about payments technology today is that it has already been simplified to its lowest common denominator. At the end of the day, payments are just pieces of information relayed on a string. In Africa, new payment platforms such as Opay, Wave, Flutterwave, and ZeePay all use existing telecommunication networks to conduct cross-border payments. It is as simple as that.

A little-known fact is that even Facebook – despite its Diem fiasco – already has its own payments feature, which has existed in its Messenger app since as long ago as 2009. Facebook Pay, which was formally launched in 2019,[92] was reported to have processed over US$100 billion worth of payments in over 160 countries and 55 currencies in the 2020-2021 12-month period alone.[93] Its Diem project was just juvenile grandstanding that served only to alarm central bankers and push them into responding in a tizzy.

Central banks' real competitors have always been stablecoins, built from the same mold as cryptocurrencies. As at the end of 2021, there were more than 73 stablecoins worldwide, carrying US$176 billion in value on a number of popular global currencies, including the US dollar, pound sterling, and Euro.

Stablecoins, unlike cryptocurrencies, are pegged dollar-for-dollar against the underlying currency such that they were technically the original digital version of the currency, long before the advent of CBDCs. In fact, by insisting that they should also be regulated as a deposit-taking institution, the US Federal Deposit Insurance Corporation (FDIC) actually created an opportunity for stablecoins to become banks on a token.

Both Randal Quarles, the vice chairman of the Federal Reserve, and Mark Carney, former governor of the Bank of England, have made statements to the effect that CBDCs are superfluous if stablecoins can be supported by a central bank balance sheet.[94] A recent working paper released by the Federal Reserve also asked a lot of questions about the efficacy of CBDCs against that of stablecoins in the areas of personal data protection and privacy.

The real power of stablecoins is the way in which thousands of

---

[92] K. Webb, "Facebook's new payment service will let you send money without fees across Facebook, Instagram, WhatsApp and Messenger", *Business Insider*, 13 November 2019. Available at https://www.businessinsider.com/facebook-pay-payments-instagram-whatsapp-messenger-send-money-2019-11.

[93] A. Rolfe, "Facebook digital wallet Novi ready for market launch", *Payments Cards and Mobile*, 19 August 2021. Available at https://www.paymentscardsandmobile.com/facebook-digital-wallet-novi-ready-for-market-launch/.

[94] "Fed Vice Chair: Stablecoins could make CBDC efforts superfluous", *Ledger Insights*, 29 June 2021. Available at https://www.ledgerinsights.com/fed-vice-chair-stablecoins-could-make-cbdc-efforts-superfluous-digital-dollar/.

programmers worldwide are able to create financial applications on them, facilitating a wide variety of transactions that mimic stock exchanges and trading as well as deposit and lending platforms.

Stablecoins such as Tether (also called USDT) already function as non-state-sponsored, externalized versions of the US dollar. Tether reportedly hit US$3.55 billion in daily transfer value against PayPal's US$2.94 billion per day.

The remarkable feature in all this is that not only are there at least 37 US dollar-denominated stablecoins today, anyone can issue a stablecoin pegged to any currency in the world. The real challenge is for whoever issues a stablecoin to get it accepted.

The collapse of the Luna blockchain token (tied to the Terra stablecoin) in mid-2022 is the first of many to come. It is a foreshadowing of just how many will routinely fail for any number of reasons. In Luna's case, this was because the algorithm it was based on created an untenable market for itself that collapsed. Over time, we will come to an understanding of the working models that will survive and those that will scale and dominate.

Because they value control, central banks are not taking advantage of the open-source application development that is possible with full-function cryptocurrencies. In such a universe, CBDCs risk becoming nothing more than a state-run information system, sidelined within an actively evolving digital ecosystem.

CBDCs can only succeed by giving unprecedented power to central bankers, over and above those given to the legislature, judiciary, or executive. In the good old days of the Weimar Republic, the sheer volume of bank notes being printed and distributed in Germany was the most visible indication of runaway inflation. The effect of a growing electronic payments network is that it hides and redistributes a lot of the excess currency in circulation such that they do not show up in a physical way.

Central bankers will also come under scrutiny for the way they redefine GDP, inflation, and other economic measurements in a changing world. The world is undergoing a fundamental shift in economic models, and countries will suffer dramatically if their currencies are devalued on the weight of their own monetary policies.

At the end of the day, the battle between CBDCs and stablecoins is a philosophical one, between a libertarian world and one managed by regulation and the state. Both have their pros and cons, but if society is headed towards greater personalization of finance and devolution of power to the individual, then it is the libertarian version that will prevail.

Several CBDC projects are simply outsourced to technology companies, while others are funded entirely in-house by taxpayers. The most recent laboratory code test on an 'OpenCBDC', conducted between the Federal Reserve Bank of Boston and the Massachusetts Institute of Technology (MIT), is indicative of these developments.[95] It incorporates all the functionalities of a stablecoin, API, and open-source computing to make the CBDC a living, breathing infrastructure that can be edited by any of its users.

A development like this – if it finally takes place – will turn the Federal Reserve into a very different kind of central bank, one that allows open participation in the use of digital currency for any number of personalized purposes. In such a case, it will be the central bank itself which has been transformed.

The geek army

For every team of central bankers designing and implementing CBDCs, there are armies of application developers tweaking away at different cryptocurrencies and solving a whole range of problems, which improves the technology every day.

Bitcoin alone has 76 million users, of which 46 million are Americans. 106 million people around the world used cryptocurrencies in 2021,[96] but

---

[95] O. Adejumo, "Boston Fed and MIT See Promising Results in CBDC Code Testing", *Be In Crypto*, 5 February 2022. Available at https://beincrypto.com/boston-fed-and-mit-see-promising-results-in-cbdc-code-testing/.

[96] J. Haworth, "How many people own bitcoin?95 Blockchain Statistics (2022)", *Exploding Topics blog*, 18 March 2022. Available at https://explodingtopics.com/blog/blockchain-stats.

only an estimated 1.36 million people have used decentralized finance (DeFi) on the Ethereum platform. This does not include the other platforms that use Ethereum, such as Binance, which suggests that the real number could be even larger although it is still a niche market and growing.[97]

One of the ways in which DeFi is measured today is called Total Value Locked (TVL). Estimates range from between US$85 billion (if you take just the value in the cryptocurrencies themselves)[98] and US$250 billion (if you take into account total assets locked inside the major DeFi protocols where the actual transactions are taking place).[99]

DeFi is not easy for the uninitiated to pick up. One reason it is not very well understood is because it is still being driven by thousands of young technology nerds and computer geeks who are fluent in programming and application development. Their singular focus – which makes them a force to be reckoned with – means those who have invested in cryptocurrencies are also likely to be totally immersed in it, sometimes right down to a specific cryptocurrency. Many make a living buying and selling DeFi loans from the comfort of their parents' living rooms.

By contrast, most lay people can't even get past how the consensus mechanism works. Then there is the problem of fraud and theft of digital assets online. Until more user-friendly interfaces are built, non-technical users will have difficulty appreciating these platforms.

Web-based protocols like Anchor, B2C2, and FTB recreate the same financial products as a bank does, but on a token. Anchor uses a stablecoin called Terra which generates income from a lending and deposit product embedded in it. The lending is fully collateralized by another token called bAsset, which includes a mechanism to liquidate bad loans.

The tokens support its investors, be they lenders, borrowers, bad loan

---

[97] F. Klauder, "How many people use DeFi?", *DeFi Times* newsletter, 7 June 2021. Available at https://newsletter.defitimes.io/p/how-many-people-use-defi.

[98] "DeFi TVL in the Ethereum blockchain", via Statista.com (accessed 12 January 2022).

[99] M. Trajcevski, "DeFi surges by 1,2000% in 2021, $240 billion Total Value Locked in Defi", *Dailycoin*, 31 December 2021. Available at https://www.investing.com/news/cryptocurrency-news/defi-surges-by-1200-in-2021-240-billion-total-value-locked-in-defi-2728005.

liquidators, or liquidity providers, as the antithesis of an institutionalized approach to finance. A platform called Ramp Defi, which carries both lending and deposit assets on its stablecoin token called rUSD, was able to raise US$1 billion in total market value.

A developer, Witek Radomski, pushed for a token standard in Ethereum called ERC-1155, which eventually made it possible to combine fungible and non-fungible tokens in the same smart contract. Platforms like Enjin, Worldwide Asset eXchange, TokenScript and Loom, based on Ethereum, support tokenizing of in-game currencies and NFTs and making them tradable across platforms.

Cryptocurrencies are fast developing interoperability and smart contracts and carrying fungible and non-fungible assets, along with many functionalities as there are programmers to create them. The benefits of cryptocurrencies are so overwhelming that CBDCs will have a hard time just keeping up.

In the insurance industry, insurance contracts can be stored on digital smart contracts, making the former more liquid and tradable as assets in their own right. Mutual funds invested in cryptocurrencies as an asset, and later as a mutual fund complete with blockchain architecture, are possible developments in the evolution of cryptocurrencies as financial products.

The Bank for International Settlement (BIS) came up with an excellent paper in December 2021, describing exactly how decentralized finance works in both accurate detail and in a manner that traditional bankers can understand.[100] Unfortunately, it also came to the hilarious conclusion that decentralization is an "illusion" and that DeFi has to be regulated on the basis of "same risks, same rules".

First, the BIS researchers did not stop to ask why there was so much technology talent in DeFi or what these talents were doing. This would have given the regulator an idea of why this industry came into existence in

---

[100] S. Aramonte, W. Huang, and A. Schrimpf, "DeFi risks and the decentralization illusion", *BIS Quarterly Review*, 6 December 2021. Available at https://www.bis.org/publ/qtrpdf/r_ qt2112b.htm.

the first place or where it is headed. Nor did the researchers question why blockchain players like Tezos, Solana, and Provenance, which carry tradable assets on their cryptocurrency tokens, have been confidently transitioning from 'permissioned' to 'permissionless' models where participants in their marketplace do not need to know each other. Decentralization is not an illusion: it just requires a different lens from that usually applied to traditional finance to appreciate how it works.

Metakovan is the avatar name of Vignesh Sundaresan, a billionaire Tamil cryptocurrency investor who shot to fame when he splashed US$69 million on an NFT of a digital painting by an American artist called Beeple. It was the highest sum ever paid for an NFT at the time.[101] He prominently displayed the NFT in his "metaverse", an entirely digital exhibition space.

The central feature of Metakovan's rags-to-riches story is that all his investments were held in cryptocurrencies only, despite originally coming from a poor family. He had no other assets, not even a property or a vehicle in the real world at the time of his historic purchase. Such is the extent of his singular focus, which appears to be a defining characteristic of his generation. The vlogger Nuseir Yassin put it succinctly when he said, "Never bet against dedicated people."

Many crypto-skeptics' criticisms, including the significant energy consumption used for staking, transaction speed, interoperability, data security, and privacy, would be solved much faster when central bankers finally get their act together on CBDCs.

In any case, the scenario currently taking shape is that the world might have a range of both CBDCs and cryptocurrency-based models in the future, with CBDCs mimicking the latter. Interoperability between CBDCs will be nearly impossible to achieve, if only because they will be ideologically aligned in blocs that might broadly mirror the trade agreements signed by different countries in the 2000s.

---

[101] A. Berwick and E. Howcrot, "From Crypto to Christie's: how an Indian metaverse king made his fortune", *Reuters*, 17 November 2021. Available at https://www.reuters.com/investigates/special-report/finance-crypto-sundaresan/.

The biggest threat for all forms of digital payments, be they cryptocurrencies or CBDCs, is a single point of failure. In the days of cash, money was dispersed across a range of financial institutions. If fraudulent cash was deposited anywhere, it would not affect the integrity of other financial institutions in the system.

But in digital currencies of any form, one software or cryptographic flaw or an attack can destroy an entire banking system, one example being the HeartBleed bug which caused massive disruption worldwide in 2014. For this reason, a multi-system payment and financial model is desirable in the networked world. As I will discuss in the final chapter, safety in a digital ecosystem depends on developing a distributed network with no single point of failure.

Cryptocurrencies are not without threats and weaknesses. The advent of quantum computing is as much a threat as it will be an opportunity for cryptocurrencies to extend their uses. Whatever the outcome, technical competencies will definitely be an asset in being able to navigate the future.

The venture capitalists

Writing as I am during the Russian invasion of Ukraine in 2022, it bears remembering that the venture capital (VC) industry was a child of war. It was the brainchild of Georges Doriot, an academic who served as lieutenant colonel in the US Army Quartermaster Corps during World War Two.[102] As the wartime director of military planning, he devised a program to provide state funding to entrepreneurs to solve logistical and technological problems in the military.

After the war, he returned to Harvard University and co-founded the American Research and Development Corporation, which became one of the first private sector venture funds to support businesses set up by returning servicemen. One of its major success stories was when the US$70,000 it

---

[102] S. Kirsner, "Venture capital's grandfather", *The Boston Globe*, 6 April 2008. Available at https://www.boston.com/business/articles/2008/04/06/venture_capitals_grandfather/.

invested in the Digital Equipment Corporation (DEC) in 1957 ballooned to US$38 million during the company's initial public offering in 1966.[103]

This piece of history becomes relevant again today with the war in Ukraine. With Russia's invasion, the role of the state in funding innovation is regaining importance as many countries increase their military spending yet again. The Rand Corporation, Southwest Research Institute, MIT Lincoln Laboratories and MITRE (for cybersecurity) all served as prototypes for the VC industry that we know today.

Since the days of the microchip in the 1970s, Silicon Valley venture capitalists have had an illustrious history of taking bets which went on to shape breakthroughs in technology. They are perpetually in the news for brokering this and that deal, such that they are seen as kingmakers who decide on the technology that will define our world.

This is true of technology generally. But when it comes to innovations in finance, VCs follow; they don't lead. The perception that VCs determine the innovations that shape the future of finance is totally understandable, but mistaken.

The same VCs who bet on deep technologies such as DNA-sequenced personalized medicine, autonomous vehicles, and AI are more circumspect about the finance industry. They are deferential towards the regulation that defines this industry in a way that they are not about almost any other.

Moreover, because VCs are most active when there is a lot of cheap money in the market, they tend to seize up when interest rates go up. Finance is especially interest rate-sensitive because of high capital and cost-of-funds issues that are more important than the technology. Innovation in finance looks very different when the cost of funds rises.

VCs view finance with the same lens as the platform industry. Here, they generally try to replicate the platform focus that has worked well in other industries. As long as entrepreneurs are focused on migrating existing

---

[103] S. O'Sullivan, C. Ebersweiler, and B. Joffe, "70 years of VC innovation", *TechCrunch*, 9 November 2017. Available at https://techcrunch.com/2017/11/09/70-years-of-vc-innovation/.

payments, investment, trading, or insurance products onto platforms, they stand a good chance of being funded by VCs. But at the back-end, nothing really changes in the finance industry, which continues to dish out the same products and processes as it has done for the last 30 years.

The fund management industry, focused on innovation in finance, betrays another aspect of the limitations they operate under. The 48 companies on the KBW Nasdaq Financial Technology Index (KFTX), which was started in 2016, include old-school financial technology companies like ACI Worldwide and Fidelity National Information Services, Both of these make money from maintenance contracts to keep mainframe technology alive. Although the index is a moving target that spans a mixed bag of old and new players as it evolves, its current list also includes Fair Isaac and TransUnion, as though oblivious to the impact that AI has had on this space – which ought to put a discount on these players as investments today.

Western Union, Visa, and MasterCard are payment companies from the days of the dinosaurs. Further down the list are players like Lending Club and Square, which are pursuing projects that could potentially disrupt the incumbents.

The fund managers are the same. The prospectus for Cathy Wood's Ark Fintech Innovation ETF investment fund, set up in April 2019, itemizes the categories it is invested in– transaction innovations, blockchain, risk transformation, frictionless funding platforms, customer experience, and 'new intermediaries'.[104]

Unfortunately, the ARK portfolio currently does not have enough credible players to populate each of these categories. The fund, with US$674 million in assets under management (AUM) appears to be doing well on the surface, its net asset value (NAV) having risen from about US$20 at inception to a high of US$51 in January 2021. However, on deeper examination, it is clearly buoyed by players who still generate their income from old-school business models.

---

[104] Fintech Innovation (ARKF) Holdings, portfolio details by ARK Holdings, 17 August 2021. Available at https://ark-funds.com/wp-content/uploads/2021/08/ARK_FINTECH_INNOVATION_ETF_ARKF_HOLDINGS.pdf

A few players in the list might arguably be classed as fintechs – Square, PayPal, Schwab, Adyen, and Lending Club amongst them. But Nvidia, Snap, DocuSign, Taiwan Semiconductor, and Pinduoduo, which also made the list, are very far from being fintechs. Online retailers such as Mercadolibre and JD are arguably half-and-half because they do have payments and financial processing services, although they are in essence,online shopping sites. Despite its name, the mix of companies in the Ark Fintech portfolio is clearly designed to support valuations and not innovation.

The legacy payment processing companies, Visa and MasterCard, invest in start-ups themselves. They are a good bulwark in any investment portfolio involving finance because they bridge both old and new sources of income. But both are also fair game for disruptors with a cloud-based platform that can help onboard anyone, anywhere, to simplify the payments industry down to its basic functions – sending a payment via a text message.

Every single one of Visa and MasterCard's 16,300 member financial institutions worldwide today still has to install their own credit card application software, usually ACI's VisionPlus, along with hardware connected to the card company's antiquated processing network in an age when cloud-based, plug-and-play models are available.[105]

VCs have also been more compliant with finance regulators than they have been with regulators in telecommunications, autonomous vehicles, or other industries. They believe there is no way they can play in the fintech space without a license, and so reward their companies for securing, rather than circumventing, the need for one.

Similarly, fintech funding takes the path of least resistance when it comes to dealing with financial regulation. VCs are wont not to argue with financial regulators; they neither understand them nor want to be caught with punitive fines.

Ant Group, the fintech arm of Alibaba, was supposed to have been publicly listed at US$280 billion in 2020. Until the Chinese government

---

[105] "Annual Report 2017", Visa. Available at https://s1.q4cdn.com/050606653/files/doc_financials/annual/2017/Visa-2017-Annual-Report.pdf.

started clamping down on its fintech players, the lion's share of fintech funding went to this one country. But as soon as the regulators started tightening the screws, the VCs evaporated. After Ant Group's IPO was canceled, the VC fintech funding shifted to Southeast Asia and India. The money simply moved on.

VCs also tend to lose their verve when it comes to identifying true revolutionaries. Most take a herd mentality, simply moving from one fad to the next. The irony is that the more fintechs there are doing the same things, the cost of an actual breakthrough increases dramatically.

Using the pharmaceutical industry as a case study, MIT's Andrew Lo has pointed out that as more patents were registered for incremental transformations, the harder it became to find funding for real breakthroughs in pharmaceuticals.[106] Investors become concerned about the time and effort put into funding breakthrough research and whether innovation would generate sufficient return for the risks incurred.

Most of these companies add to, not reduce, complexity in finance. Risk management processes are being made more complicated, not less, because of the sheer volume of funding available. Any reasonable bank or service provider has to deploy several slivers of fintech solutions to benefit meaningfully from the transformations that are possible in credit profiling, risk, or payments.

Regulators in turn sometimes subject fintechs to onerous compliance, know-your-customer (KYC) and even capitalization rules, and make funding a criterion in itself to determine which ones are licenced. The fintechs themselves in turn hire expensive bankers to impress regulators. Their innovations are never in danger of reducing costs even when they claim to be promoting financial inclusion.

The result of all this is that in most countries, the real cost of credit to the unbanked remains a usurious 18-30%, even on digital channels. Seen through this lens, the digital disruptors start to look more like the incumbent

---

[106] A. Lo, *Adaptive Markets: Financial Evolution at the Speed of Thought* (Princeton: Princeton University Press, 2017).

banks they set out to replace. In the words of the writer Antonio Garcia Martinez, venture capital is "...a hedonistic world of private institutional capital of too much money and too many half-baked ideas in the hands of too few good people."[107]

At the same time, a different source of funding is on the rise in DeFi. Ethereum, where efforts were concentrated on turning it into a smart contract token capable of supporting decentralized applications, had a market capitalization of US$250 billion in late January 2022. The EOS cryptocurrency, which can process millions of blockchain transactions per second and eliminates user fees, has a market capitalization of US$5 billion.

Binance, which had US $7.7 trillion in volume transacted on its platform across over 13.5 million users in 2021, has demonstrated that its size gives the ability to navigate between different regulatory regimes despite raising the ire of US regulators.

Lumen, which very specifically supports instant global transactions and access to low-cost financial services, has raised US$11 billion. Tether, the stablecoin mentioned earlier, has raised US$34 billion even though it retains a face value of just US$. Even Dogecoin, which was essentially created as a marketing joke, managed to raise US$7 billion.

Crypto assets are now not only a store of value, but a funder of the innovations that sit on them. All these numbers are capital for use in developing new applications on these platforms and pushing the industry forward without the need for VCs. As soon as a company is able to attract this level of funding, the programming community steps up to chip in.

When it came to raising public funding, the corporate finance world went from private equity to VC to special purpose acquisition companies (SPACs). But this approach lost its sizzle fast when investors could not square the discrepancies between the sheer volume of money involved and the applications being created. The token world went from initial coin offerings (ICOs) to collectible finance to application development, which

---

[107] A. G. Martinez, *Chaos Monkeys: Inside the Silicon Valley Money Machine* (London: Ebury Press, 2016).

is closer to a world where individuals can participate in funding their own future of finance.

CHAPTER 6

The anatomy of innovation

"Software will eat all the business in the world."
Marc Andreessen

"There are decades where nothing happens; and there are weeks when decades happen."
Vladimir Ilyich Lenin

In 2008, while the US banking industry was quickly slipping into its worst-ever mortgage-driven crisis, the finance industry was too busy to notice the emergence of breakthrough technologies that would soon revolutionize society in fundamental ways.

The rise of Facebook and Twitter, but equally importantly, VMware, the cloud computing platform, Hadoop, and GitHub revolutionized coding, sourcing, and application development forever. It was also the period when data processing speed increased dramatically. The appearance of all these developments was totally unrelated to finance.

The technology platforms born around 2007-2008 went on to create social upheaval of enormous proportions, with results as varied as overhauling the way we hire taxis to the Arab Spring and contact tracing during the Covid-19 pandemic.

The iOS and Android application development platforms made mobility an essential component of all industries. But while these monumental changes were taking place in the technology world, the finance industry was still caught up nursing its wounds from 2008.

In 2008, banking regulators were still using capital adequacy models developed in the aftermath of the 1984 savings and loans crisis to tame a new crisis, this time involving banks trading in esoteric instruments with no underlying assets. The advent of Bitcoin added a new technology-based asset class which would introduce decentralized finance 10 years later, but hardly received any attention at that time. It was clearly a mismatch, but the industry could not think beyond its own limits.

Innovation often comes very late to finance. As recently as 1998, the US Securities and Exchange Commission (SEC) debated whether bulletin boards should be deemed as exchanges because they simply offered to trade. When authorized exchange-issued mobile phones were allowed on the NYSE in 2003, they differentiated players who had access to phones on the trading floor from those who did not.[108] Even the humble telephone could technically be considered a 'fintech' development of its day.

In this chapter, I discuss five elements of innovation that seem counterintuitive to a conventional understanding of finance. The ways in which these innovations evolved are worth understanding in some depth, not least because they help our attempts to project how things will play out in the future.

The post-Bretton Woods creations

The finance industry that we know today started on 15 August 1971. That was the magic date when President Nixon announced that the US was abandoning its convertibility to the gold standard on weekend television. It marked the end of the Bretton Woods agreement, which many trading nations had hitherto been party to in order to stabilize the price of money. That was the date on which the industry began its long journey to where we are today.

---

[108] "NYSE mobile phone options now available to traders", *Mobile Commerce Press*, 30 June 2016. Available at http://www.mobilecommercepress.com/nyse-mobile-phone-options-now-available-traders/8522622/.

Up to the end of the Bretton Woods era, there used to be a saying in banking that a banker woke up in the morning, paid 2% for his deposit, made a loan at 4% in the afternoon, and was on the golf course by 5:00PM. Bankers led very predictable lives before the US finally abandoned the gold standard.

By 1973, when the International Monetary Fund (IMF) formally ended the gold parity,[109] the world had entered the age of the floating exchange rate mechanism, which would go on to have a profound influence on the assets and liabilities of financial entrepreneurs.

The price of money, regardless of currency or country, went from something as fixed as gold to fluctuate with any number of ephemeral factors, including inflation, exchange, and interest rates. In doing so, the face of finance was changed forever. Over time, it became pegged to derivatives, futures, and indices. Eventually, money will be pegged to indicators that have nothing to do with any underlying asset, securities, or even the ability of countries to meet their commitments.

Bankers started to learn that the cost of funds, even domestically, was subject to increasing uncertainties driven by supply and demand factors outside their control, just like the ice merchants did before the advent of the refrigerator. By the time ice arrived in the bars of Havana from the ice fields of Boston, a lot of its value would have melted away. This is exactly what monetary transactions face today.

The groundwork for this was laid before the end of the Bretton Woods regime. Entrepreneurs like Bruce Bent and Henry Brown established the first money market fund in 1971, getting around restrictions on banks by copying the idea of a *contra garantia* (an escrow account) from an earlier European innovation in 1968.

After Bretton Woods ended, Walter Wriston, the erudite chairman of Citibank in the 1970s, created negotiable certificates of deposits (CDs) as a way of getting cheaper corporate deposits around Regulation Q. Collateralized debt obligations (CDOs) were also invented around this

---

[109] J. Rickards, *Currency Wars: The Making of the Next Global Crisis* (New York: Portfolio/Penguin, 2011).

time as a way of getting around Regulation Q. The now-forgotten regulation forbidding paying interest on checking accounts was only lifted in 2011. Wriston also pioneered the practice of lending to corporations against cash flow rather than against hard assets in the late 1970s, advancing the trend towards financing intangibles.

When Merrill Lynch introduced its Cash Management Account (CMA) in 1977, Fortune magazine called it "the most important financial innovation in years".[110] The CMA enabled customers to sweep all their cash into a money market mutual fund, and the brokerage threw in a chequebook and a credit card to make it look like a full-service banking product.

The first rumbles of a data-driven industry also started in the 1970s. The first index fund was started on 1 July 1971 by William Fouse at Wells Fargo, together with notable industry economists like Harry Markowitz, Bill Sharpe, Merton Miller, and Eugene Fama, with just US$6 million. According to Fouse, the Wells Fargo team were viewed as madmen at that time. "It was a hotbed of investment radicalism," he wrote in a 1980 *Institutional Investor* article.

In 1976, John Bogle set up his own index funds business, where fund managers invested in indices instead of the underlying assets. Bogle was passionate to keep the cost of trading as low as possible for retail investors. This commoditization of financial products continues ruthlessly to this day.

A futures market for foreign currencies was introduced between 1970-1972, followed by one for interest rates in 1975 by none other than Richard Sandor, who contributed one of the forewords to this book. When he launched the futures market for interest rate derivatives, it did not make sense as Treasury bond prices were very stable – although interest rate margins eventually became widest in the late 1970s. Credit goes to Sandor

---

[110] "The Firm's Cash Management Account is Dazzling a Lot of Well-Heeled Customers - And Scaring the Competition. *Fortune*, October 1980, pp. 135-144, cited in E. K Clemons and M. C. Row, "The Merrill Lynch cash management account financial service: a case study in strategic information systems", Proceedings of the Twenty-First Annual Hawaii International Conference on System Sciences (1988), Vol.IV, Applications Track. Available at https://ieeexplore.ieee.org/document/11972.

for his foresight: this innovation gave rise to subsequent developments in the expansion of credit products.

All of these activities had one thing in common: to keep the cost of funds in their respective businesses as stable as possible even as the investment industry was beset by greater uncertainty, especially inflation.

Between 1977-1981, cumulative inflation was over 50% and the value of the dollar halved, making it attractive to invest in hard assets like property and gold.[111] As Henry Kaufman, the famous Dr. Doom, pointed out at the time, inflation made bank lending even more profitable.

Home mortgages eventually became the anchor product of many main street banks, first in the US and then the rest of the world. Today, the lack of inflation is turning bank lending into a cost for banks, not a source of income, unless they hedge their interest margins. This required a different kind of innovation to bypass dwindling credit costs.

As increased regulation, the rising cost of capital, and narrowing margins started eroding the asset-liability business, investment banks began the practice of securitizing mortgage assets and freeing up their balance sheets to take on more loans, to the effect that banks were no longer carrying the assets on their books and the assets themselves were becoming increasingly financialized. Mortgages were sold in tranches, and the derivatives created out of them were traded in their own right.

Similar regulations around the world sped up the preference for online, real-time, fully automated trading and reduced costs. Simultaneously, they disintermediated the brokers to create a larger and more liquid marketplace for the new securities being created.

In the UK, regulators introduced what became known as the 'Big Bang' package of legislation in 1986. This included the abolition of the single capacity rule and fixed commissions for trades, while the introduction of screen-based quotation systems further commoditized the industry by regulation.

---

[111] J. Rickards, *Currency Wars: The Making of the Next Global Crisis*, above at 108.

Subsequently, the first ETFs (exchange traded funds) – index funds constituted as a stock instead of a fund – were launched in Canada in 1989 as a transparent, low-cost, and uncomplicated way of tracking indices by owning the underlying assets directly on behalf of shareholders.

Nathan Most and Steven Bloom designed and developed the US S&P 500 in January 1993, which remains the world's largest ETF to this day. The industry grew from nothing to US$2.99 trillion by December 2015, with flows of US$55 billion per month. Every step of the way, finance was evolving from trading in something very tangible to the complete opposite.

Meanwhile, innovations in the 2000s took on a sinister twist. While credit default swaps (CDS) were first introduced in 1994, ostensibly as insurance against default or a credit event on a collateralized debt obligation (CDO) or bond, the investment bankers who conceptualized CDSes did so to profit from trade in both directions.

In essence, it wasn't risk management anymore. By the 2008 banking crisis, the CDS market had grown to about US$70 trillion, and CDSes were widely traded as an asset class of its own. Over time, all sorts of different financialized tools were invented, many of which had less to do with managing risk or reducing costs than profiting off investors whether the market went up or down.

China does not get as much credit for innovation in finance as it should. When Chinese financial institutions created trust companies to get around stringent borrowing limits of their own, it was called "shadow banking" by Western media and given a sinister twist. Despite this, many of them were able to move fast and cheaply, disrupting traditional channels to extend credit to the masses in a very short period of time.

This long list of post-Bretton Wood innovations can be characterized by three key features: they destroyed costs, commoditized products, and created new business. By these standards, very few of the developments in fintech today would qualify as true innovations.

For example, the buy-now-pay-later (BNPL) platforms have existed for a long time in the traditional credit card industry, but they are now being put on platforms and processed with more analytics to trigger addictive consumer behavior. However, their real selling feature remains the promotional rates being offered.

At best, this is an old business under a new name; at worst, it is an abuse of analytics to engender addiction. But at the back-end, BNPL transactions are still processed in the same good old-fashioned way that the credit card industry was, except on an app rather than a physical card.

Innovations in finance can be characterized as innovation only when they take place on the balance sheet. Many so-called innovations pursued by fintechs today in fact *undermine* the balance sheet by way of subsidized loans and deposit rates, funded by VCs who are able to absorb the losses generated. The days of real innovation in finance will return when the technologies being created drive down prices on the balance sheet without any funding help.

The triumph of capital over labor

The origins of the rise of the fintech phenomenon are worth understanding in substance. It was not all about technological innovation at all, but rather a story about the triumph of capital over labor. By examining these historical threads, we can trace the evolution of the fintech fiction across three acts – and it is not a complimentary tale.

Act One concerns 'shareholder value', the flag raised by US corporations way back in the 1990s in their fight against organized labor. This resulted in outsourcing work to developing countries, leading to the consequent decline in real wages that paved the way for the middle-class crisis the US is now mired in.

Had it been argued in 1996 that the outsourcing of work to developing countries by players like Jack Welch of GE or John Reed of Citibank was really a battle of capital over labor, it would have fallen on deaf ears, but this phenomenon nonetheless cast a long shadow over the US economy. The country has since had to contend with the twin forces of years of stagnated wages and the rise of capital markets as the main source of wealth, to the benefit of capitalists alone.

The early 2000s were ignominious, with thousands of bank employees losing their jobs year after year due to the migration towards outsourcing, open-source computing, and other alternatives in a bid to cut operational costs.

It was a difficult time for labor in all of the developed world in general, with the entry of China into the World Trade Organization (WTO) as well as the internationalization of cheap IT skilled Indian workers harnessed from the Y2K era. Coupled with the increasing demand for capital by regulators, cost management became a matter of survival for financial institutions around the world.

Act Two concerns the rise of thousands of 'start-ups' unwittingly set up by thousands of displaced workers to absorb the operating costs of the financial institutions they used to work for. The industry had a gravitational pull on its ex-employees, consultants, and hangers-on, all imagining they were in a position to solve legacy problems that had never gone away.

Even today, fintechs are routinely made up of ex-employees wanting to help their former employers lower costs – already saved through their own retrenchments – even further. This is displacement activity, not innovation.

The advent of Java C++ programming turned almost every bank problem into another excuse to mindlessly automate the obvious. In 1997, Elon Musk, in creating the failed X.com bank, insisted that it was possible to do all the coding for an internet-only bank totally on C++, invented just ten years earlier.

His colleagues were skeptical, but he had planted the seed for what was to become the fintech industry. Almost all programming in the fintech world today is done on C++ or Linux, the underlying open-source coding languages that can be modified simultaneously by just about anyone.

My friend, DK Kim, a fintech expert, once called the deluge of C++-based applications in the financial services industry "Java lipstick on pigs" (Java being the platform on which the C++ code is run). Nothing in finance had fundamentally changed, except that anyone could now codify any existing banking process into a Java-based software and call it beautiful.

Fintech founders propose to externalize and absorb the cost of their former employers, underwritten by the investors of their start-ups (who then monetize their investments), when the company is traded in the private marketplace driven by venture capitalists.

A real example today goes like this. An ex-employee sets up a fintech company and charges his first bank customer as little as US$40,000 for a database innovation project as 'proof of concept'. In the past, a traditional technology company like IBM or Oracle would have charged the same bank nearly US$2 million for the same project.

The shortfall in the revenue required to deliver on the project is subsidized by the investors of the company and justified as the justified 'burn rate' at the start of a business before it actually makes money. The legacy bank gets a US$2 million value for only US$40,000, which shows up as a lower cost-to-income ratio on its balance sheet, contributing to the incumbent banking industry looking even more profitable than it ever was.

Fintech conferences feature rows of exhibition booths of software solutions, each purporting to solve one unique problem as a standalone software. This adds to , not reduces, the complexity of the 'technology stack' that banks eventually end up with. The fintech itself is prevented from scaling because they tend to be specific to one or two banks and are not able to integrate with other fintechs. Each one becomes a one-purpose solution designed to solve one problem at a legacy bank.

Each bank will have its own set of fintechs that it works with, ones that other banks would avoid due to conflicts of interest. As a result, the technology itself becomes commoditized or obsolete very quickly. The owner's only recourse then is to subsequently attempt to sell the company to another investor at a haircut valuation, and so the game goes on. In this way, labor is kept as a contingent part of capital, without ever becoming a cost of the balance sheet to the traditional bank.

For these reasons, capital wins over labor. Thousands of fintech start-up entrepreneurs risk their careers in the hope of becoming moguls themselves. Some become serial entrepreneurs, flipping one useless company after another – but many go back to becoming highly paid employees in a traditional bank or the next well-funded fintech.

In the meantime, salaries in traditional banks continue to escalate as regulators load even more compliance and licensing costs. Ironically, this makes working at a traditional bank more desirable than starting a fintech company, which most people do only when they lose their jobs or have become sufficiently wealthy from their regular bank jobs.

The incumbent banks, on their part, organize 'hackathon' sessions out of their marketing, not technology, budgets. The best ideas from a deluge of wide-eyed smart young people are routinely absorbed into the banks, with no recourse for the entrepreneurs themselves.

Even governments get in on the act, promoting entrepreneurship on the one hand but tightening regulation with the other such that fintechs don't ever get to upstage the incumbents, no matter how hard they try.

The few who become fintech billionaires achieve this based not on the platforms they build, but their ability to raise and flip funds. The rest of the industry, whose focus is on software, has to contend with poverty – the inability to meet rent, salaries, or their kids' school fees, and encountering job losses several times over in their careers. The industry is far more prosaic than it is made out to be.

The ravages of zero marginal cost

Many in the finance industry are influenced by the assertion, made by the futurist Jeremy Rifkin, that we are on the cusp of a world which costs practically nothing. In his book, *The Zero Marginal Cost Society*, he argues that developments like the Internet of Things, solar and wind energy, improved AI and robotics, 3D printing, and improved shipping and logistics with smart GPS sensors embedded in packaging will all serve to bring the marginal cost of production down to zero.

The academics Boyan Jovanovic and Peter Rousseau, the authors of *General Purpose Technologies*, posit that transformational technologies should achieve three things: deliver dramatic cost declines, impact many industries and geographies, and serve as a platform for more innovation.[112]

These are very seductive propositions that work well in manufacturing and other industries with tangible products and services that depend on production. It is tempting to apply them to finance, except that in this industry, the cost of funds is persistently high and the cost of labor persistently inflated because of regulatory costs.

Deep down, every bank CEO suspects that no matter how hard they try, the cost of business will creep up on them so long as they are organized as institutional businesses with hierarchies and departments, even as their income is decimated by rising margins, competition, and regulation.

In the production of financial services, every revenue stream is loaded with compliance as well as customer acquisition and retention costs, such that digitization increases rather than lowers the costs of onboarding and retaining new customers efficiently. But the single most significant cost in financial services is salaries, which in many countries have been inflated far beyond the true worth of the work that finance employees do.

It would be reasonable to think that the use of AI in chatbots and robo-advisors would lower costs and enable differentiators. But what happened was that soon enough, every player, big and small, old and new, was able to offer the same platforms at commoditized prices such that these were no longer competitive advantages.

The fixed cost of organized labor and the infrastructure to manage it are not zero, and herein lies the dilemma. In 2018, an AI company called Taiger claimed that it could help banks save up to 85% in costs through the use of a chatbot, an enterprise search tool, and an information extraction tool.[113]

---

[112] B. Jovanovic and P. Rousseau, "General Purpose Technologies", chapter in *Handbook of Economic Growth*, vol. 1, part B, pp. 1181-1224. Available at https://econpapers.repec.org/bookchap/eeegrochp/1-18.htm.

[113] C. Y. Min, "AI firm Taiger gives clients more bite in slashing costs", *The Business Times*, 6 March 2018. Available at https://www.businesstimes.com.sg/sme/ai-firm-taiger-gives-clients-more-bite-in-slashing-costs.

The problem was right there in Taiger's own pitch: that 85% in reduced costs was the ceiling on the income to their own business. Because there are only so many banks in any one market, by 2020, AI-driven bots became so commoditized that Taiger lost its own competitive justification.

Historically, the commoditization of the manufacturing process has not created immediate profits for new players. It turned it into a market share war for its own sake. When Henry Ford introduced the first assembly line cars, it destroyed prices for all kinds of vehicles, from horse-drawn carriages to combustion engines, for years to come. His subsequent competitors had to be well-capitalized to compete for market share.

Every new digitization effort today in the finance industry is promoted as a cost-reduction exercise that it never is. Data has a way of compressing and commoditizing the output of the finance industry but without reducing costs for the institutions themselves. Ironically, it destroys the very institutions trying to profit from it.

At the beginning of the 2010s, algorithmic trading techniques appeared to provide a promising lead against traders who were not invested in speed and analytics. But as the high-frequency trading (HFT) industry evolved, the market was open to anyone who could invest in systems, and it became crowded in due course.

More intelligence was increasingly needed in areas like forecasting and decision-making to maintain a lead and, therefore, the right to charge a premium. The journalist Isabella Kaminska has pointed out the law of diminishing returns applies for any institution built on the use of data, even when invested in algorithmic trading in pursuit of a competitive advantage.[114]

Acquiring data was not in itself the problem. In no time at all, other challenges arose: there was a competitive limit to the speed of a trade (you could not possibly go faster than the speed of light) and so on. Eventually, all formulas started to look the same, and players were all subject to the same

---

[114] I. Kaminska, "HFT as an insight into where fintech is going", *Financial Times*, 28 March 2017. Available at https://ftalphaville.ft.com/2017/03/28/2186482/hft-as-an-insight-into-where-fintech-is-going/.

regulatory controls, putting them back on the same starting point.

Undeterred, HFT traders started looking at new algorithms, techniques, and even new data types and angles to retain their edge. Machine learning and artificial intelligence all looked promising.

However, by 2014, a large number of HFT firms were either in liquidation or had merged with other firms because of intense competition. As high speed became more accessible to all traders, it not only reduced differentiation,[115] but perhaps, more ominously, added the very costs that the players thought they had overcome.

In the US alone, HFT revenues fell as much as 85% over several years, going from US$7.2 billion in 2009 to US$1.1 billion in 2016. TABB Group, a consultancy, has estimated that revenues slid US$900 million in 2018 alone. Then came the mergers.

Quantlab's acquisition of Teza's assets in 2017 was not successful in creating sufficient scale and market share to counter the rising costs and lower margins in this industry. Other players ventured to extend these services down to retail customers, which incurred its own set of costs and problems.

After 2014, the notional value of derivative trades went through an interesting correction. This was primarily due to the fall in oil prices, which accounted for as much as 35% of the derivatives trade and had lost 55% of its underlying value. But it was also driven by new technologies that reduced the size of the trades, making it possible for more players to participate and creating more liquidity that was able to affect trade volatility.

News information platforms such as Markit and inter-dealer broker Creditex were able to shrink trades to one-tenth the size of the gross notional market through more accurate and current pricing – another step in the growing financialization of everything.

In a similar development in retail payments, when the German fintech company Wirecard imploded in 2020, it was discovered that the cost of

---

[115] J. Rennison and J. Dye, "Ex Deutsche Bank traders have Libor-rigging convictions overturned", *Financial Times*, 27 January 2022. Available at https://www.ft.com/content/2bba9f8d-12f7-4f7a-ba59-f49555f7f01d.

processing payments had collapsed a long time ago. Wirecard had bought the transaction processing businesses of Visa and MasterCard in several regions in the hope that scale could ameliorate the fall in transaction costs.

Even so, the company still had to outsource the transactions to several even cheaper processing companies because the margins in payments processing had practically collapsed. Today, card companies make considerably more money from the marketing activities they manage for their member banks globally than they do from transactions. In fact, the actual transactions are increasingly tangential to the new business models arising in payments.

The idea of zero marginal costs continues to elude traditional finance players. Despite this, hope springs eternal, and the proliferation of digital-only banks around the world continues to be based on the dream that costs can be amortized by digital. Clearly, the real battle in the finance industry remains on the balance sheet and the zero marginal cost of technology augments, not replaces, that core tenant.

Blockchains, killed in the back office

Every few years, a supposedly era-defining technology is flaunted heavily in the financial services industry. Nobody is allowed to criticize it. CEOs are made to feel like idiots if they do not invest in it. A few years later, the fever will subside as mysteriously as it appeared and consumed the industry.

There are two blockchain crazes in finance today. One is the decentralized, permissionless version that is going from strength to strength, driven mostly by young people working outside traditional financial institutions.

The second blockchain craze, called the 'permissioned' version, involves finding every conceivable way to keep blockchain within the control of licensed institutions in finance. One will succeed. The other will fail.

Blockchain has tremendous potential to transform both how we validate and execute all kinds of transactions as well as how institutions are organized. At a basic level, blockchain technology is a continuation of the evolution of data from the days when it sat inside individual computers to the present, where it is stored on a shared ledger.

Newspapers around the world have extensively covered all kinds of blockchain projects in the world of finance. But almost all known blockchain projects in traditional financial institutions are for "permissioned" transactions. In other words, they are between known customers who are manually approved to participate in a transaction or ecosystem.

The real challenge is that traditional financial institutions are still haunted by their 'front office, middle office, back office' demons, and are trying to retrofit blockchain to support this outmoded way of thinking.

It seems like only yesterday when this phrase first swept the industry, during a time when trading floors started generating a lucrative source of new income via derivative trading activities.

The US$1.5 billion failure of Barings Bank in 1995 involved the tale of Nick Leeson, a 'front office' trader who had access to both the 'middle' and 'back office' concepts that were brand new at the time. The trading house was divided between the 'front office' where the traders made their trades, the 'middle office' that processed them, and the 'back office' where the trades were settled.

Each division was supposed to be managed separately so that traders could not falsify trades. Leeson, however, could access all three in the Singapore branch of the bank, far away from the main office in London, and set about falsifying his losses until he was caught. But the nightmare did not stop there. The phenomenon kept getting larger over the years.

In 1996, Yasuo Hamanaka of Sumitomo Corporation incurred $2.6 billion in trading losses and was sentenced to eight years in prison. In 2008, Jérôme Kerviel was convicted for trading losses at Société Generale to the tune of US$7 billion. In 2011, Kweku Adoboli, a director of the UBS Global Synthetic Equities Trading team in London, lost US$2 billion.

All three cases involved fraudulent transactions. All three men claimed that their bosses should have known about their trades. All insisted that they were motivated to generate profit for their banks and not for themselves. It's a story that repeats itself every year somewhere in the industry.

Because of this recurring nightmare, financial institutions and large corporations have invested billions of dollars in computer systems and an army of compliance and risk managers for fear of losing control of the middle and back office. Regulators reinforce this fear by putting in place punitive measures to ensure such fraud does not happen again.

The most visible manifestation of this fear is that financial institutions are unable to dismantle their armies of compliance and operational risk management employees. In all bank blockchain projects, compliance teams are still there and growing. It is as if blockchain technology never existed, let alone changed anything.

The governance structure that blockchain architecture offers runs counter to the entire idea of 'front office, middle office, back office'. To say that the middle office becomes a field of APIs, or that the back office becomes an unmanned reservoir in the cloud through big data and artificial intelligence, is akin to driving a powerful automobile with a horse hitched to the front.

Against this background, the way blockchain technology secures the integrity of transactions is ideologically incompatible with the self-preservation instincts of financial institutions today. For this reason, there are almost no 'permissionless' blockchain initiatives, pilots, or projects anywhere by traditional financial institutions or their regulators.

Moreover, the salaries paid to compliance and risk managers create a self-preservation instinct. Compliance and operational risk management jobs are paid very well in finance, more than in any other industry. This alone creates a cycle of self-justification, with employees seeking to create reasons for their continued existence.

Even technology companies like IBM, R3, and Hyperledger are reluctant to dismantle the 'enterprise' nature of big business. They build blockchain technology stacks carrying the same compliance and risk management infrastructure as in the pre-blockchain era.

On top of this, almost every bank-led blockchain project is proprietary to that institution, creating interoperability issues that have not even started to be discussed in the industry.

The industry took about 20 years of useless conferences to derive standards for interoperability, in what eventually became the SWIFT payment standards. Although the blockchain industry as a whole has been able to create interoperability in two short years, the finance industry is insistent on rebuilding its own iteration of this.

Attempts by banks to push through trends in supply chain or invoice financing for small businesses through the use of blockchain forget the lessons learned from the days of electronic data interchange (EDI) technology.

Bank-owned EDI consortiums like Bolero and the many bill presentation platforms in the past failed not because of technology, but how their members perceived the other financial institutions involved in transactions. Intermediaries do not like other intermediaries.

Blockchains developed by non-bank, third-party contractors like BlockApps and Consensys have a greater chance of extending into areas like trade finance than any bank-sponsored or dominated consortiums because they are not as selective as banks are in how they onboard participants and create interconnectivity with other platforms.

Signifyd, an API that offers fraud analysis by aggregating retail transactions across hundreds of companies, allows its users to contribute and benefit from collective learning better than any individual financial institution can. For blockchains to be fully functional, full and open participation by everyone and anyone is key, with each user contributing mutually validating information to the network.

It is for these reasons that the transformation of the industry will need to come from outside finance. A wholly different set of rules, which I call the 'symmetry of deception', will need to kick in. It is to these that we now turn to understand how all industries will eventually embrace blockchain technology.

The symmetry of deception

A phrase we are all too familiar with today is the 'symmetry of information', where all parties to a deal strive to get equal access to information. In this regard, car-sharing services like Uber and Lyft are firmly developments in their own industry, where stakeholders reveal their location, resources, and intentions in a symmetric manner.

In the old days, the crime was in the actual trade. In 2013, Panther Energy Trading and its owner, Michael J. Coscia, were fined US$2.8 million by the Commodity Futures Trading Commission for using sophisticated computer algorithms to illegally place and quickly cancel bids on commodity contracts in a practice known as 'spoofing', which had been categorically banned by Congress in 2010.[116] Their act was fraudulent, the practice was outlawed, and there was nowhere to hide.

During the Poly Networks heist of 2021, cyberthieves stole US$600 million worth of cryptocurrencies – only to return about half the amount in the next few days because they realized that they were being tracked.[117]

In 2022, in one of the biggest busts by the Federal Bureau of Investigation (FBI) to date, Ilya Lichtenstein and Heather Morgan stole 119,754 Bitcoins worth US$4.5 billion from Bitfinex and hid them on the Amazon cloud platform.[118] Both were active members of the cryptocurrency community. These points are being amply played out in the most recent cryptocurrency thefts.

Deception requires a different treatment. As we slide into the networked phase, parties share only information that they want to reveal, without also revealing their respective intentions. This is what I call the 'symmetry of

---

[116] S. Brush and L. Fortado, "Panther, Coscia Fined Over High-Frequency Trading Algorithms", *Bloomberg*, 22 July 2013. Available at https://www.bloomberg.com/news/articles/2013-07-22/panther-coscia-fined-over-high-frequency-trading-algorithms-1-.

[117] A. Kharpal and R. Browne, "Hackers return nearly half of the $600 million they stole in one of the biggest crypto heists", *CNBC*, 11 August 2021. Available at https://www.cnbc.com/2021/08/11/cryptocurrency-theft-hackers-steal-600-million-in-poly-network-hack.html.

[118] S. Lynch, R. Satter, and L. Cohen, "U.S. accuses couple of laundering $4.5 bln in bitcoin tied to 2016 hack", *Reuters*, 10 February 2022. Available at https://www.reuters.com/technology/us-arrests-couple-allegedly-laundering-45-bln-crypto-tied-bitfinex-hack-2022-02-08/.

deception'. All transacting parties share the relevant information but keep their respective motives to themselves. By contrast, in the Bitfinex episode, the thieving couple stored their information on the cloud in plain sight.

Clay Shirky has explored the concept of 'algorithmic authority',[119] where falsehoods are checked by the active participation of the users themselves. In other words, the more participants there are, the greater their ability to detect and curate malicious intent. This will require transforming the way we interact.

We see this already in social media, where people feel like they are all connected to each other, but only reveal the parts of themselves that they want their peers to see. Everyone assumes that their intentions are mutually transparent, but in a digital world, all parties to the network can be pursuing several different motives simultaneously.

Given the superior technological alternatives available to the individual in the networked phase, any individual can manage several realities simultaneously. The key risk factor in the networked world is deception, rather than corruption or exploitation. (I attribute this phrase to the social scientist David Ronfeldt, whose theory I will expound on more fully in the final chapter.)

One example of deception is in options trading. You know when someone has bought a lot of put or sell options on a stock, but you have no idea whether he is long or short on the stock. You may have access to the facts but not his motives.

The integrity of information sharing in the networked phase rests on all parties' bona fide participation; they have no reason to rob each other. But outside of that, no party has the right or even the ability to check on the intent of the other. This is where the opportunity for deception arises.

Deception can also be malicious, as seen in the attacks on 'flash loans', a decentralized finance product. In one such example, two attacks on the bZx lending platform in February 2020 allowed the attacker to drain hundreds of

---

[119] C. Shirky, "A Speculative Post on the Idea of Algorithmic Authority", blogpost on shirky.com, 15 November 2009. Available at http://www.shirky.com/weblog/2009/11/a-speculative-post-on-the-idea-of-algorithmic-authority/

thousands of dollars' worth of Ethereum cryptocurrencies from the platform.

These were not cyber-attacks involving the theft of an actual asset, but rather a situation where the attacker took advantage of a bug in the system to profit from it. Instead of just buying low and selling high, the attacker (or attackers) used the borrowed funds to manipulate markets that were unusually vulnerable. Patching these bugs before the next one emerges requires technology, not banking, skills.

Under such an approach, patch solutions are not mere corrections of errors but a self-learning system that becomes smarter after every breach. They allow participants to continue actively interacting with each other, without also requiring huge intermediaries to keep an eye on transactions.

Blockchain technology may appear to facilitate the integrity of the audit trail because the information is held by all transacting parties. No transacting party is able to compromise the integrity of the audit trail. But the intentions of the parties are not reflected in the blockchain. In other words, something might look like a trusted transaction, but can be a perfect conduit for carrying out deceptions.

This has a bearing on the way that cybersecurity infrastructure is being built in the networked world. There is a thinking that artificial intelligence detects patterns and therefore can detect deception. It does not, because the deception is not in the pattern: it is in parties' intangible, invisible intentions. The way to protect against this is to increase, not decrease, participation – to amortize potential damage across the collective intentions of as many participants as possible.

In the same way, algorithms are subject to deception, not fraud. Fraud denotes intention and can be programmed into or detected by algorithms. Deception exists outside stated intention and has to be accounted for differently. Something can be deceptive but not fraudulent (unless a crime is established), but perpetrators can still secure a pecuniary advantage that they may not have been entitled to. The innovation required to overcome financial crime in a networked world is completely different from anything established in the past.

CHAPTER 7

The institution crumbles

"Too big to fail isn't a policy; it's a problem."
Ben Bernanke, former chairman, US Federal Reserve

"How did you go bankrupt? Two ways. Gradually, then suddenly."
Ernest Hemingway, *The Sun Also Rises*

What are the defining institutions of our day, and what will be the ones of the next 10 years? In 2000 BC, it was arguably the temple; in the late Bronze Age, the military; in the Middle Ages, the nobility. It was the merchant army during the Renaissance, the state-sponsored trading house in the colonial era, and, just 20 years ago, the publicly-traded multinational corporation.

Why, then, do we think that traditional banks and financial institutions will remain the same as we know them today? In fact, the largest financial institutions today are not even banks any more. The largest bank in China, ICBC, has just US$3 trillion in total assets. Blackrock, the asset management company, runs US$5 trillion worth of assets and another estimated US$2 trillion worth of discretionary assets.

At the start of 2022, James Gorman, the CEO of Morgan Stanley, committed his bank's wealth management business to shooting for US$10 trillion worth of assets under investment.[120] The problem is that growing to such a size is no longer a matter of gaining market share against other competitors, but creating new products and assets that do not yet exist.

---

[120] J. Franklin, "Morgan Stanley lifts profitability target as it seeks $10tn in client assets", *Financial Times*, 19 January 2022. Available at https://www.ft.com/content/b7c1961f-09c4-4109-8c25-89acb00264b9.

Adam Smith originally called the institution the most unproductive form of organization. When writing the *Wealth of Nations* in 1776, at the start of the Industrial Revolution and modern capitalism, he thought that the most efficient way to trade in skills and labor was to be self-employed. According to him, "negligence and profusion" would result if society were organized like a corporation.

Nonetheless, the body corporate still became the primary entity by which we trade in goods and services. It was only in 1937, when the market economy was well established, that a young economist named Ronald Coase asked a very obvious question: if markets were indeed efficient and people could essentially hire workers and manufacture and distribute goods in the normal course of supply and demand, instead of between corporations, why did we still need companies?

Coase went on to answer his own question in his now-famous 1937 paper, *The Nature of the Firm,* and other writings.[121] He pointed out that despite Smith's maxim that the market could discover the best price most efficiently, the economic cost of finding information was high. As a result, the body corporate was the better way to make business more predictable in terms of costs, value, timing, and delivery.

Despite Bill Gates' 1984 proclamation that "banks were dinosaurs", the script that subsequently played out was very different from what he imagined. It was the hunter who became the hunted. Technology companies – including Microsoft – were themselves transformed, reorganized around armies of open-source coders who no longer needed to work inside large organizations to build software products.

Technology players had to overhaul their original business models several times over, going from software sellers to subscription platforms and eventually community builders in the cloud. Microsoft today is an entirely different organization from what it was in 1984. Other technology companies, from Adobe to SAP, also morphed into cloud-based communities, deriving

---

[121] R. H. Coase, "The Nature of the Firm", *Economica* vol. 4 pp. 386-405 (2018). DOI: 10.1111/j.1468-0335.1937.tb00002.x

income from bringing their coders and users together into one interactive ecosystem.

Device use evolved too, going from desktops to laptops, tablets, and mobile. A Goldman Sachs research paper has pointed out that while Microsoft accounted for 97% of all operating systems on any computing device in 2000, this figure dwindled to only 26% in 2013 as the range of personal devices exploded. It will change again when devices move from mobile to the Internet of Things, by which time the actual devices in question will become irrelevant.

Continuing with the development of the open-source universe, in February 2017, Microsoft first migrated its Windows development from Perforce, another proprietary version control system, and eventually bought GitHub in 2018. IBM bought Red Hat, another open-source platform, in 2019.

The players making these acquisitions had suffered massive fallout in their existing business models. IBM had seen its quarterly revenue fall for 23 quarters before finally announcing plans to separate its cloud and legacy businesses in 2020. In other words, it had to be transformed if it was to survive.

These developments also beg the question if we will ever see the disintermediation of any business created on open source from the reaches of the incumbent players that absorb them, including financial services.

The balance sheet never lies

I have stated several times in the book already that innovation in finance is defined not by technological developments, but what takes place on the balance sheet. In his classic book *Bits, Bytes and Balance Sheets*, Walter Wriston suggested that all balance sheets tell a story. To track changes taking place in any business, read their balance sheets like you would a score sheet to play a song on the piano.

The story of Deutsche Bank, one of several global banks that went through a metamorphosis over the 1990s and into the 2000s, is an object lesson in how the balance sheet captured the story of poor decisions and leadership in finance, characterized by megalomania and sheer stupidity.

Deutsche Bank's balance sheet rose from 573 billion Deutsche marks (about €292 billion) in 1994 to €2.2 trillion in 2007, a ripping growth by any measure.[122] It was not, however, achieved organically.

In 1994, most of Deutsche Bank's earnings came from traditional, organic, domestic commercial banking. In 1999, it soldered on Bankers Trust, a global investment bank that mainly operated from London, and culturally and intuitively a very different organization from the parent bank in Frankfurt.

The 1990s proved to be very profitable for several Anglo-Saxon banks in their respective domestic businesses, particularly in the UK, but also in Germany and the Netherlands. This might have continued had their leaders' egos not got the better of them. Buoyed by their success in the domestic markets, they started harboring ambitions of becoming global investment banks.

By 2010, investment banking had climbed to account for 50% of Deutsche Bank's profits. However, it also consumed 50% of the bank's equity and 75% of leverage assets. It was guzzling capital like almond orchards consume water.

Similarly, on the costs side, from 1994 to 2015, Deutsche Bank's employee size grew only 30%, but total salaries rose by 200% to €13 billion in the same time. Most of this rise was paid out to the new investment bankers and markets teams.

In 1994, more than 75% of its employees were based in its home country, Germany. By 2001, more than 50% were based in the UK and the US, and by 2007, fully two-thirds of the bank's employees and income were from outside Germany. It became technically a UK-domiciled bank.

Culturally and operationally, these were completely unsustainable

---

[122] Ullrich Fichtner, H. G. (2016, October 22). How a Pillar of German Banking Lost Its Way. *Der Spiegel*.

numbers. It had gone from being a conservative Germanic institution to one driven by English-speaking, Anglo-Saxon mores imported from employees based in London and not Frankfurt.

Between 2001 and 2015, the global markets division of Deutsche Bank earned €25 billion after tax. But since 2012, the bank has been paying at least €12 billion in fines, long after the investment bankers had been paid their bonuses and left the bank.

For years, it begged asking if that journey was ever worth it in the first place. Deutsche Bank eventually started the long journey back to refocusing its balance sheet on its European roots, but the Germany it returned to was not the same Germany of the 1990s.[123] It was time for a new chapter to begin.

Deutsche Bank's story is not unique. The balance sheet of the other so-called global European banks, like RBS, Lloyds TSB, and ABN Amro, made a similarly dramatic transition between the 1990s and the banking crisis of 2008. None of them thought there were limits to just how large and dominant they could become.

In the US, a similar transition started when Citibank and Chase Manhattan pushed for the repeal of the Glass-Steagall Act of 1932, which kept US commercial banks from engaging in investment banking.

The Act was replaced by the Gramm-Leach-Bliley Act of 1999, allowing these banks to merge their investment bank and securities businesses. Before long, all the major US banks started accumulating dangerous levels of derivatives on their balance sheets.

In the mid-1990s, the combined assets of what is now known as the Big Six group of large financial companies in the US were less than 20% of GDP, with no bank being larger than 4% of GDP, inclusive of their off-balance sheet liabilities.

By the late 2000s, the six largest banks controlled over 60% of GDP combined, triple than what they did a decade ago, mainly because of their

---

[123] M. Arnold, "Boost for Staley's as Barclays investment bank outperforms rivals", *Financial Times*, 27 April 2018. Available at https://www.ft.com/content/97250344-491e-11e8-8ee8-cae73aab7ccb.

huge trading books. Today, the top four US banks control 50% of the total assets of the country's banking system.[124]

The concentration risk argument is distorted because the composition of assets in larger institutions differs from smaller ones. When they are small, their assets are composed mainly of plain loans. But when they are larger, it is usually because they have a large trading book.

The valuation of the trading books of any bank in the world is mainly notional and has nothing to do with any real underlying assets. At one point, speculation on Deutsche Bank's total derivatives exposure was anything between US$45 trillion and US$60 trillion.[125]

The derivative books of US banks were of similar magnitude relative to the size of the institutions. These numbers could destroy entire countries, let alone banks, and they were not based on any objectively verifiable estimates. Warren Buffet once called them "financial weapons of mass destruction".

In the US, the Dodd-Frank Act of 2010 and the accompanying Volcker Rule were among the better attempts to reign in derivatives trading for its own sake, not for hedging and not for their customers – not that they limited US banks' capacity for self-sabotage.

In 2012, four years after the US banking crisis and long after legislation was put in place, JP Morgan, a global bank, incurred losses estimated at over US$9 billion in credit default swap trades, described as "derivatives of derivatives", in the so-called London Whale incident.

Almost every year, there is a derivatives-related scandal affecting one bank or another. It can be assumed that all the major banks have larger derivatives exposures unaccounted for in their balance sheets to this day. Despite the attempts to rein them in, banks simply became a different beast: not just large on the balance sheet, but almost ungovernable from a management perspective.

---

[124] A. Phaneuf, "Largest US Banks by Assets in 2022", *Insider Intelligence*, 2 January 2022. Available at https://www.insiderintelligence.com/insights/largest-banks-us-list.

[125] M. Bird, "Understanding Deutsche Bank's $47 Trillion Derivatives Book", *The Wall Street Journal*, 5 October 2016. Available at https://www.wsj.com/articles/does-deutsche-bank-have-a-47-trillion-derivatives-problem-1475689629.

The network age will add another layer of complexity to the balance sheet of traditional banks. Some will be carrying cryptocurrencies and other esoteric assets. Others will carry exposures to factors outside their control. But studying a bank's balance sheet will give us the best indication of the kinds of issues it will face and the kind of beast it really is. It never lies.

The ring-fencing riddle

Building on the theme that the balance sheet is the best indicator of a bank's profile, attempts to manipulate it just because technology enables us to do so will not necessarily result in workable solutions.

After the 2008 banking crisis, regulators in the US, UK, and Europe went into a frenzy trying to ring-fence banks' traditional and organic domestic business from the investment banking portions that got them into trouble. It may well have been a case of closing the stable gates after the horses had bolted and technically impossible to achieve, but they tried.

The UK eventually responded with its own ring-fencing legislation in a Banking Commission Report under the auspices of Sir John Vickers. It was an attempt to bring banking back to basics by limiting what banks could or could not do on their balance sheets. It was made possible because regulators simply assumed that the technology allowed them to do so.

A host of 'challenger' banks in the UK, like Atom, Monese, Monzo, Osper, Starling, and Tandem, and mobile-only banks in the US like Simple, Moven, BankMobile, and GoBank, boasted of being able to onboard large numbers of customers using advanced advertising campaign matrices run by an army of social media experts. India created a similar category called "payment banks" that could collect deposits but not issue loans.

The introduction of chatbots, mobile apps, and so-called robo-advisors could routinely onboard 60,000 - 100,000 new customers a month for banks and brokerages, numbers that could not be achieved in the physical realm. The technology appeared to offer the possibility that if origination costs were kept low, it would make the ring-fenced businesses commercially viable.

The so-called 'neo-banks' in the UK and the payments banks in India encountered this conundrum as well. Although they were licensed to collect all the deposits in the world, they were also ring-fenced from profiting from this.

Old-school commercial banks used to manage their cost-of-funds by using profitability from the proprietary trading book to transfer the price of their core deposits. However, challenger banks in some markets today incur incredibly high operating costs on acquiring their deposits without being able to deploy them as a traditional bank does – because the lending side has a mismatch of tenure, capital, and liquidity levels of its own.

But ring-fencing also created other problems. The first is an existential one: financial institutions which do not have both sides of the balance sheet invariably lack the discipline that comes with knowing their customers on both sides to keep their business sustainable.

The ring-fenced institutions knew how to get the liabilities (deposit) side of the balance sheet right, but not the asset side. Over time, the industry became akin to one huge social media project, where those with skills in making the mobile experience 'frictionless' became the most authoritative professionals.

But without profitable lending, trading, or investment business on the other side of the balance sheet, all the social media talent in the world only became a huge cost to the digital banks licensed to play this game.

They had not figured out how to monetize the deluge of customers they were onboarding. The deluge itself was ephemeral, with every new player generating even better onboarding numbers than the ones just a few weeks before.

It soon became cheaper, faster, and highly commoditized to originate these kinds of numbers, despite the fact that almost none of the challenger banks in the UK or the payments banks in India were ever profitable as standalone businesses.

From the banks that have been publishing their balance sheets, we can see that the innovators were strong deposit-takers on the liabilities side of things without a strong corresponding revenue-generating asset – although, this said, they were not allowed by law to grow this.

Under the traditional banking model, there were considerable cross-subsidies between different business lines. If one was unprofitable, it could still be justified as a necessary service to secure the others. But when the regulators created these ring-fenced players, it created fintech technology mismatches at several levels that were not immediately obvious.

Another form of ring-fencing involved the launch of digital banks around the world. Many countries licensed digital-only banks with lower capital requirements than traditional banks in exchange for limits on the types of business they are allowed to do. However, a recent report from the consulting firm BCG suggested that more than 95% of digital banks globally are not profitable.[126]

It is not an exaggeration to say that it takes only about ten people to start a digital bank today. It is virtually possible to do this in a garage at the lowest possible cost. All the technology required to run a digital bank today can already be set up or bought on the cloud. In several countries today, a digital-only bank license can be secured for a paid-up capital of just US$10 million.

But the add-ons like people, process, and compliance costs required to start a finance platform today bring things right back to the same, if not higher, cost structures of the traditional banks they were intended to replace.

Regulators throw in an encyclopedia full of rules that come from traditional banking and can only be met by applicant banks employing armies of management consultants, technology vendors, and 'experienced' former bankers, all at high costs. The consulting fees alone are another US$30 million. By the time the first digital bank is up and running, at least 1,000 employees would have been hired to run the project.

The digital bank then takes 3-5 years to get on its feet, burning

---

[126] J. Choi, Y. Erande, Y. Yu, and C. J. Aquino, " Emerging Challengers and Incumbent Operators Battle for Asia Pacific's Digital Banking Opportunity", *Boston Consulting Group* report, 7 June 2021. Available at https://web-assets.bcg.com/53/42/92f340e345dab62aa227fd53ccd4/asian-digital-challenger-bank.pdf.

billions of marketing dollars in the process, but will never match the number of customers of the incumbents. Its activities fail to generate any transformational value that can be plugged back into the real economy, beyond more churn activity for activity's sake.

There are a handful of exceptions. The digital-only bank in Korea, Kakao Bank, has been profitable since its inception because its core business was in foreign exchange. The digital-only banks in China have been profitable because any bank that could gather deposits cheaply could lend them to other banks in the inter-bank market at a good net interest margin.

To the extent that these products and income concessions exist in other parts of the world, some digital banks will be profitable due to very specific products or access to funds. The rest, unfortunately, will find it nearly impossible to compete against the incumbents on price or scale.

The liquidity sitting outside

One important reason financial products will look very different in the networked world from how they do today is that financial liquidity, the essence of the industry's resources, will increasingly sit outside of formal institutions. It sounds like a technology issue, but it is really a balance sheet one.

Financial liquidity is a child of information. When information rested on balance sheets, liquidity was to be found in balance sheets. When information was to be found in the markets, liquidity was to be found in the markets. When information is floating around the networks, liquidity will be found in the networks. Institutions will simply have to adapt.

Today, regulators and economists alike both see that liquidity – and the leverage ratios that affect it – sits only inside the balance sheets of financial institutions. They cannot imagine a world where financial liquidity exists *outside* the balance sheet and has to be managed as such.

Central banks, treasuries, and regulators around the world use the banking industry's balance sheets to manage entire economies by imposing reserve requirements, capital charges, and leverage ratios on financial institutions when massive amounts of liquidity exist outside the industry in corporations, funds, and ordinary people's pockets.

The very detailed and complex global liquidity or capital requirements for financial institutions was hijacked by politicians sitting around the Financial Stability Forum after the 2008 banking crisis, trying to control systemic problems that existed in their imaginations.

The Bank for International Settlement (BIS), the master global regulator, has a rule in Basel III that requires a liquidity coverage ratio, whereby banks must maintain enough liquid assets to meet their needs for an arbitrary 30 days in a crisis.

Concepts like the BIS's Net Stable Funding Ratios (NSFR) and the EU's Additional Liquidity Monitoring Metrics (ALMM) are just subjective indicators supporting an accounting fiction around assets whose valuations increasingly fluctuate over a multitude of issues.

Precisely because of the difficulty of keeping up with the proliferation of rules, there is the added complication of 'internal models' – yet another fiction assigned by regulators to be managed by the bank directly to keep them internally focused.

Financial institutions find that they have to leverage their balance sheets to maximize return on investments (ROI) on the business.[127] Leverage is a double-edged sword to maximize capital and provide liquidity, or a three-edged one if we take into account the fact that leverage both needs and creates liquidity.

We have to think about capital markets, bank deposits, lending, and investments in liquid assets, all together and all at the same time.[128] Outside this genie's lamp, short-term funding has been falling over the years, and

---

[127] A. K. Kashyap, R. Rajan, and J. Stein, "Banks as Liquidity Providers: An Explanation for the Co-Existence of Lending and Deposit-Taking", *Journal of Finance* vol. 57(1) pp. 33-73 (2002). Available at https://scholar.harvard.edu/files/stein/files/liqpro-jf-final.pdf.

[128] H. DeAngelo & R. M. Stulz. "Liquid-claim production, risk management, and bank capital structure: Why high leverage is optimal for banks", *Journal of Financial Economics*, 116 (2), pp. 219-236 (2015).

whatever is still in the market is increasingly collateralized and therefore more expensive.

Ironically, because of a pecking order where the largest players have greater access to cheaper and larger sources of liquidity, even in the strongest economic conditions, there can still be small players who suffer chronic liquidity problems and have to pay a premium just to stay afloat.

As one can imagine, all these result in counterparty risk rising to more than ten times the capital that regulators are asking banks to put aside to survive liquidity risks. The leverage that banks are carrying today is owed to each other, instead of extending their lending businesses to their customers and to the real economy.

On the other hand, large banks like Deutsche Bank, Barclays, and Société Generale have in the past reduced their cash reserves (namely their holdings of government bonds, cash, deposits with other banks, and other easily liquidated assets) just to improve their leverage to achieve shareholder returns.

As a result of scrambling to meet these increasingly twisted requirements, financial institutions and corporations are left without the bandwidth to respond to the challenges and opportunities of an increasingly networked world.

The current thinking on bank leverage and liquidity is developed by the most brilliant economics and banking brains of our times, including academics and central bankers like Nobel laureate Bengt Robert Holmström and his collaborator Jean Tirole. Their theories assume asymmetry of information, namely that not all parties participating in a decision have equal access to the same information.

At the same time, there was already some recognition in basic banking models – even in the early days before the technologies we know today – that the demand for liquidity is exogenous to institutions.[129]

---

[129] D. W. Diamond and P. Dybvig, "Bank Runs, Deposit Insurance, and Liquidity," *Journal of Political Economy* vol. 91(3) pp. 401-419 (1983). Available at http://www.bu.edu/econ/files/2012/01/DD83jpe.pdf.

Way back in the early 2000s, the academic, economist, and future central banker, Rajan Raghuram, observed that the efficiency of the transmission process and the quality of intermediaries also play an essential role in generating liquidity. In 2001, he made the interesting suggestion that bank depositors themselves would be in a position to determine the quality and risk of loans if they were given more information.[130]

He was thinking about efficiency of the intermediation process. This is being incrementally improved today through the development of peer-to-peer lending, instant digital payments platforms, digital wallets, and digital money market funds where lenders or payors have direct and instant information regarding their money.

The speed of transactions also facilitates liquidity. Instantaneous payments and settlement release funds into the networks that were previously trapped by $T+x$ settlement times. However, speed is not necessarily universally desired. A whole series of intermediaries in many systems continue to prefer friction for several reasons, good and bad alike.

In markets where the intermediation industry is still poorly run, liquidity can still be realized by unlocking huge non-performing and delinquent loans still sitting on balance sheets. There are technological ways to resolve this as well.

Aspirational fintech players have alluded to the same theories. Kristo Käärmann, a founder of the online cross-border money transfer business Wise (formerly called TransferWise), once told me that the supply and demand of foreign exchange on both sides of their trades for all their currency-pairs have never had problems of liquidity since their business started in 2013.[131]

Kaarmann said that the traditional banks have liquidity issues because the entire banking payments infrastructure has large pockets of liquidity

---

[130] D. W. Diamond and R. Rajan, "Banks and Liquidity", *American Economic Review* 91(2) pp. 422-425 (2001). Available at https://www.aeaweb.org/articles?id=10.1257/aer.91.2.422.

[131] "TransferWise's Kaarman: Banks haven't really treated their users transparently", *The Asian Banker*, 13 April 2018. Available at https://live.theasianbanker.com/video/transferwises-kaarmann-banks-havent-really-treated-their-users-transparently.

trapped in opaque counterparty and capital requirements. When liquidity exists outside the institution and is easily discoverable by the user, it becomes freed up to use.

Similarly, Brad Garlinghouse, the CEO of the blockchain-based transaction services platform, Ripple, has said that the liquidity needs of banks today are managed with literally US$10 trillion worth of float that sits locked up in Nostro and Vostro accounts.[132]

The banks that dominated the derivatives trade preferred to trade with each other on proprietary platforms rather than on open exchanges with non-banks. As discussed in the earlier chapter on the Reddit revolution, there have already been instances where the extrinsic forces of retail investors have broken through to wrest the price discovery process from these closed communities.

In fact, the black box approach to managing risks is wholly extrinsic. Blackrock's Aladdin (Asset, Liability, Debt and Derivative Investment Network), which claims to be able to process all possible external risk scenarios, is probably one of the most extensive electronic risk management systems run by one of the world's largest investment management companies.

Aladdin keeps track of about 30,000 investment portfolios and supports decision-making for about US$21.6 trillion in assets (including BlackRock's own US$9 trillion assets), which at one time was about 7% of the world's financial assets.[133]

Aladdin counts amongst its clients other leading fund managers like Vanguard and State Street, as well as half the top ten insurance companies, Japan's $1.5 trillion pension fund, and several of the largest US listed companies. (Perhaps just as important is the fact that it has a revolving door with the political establishment.)

---

[132] C. Terenzi, "Brad Garlinghouse says Ripple wants to reach $2 trillion XRP liquidity", *Use The Bitcoin*, November 2019. Available at https://usethebitcoin.com/brad-garlinghouse-says-ripple-wants-to-reach-2-trillion-xrp-liquidity/.

[133] R. Ungarino, "Here are 9 fascinating facts to know about BlackRock, the world's largest asset manager", *Business Insider*, December 2020. Available at https://www.businessinsider.com/what-to-know-about-blackrock-larry-fink-biden-cabinet-facts-2020-12.

Meanwhile at the product level, more start-ups are demonstrating that there is value in being transparent and sharing data with customers. The FX market is a prime candidate for revolution; its wholesale side has been kept deliberately opaque so that the dominant players could profit from a fragmented retail FX distribution base (money-changers and small domestic banks that extend these services to their customers).

Access to information today is anything but symmetric, portending to the continued domination of big business in a digital society. Digital platforms like Google and Amazon aggregate even larger amounts of data than institutions did in the past. Each of these aggregators protects massive proprietary platforms that applications sit on and function in their own silos.

The key difference is that the data which exists outside of institutions is now more valuable than the data within them. Blockchain and API technologies demand that the institutions that rely on them extend the trust and integrity in the transaction to users. The technology companies of the world have figured this out. Most financial services players have not.

Some new digital banks are natives of this transition. In China, WeBank claims to process about one terabyte of external data every single day to develop the profile required to monitor each of its customers, akin to Tesla saying that it processes 10 billion terabytes of data for each of its cars. That said, the technology inside a Tesla autonomous vehicle depends on data that comes from outside the vehicle. It is externally focused on the road and its surroundings. One day, all businesses will be too.

But we want to be banks too

A decade after the onslaught of the supposed fintech disruptors, many of them are throwing in the towel and either acquiring a bank or applying for licenses to become banks themselves.

Lending Club acquired Radius Bank in the UK. Square and SoFi acquired banking licenses in the US. A whole array of players, including Revolut, Lunar Bank, and Margo Bank are famously doing the same in

Europe at the time of writing. The question that arises is: why are so many of the disruptors wanting to become the very banks they sought to replace?

Peer-to-peer (P2P) lenders were the first disruptors which emerged to replace banks in the early 2000s. One by one, they, along with the other 'challenger' and neo-banks, failed by aspiring to become the very institutions they were seeking to oust.

In the UK, Zopa, self-styled as the world's oldest P2P player, eventually applied to start a challenger bank alongside its original platform in 2020, saying that leverage would make it a more attractive investment for its shareholders.[134] The real reason is that it had failed in its original P2P lending business. It was onboarding only US$1 billion of loans every year in a crowded marketplace and was desperate to show its investors it could scale with minimum risk.

In all the time that Zopa was a challenger institution, it tried competing on the same basis as how banks reviewed borrowers, which resulted in merely reinforcing the existing model for doing so. It walked right into the same problems – high capital costs, leverage, proprietary data, and products – as the incumbents it was trying to replace.

Platforms alone do not determine the success of a financial services business. In finance, funding costs, liquidity, risks, and profitability are not technology issues but balance sheet ones – the site of a whole host of other battles themselves.

These first-generation disruptors failed on several counts. First, they were selling the same products as the institutions they wanted to challenge. Because they thought of loans as products in the same way banks did, they had to mimic the same elements required to deliver them, such as management, marketing, risk, delivery, technology, compliance, and collection costs, even though they were not subject to the same regulatory requirements.

---

[134] J.D. Alois, "Zopa Becomes a Bank. Fintech Announces Approval of Full Bank License as it Moves Beyond Online Lending", *Crowdfund Insider*, 23 June 2020. Available at https://www.crowdfundinsider.com/2020/06/163139-zopa-becomes-a-bank-fintech-announces-approval-of-full-bank-license-as-it-moves-beyond-online-lending/.

Very simply, they should not have been selling loans at all. But in the first iteration of the challenger institutions, the industry had no idea what loans should be replaced with. Customer credit profiles in finance are still based on historical and static credit bureau information, selling traditional loans that changed precisely nothing.

Today, virtually no fintech players question the relevance of the products they design and sell in the digital world. A mutual fund is still a mutual fund, bought and sold by brokerages and traditional fund managers as a standalone product with all its backend processes intact, including redemption delays and institutional costs. Digitizing a mutual fund business involves digitizing the delivery of the product but not the product itself. It is a theme we will explore in detail in the next chapter.

The second reason is that the two sides of many disruptors' balance sheets don't match. Although they assume they are using the same balance sheet as the incumbents, with ring-fencing rules in place, as well as the focus of innovations on the liabilities side of the business, the balance sheet of any disruptor is far more restricted than that of a fully licensed bank.

On the technology front, the user experience (UX) teams in the neophyte start-ups were geniuses. They dramatically scaled the onboarding of the deposit side of the business. The early mobile banks, Moven and Fidor, were onboarding up to 60,000 new customers per month in their time, numbers that high-street banks were not able to match.

But as soon as these customers were onboarded, the costs of maintaining and monetizing them kicked in. Moreover, as fast as a company can acquire customers, it can also lose them just as quickly to the next disruptor that comes along, whether on price or user experience. Worse, innovators get stuck with customers who become inactive very swiftly and cannot be revived after that.

The third reason is that disruptors have not yet been able to use the network effect to its fullest, in an era where the speed and volume of data can transform a product. For example, a mutual fund operating with speed and transparency could easily be rendered as a fee-paying current account linked to lifestyle choices. The disruptors did not go far enough to perfect the dialogue with customers which the platforms were supposed to enable, which brings us back to the rise of the Reddit rebels discussed earlier.

With higher and faster bandwidth in telecommunications infrastructure, quantum computing on a cloud-native platform with low latency will make the current construction of the body corporate untenable. It will also give P2P platforms' current business models a new lease of life.

Just like the first motorized vehicles were no faster than the horse-drawn carriages they were trying to replace, on top of the fact that roads were not yet tarred and the pneumatic tyres on which these heavy machines rode were still to come, challenger institutions will have to wait for some of the supporting infrastructure to be in place before their business models can become fully viable.

Sadly, venture capitalists do not take a long-term view of their investments in finance in the same way they do with technology. They cannot see beyond how current technology is applied in finance – and they are terrified of regulation. On top of this, the glut of conditions imposed by regulators not only leaves challenger institutions subservient to their traditional rivals, but limits their potential to break through.

In the meantime, developments to ensure that the transformation is capable of taking place both ways are under way. In insisting that stablecoins are regulated as deposit-taking institutions by the Federal Deposit Insurance Corporation (FDIC), US regulators are providing a back-door for some banks to be reduced to stablecoins and for some stablecoins to become banks themselves. What they call themselves is irrelevant: on the basis of their balance sheets, both are deposit-taking institutions that morphed into a new monster in the digital age.

CHAPTER 8

Reimagining the product

"Platforms do not create products. Conversations do."
Parker, Van Alstyne, & Choudary, 2016

"He is no fool to lose what he cannot keep, to gain what he cannot lose."
Jim Elliot, *Passion and Purity*

Those of us born before the 1970s will be familiar with Kodak, the company once world-famous for its iconic 35mm color film cartridges in their yellow boxes. Every tourist destination in the world, no matter how remote, would have stores selling these cartridges for manually loading into cameras to take photos.

Kodak stopped selling these film cartridges only in 2009. It was already on its way to declaring bankruptcy, which it did two years later. It had kept on producing its physical film cameras until 2004, when it was evident even in the 1990s that film was on the way out in favor of digital.

In a now-famous speech I gave in 2017, "Banking's Kodak Moment", I argued that like Kodak, the finance industry will also come to a point when it will be asking itself why it kept pushing the same products for as long as it did, when the economy was clearly moving towards a whole new realm that required new products.

Looking to the music industry, early platforms like Napster, BitTorrent, and Kazaa not only disintermediated the way that the compact discs (CD) and music stores delivered music, but set in motion a series of developments that resulted in the eventual rise of Apple and Spotify. These, in turn, became super-aggregators that spawned a totally new set of economic outcomes in the music industry.

Such a transformation has not taken place in finance yet. In fact, the finance's industry hiding behind licenses and policies to tide out the ravages of commoditization is akin to how music labels introduced digital rights management (DRM) in a hopeless attempt to protect intellectual property rights from appropriation by the likes of Napster and BitTorrent.

The music label companies then were still holding on to the world of CDs and other media at a time when these were being taken away, and the benefit of a fully digital music industry was not clear to them. In the same way, the effect of licenses in financial services prevents the industry from imagining a brave new world that is already on the horizon.

Today, conventional belief is that digitization is leading finance and other industries towards Rifkin's concept of zero marginal costs, discussed in an earlier chapter. Many CEOs think that if they have a digitalized product, it will cost them nothing and the incremental revenue is all profit.

The truth is that the majority of fintech innovations eventually fail due to the unexpected costs of running digital products. At the end of the day, digitizing the same financial products from the legacy world still requires armies of marketing and sales teams (which never meet their targets) as well as compliance and funding costs, all in a finite marketplace.

Applying too much technology to an incumbent system only reinforces the status quo. It is not the way to create the future. A standard mortgage on a house in a quiet neighborhood of a reasonably small country does not need the AI that banks are purporting to pour into their products. The products themselves have to change, but this is simply not what is happening today.

Mapping the birth of new products

Of the 66 fintech unicorns in the world, estimated to be worth US$230 billion in investment value as of April 2020, almost all of them are pursuing better and smoother deliveries of the same deposits, loans, and investment products that we have always known.

By enabling banks to sell the same old products, focusing on the data held within institutions and failing to tap user-generated content, the fintech industry only adds layers, clutter, and complexity at multiple levels. They make current financial products more, not less, expensive and cumbersome.

With a few exceptions, the finance industry has not been building on the opportunities that are being thrown at it from the network effect of the digital economy. The UK's Open Banking Working Group is an excellent concept for opening up financial services to all players. Having said this, the players who should have benefited from the Open Banking model assumed that customers wanted the same banking products the industry has been selling all along. They have underestimated the potential of APIs to personalize products that never existed in the past.

Let us consider several examples. The product at the core of Lemonade, a unicorn fintech company valued at around US$2 billion, is at its heart still a traditional, regulated insurance offering, albeit being one sold faster and more smartly than before.

The product inside a Stripe payment is digitally smooth and effortless, but still, in essence, the same traditional credit card processed by Visa and MasterCard 30 years ago. So is Rapyd, which is purportedly helping small businesses with digitizing old-fashioned payments.

By keeping Visa and MasterCard out of China, the Chinese platforms Alipay and WeChat Pay introduced a whole new universe of connected supply chains that transformed lifestyles forever, but the West did not catch on to this trend. Every product was siloed, existing in its own little column and unconnected to other products.

Robinhood, for all its claims of revolutionizing retail investing, is still an equities brokerage service. Avant claims its loans are cheaper – but it can't technically manage this because it sells the same old-fashioned loans as traditional banks, and will be slapped with the same compliance, risk management, marketing, and operational costs as the latter. To get around this, it just targets higher-risk customers to whom it can still charge a premium.

These companies might repackage their products, onboarding millions of customers quickly by cross-subsidizing the costs involved with another side of the business, but their products are ultimately the same as those carried by traditional, non-digital players.

Trying to create a digital mousetrap around the same products as before is digitization, not innovation. Worse, predatory pricing tucked away somewhere in the business model is not innovation but enticement. It is predatory, replicating everything that is wrong with finance in the digital age without bringing us any closer to the personalization of finance.

Transforming the finance industry cannot mean selling more of the same deposits, same lending, same mutual funds, or same capital market deals. If the products they sell today have not changed, nothing has.

Table 2 suggests a visual evolution of financial products that tracks the transitioning in the technology platform. It takes into account various points which have been made in this book, namely, that assets will become increasingly ephemeral, that individuals should be able to design their own products, and that the products themselves will become increasingly device agnostic.

Tom Lee, the economist and managing partner of the hedge fund research company FundStrat with a solid track record of predicting stock market performance, points out the confluence of the network effect on a wider range of assets as creating new economic trends that we still don't quite understand. In an increasingly networked world, wealth becomes an asset when it is shared, not hoarded. The data that indexes the relationship between all of the different data points becomes a product in its own right.

As we enter the personalization phase, products will be increasingly device-independent, which requires us to basically throw out the credit card and ATMs mindset. When devices are interconnected and interacting with a lot of profile data in the Internet of Things, the owner of said data will be in a better position to design their own products.

The following sections challenge today's bankers to give up their most treasured products; to reimagine products that are more "refrigerators" rather than the "ice boxes" that they have been selling. It requires a bold assertion of where the future is taking us and a willingness to give up the familiar for untested products that have never existed on balance sheets before.

Dump the deposit account

The bank deposit account is the Kodak equivalent of the financial services industry today. This is the one product that banks can't imagine giving up, ever.

The response to the suggestion to give it up will probably be incredulity at multiple levels. But around the world, customers have generally moved *out* of deposits. The mutual fund industry in the US is now worth US$29.3 trillion in assets under management (AUM). This is 62% more than all the deposits in US banks combined, which currently stands at US$18 trillion.[135] (The US itself accounts for 40% of the world's mutual fund industry, although much of the profit of fund managers comes from outside the US.) Fund managers like Blackrock and Blackstone are much bigger than the world's largest banks.

More importantly, the global mobile wallet market, which was valued at US$1.54 trillion in 2020, is projected to reach US$11.83 trillion by 2028,[136] growing at a compound annual growth rate of 29.1% from 2020 to 2027.[137] The mobile wallet is the most dynamic replacement for the humble deposit, as it can be integrated directly into the everyday lifestyle needs of depositors.

Banks can also choose to play the field by providing fee-based Nostro account services to all kinds of digital wallets. Stablecoins, as a form of

---

[135] "United States Total Deposits for June 2021", via CEICData.

[136] "Mobile Payment Market Size, Share and Covid-19 Analysis", Fortune Business Insights report, January 2022. Available at https://www.fortunebusinessinsights.com/industry-reports/mobile-payment-market-100336.

[137] "*Mobile Wallet Market by Type, Technology, End User and Industry Vertical: Global Opportunity Analysis and Industry Forecast, 2020-2027*", Research and Markets report, April 2020. Available at https://www.researchandmarkets.com/reports/5118741/mobile-wallet-market-by-type-technology-end?utm_source=dynamic&utm_medium=CI&utm_code=9jzr3m&utm_campaign=1408567+-+Global+Mobile+Wallet+Market+(2020+to+2027)+-+by+Type%2c+Technology%2c+End-user+and+Indus.

Table 2: A product map

	Before 1991	From about 1991	From about 1999	From about 2010	From about 2020
Development of the internet/Web stages	Early internet	Web 1.0	Web 2.0	Web 3.0	Personalization
	Computerization	Netscape	World Wide Web/ Social Web	Semantic Web	Emotional Web
			User-generated social media; Google, Facebook, Amazon	Mobile-led, advanced platforms using AI, machine learning, always present, open-source	Device independence, Internet of Things, interconnected blockchains and tokens
Finance	Finance 1.0	Finance 2.0	Finance 3.0	Finance 4.0	Finance 5.0
	Collateralized loans	Collateralized loans	Collateralized loans	Collateralized loans	"Asset-lite" co-ownership models – subscriptions, time-shares, leases, real-time P2P lending, etc.
		Consumer credit	Consumer credit	Consumer credit	
		BNPL	BNPL	BNPL	
				P2P lending	
				Online brokerage	

Platforms and products	Cash payments	Batch- processed debit and credit cards	Real-time credit and debit cards Online versions of card payments (Paypal)	A range of real-time digital and mobile payment wallets – Alipay, WeChat, Apple Pay, cryptocurrencies	Token-based, device independent, peer-to-peer Value and smart contract exchange – cryptocurrencies, banks trade in data enrichment business (e.g. Veracity)
Assets	Asset-based wealth – property, shares	Asset-based wealth – property, shares	Asset-based wealth – property, shares transacted online	Alternative assets, cryptocurrencies, gaming tokens, collectibles, NFTs	Intangible asset classes that are personal to the holder – time, work, relationships, virtual assets in the metaverse

Source: Emmanuel Daniel

deposit-taking platform, went from about US$1 billion in 2018 to about US$160 billion today and growing.[138]

As discussed in previous chapters, stablecoins have a whole range of uses, including investing in digital assets such as tokens and NFTs as well as paying for a whole range of activities in the burgeoning DeFi sector.

But even in the traditional world, the success of the then-Ant Financial's Yue Er Bao, the online money market fund founded in China in 2013, is still the gold standard for turning the humble deposit account into a more active investment one. It raised more than US$100 billion in AUM in its first year alone.

Valued at 1.5 trillion RMB (US$235 billion) in 2018, Yue Er Bao was the world's largest money market fund at the time,[139] although it subsequently declined by more than 55% after that due to more restrictive regulation as well as Ant Group beginning to sell other funds on its platforms – both signs of a maturing market.[140]

Yue Er Bao's parent wealth management business currently has 2.2 trillion RMB (US$345 billion) in AUM, and its payments arm has 622 million users. Speed and convenience turned Yue Er Bao into a virtual sweep current account that moms and pops could transact with on their mobile phones – a true product innovation not seen in finance since the 1970s.

Yue Er Bao started out as a 'conversation' with users of Alibaba merchant accounts, where they held money in a Nostro account but did not know where to park their excess funds. Western analysts did not catch the significance of this, watching it with suspicion and hunting for flaws in the product.

---

[138] V. Subburaj, "Stablecoins: What are they? And how are they redefining the crypto ecosystem?" *The News Minute*, 30 December 2021. Available at https://www.thenewsminute.com/article/stablecoins-what-are-they-and-how-are-they-redefining-crypto-ecosystem-159324.

[139] H. Sender, "Ant Financial extends dominance in Chinese online finance", *Financial Times*, 17 May 2018. Available at https://www.ft.com/content/fde8fe0c-5830-11e8-b8b2-d6ceb45fa9d0.

[140] Q. Yue and D. Jia, "China curbs money market funds, amongst them Ant's Yue Bao", *Nikkei Asia*, 17 January 2022. Available at https://asia.nikkei.com/Spotlight/Caixin/China-curbs-money-market-funds-among-them-Ant-s-Yu-e-Bao.

Jiko, a highly commendable fintech effort built on the same model, is a tiny cousin to Yue Er Bao in the US. The basic idea is the same, except that Jiko offers a timid and tentative approach of investing customer deposits in very conservative and ever-shrinking US treasury bills. Treasury bonds had a 3.3% return on investment in 2019, which dropped to negative levels in 2020 during the Covid-19 pandemic.

Jiko could have offered multiple options of other asset classes for its customers to choose from, but it did not. The Chinese platforms were prepared to be bolder, faster, and far more integrated as digital sweep accounts, even ahead of the regulatory curve.

Yue Er Bao was an equal player in the interbank funding market, making it possible for it to profit from selling funds to smaller banks, without which the product would not have succeeded. The technology was just the enabler.

Jiko, on the other hand, was never going to be admitted to the funding market in the US unless it became a bank – which it did. Jiko recently became the first fintech in the US to buy a bank, just ahead of Lending Club, a fintech P2P player that also wanted a banking licence for different reasons.

Technology enables many non-finance players to become technically deposit-taking entities – telecommunication companies, supermarkets, utilities, mass transport companies, and even gaming platforms. In some jurisdictions, being incorporated as a deposit-taking company is more capital-efficient than being incorporated as a bank.

Today, despite year after year of massive cost-cutting measures, the deposit business represents a huge compliance and cost of funding millstone around the necks of traditional banks, just like the 35mm film that eventually dragged down Kodak.

Where there are too many deposits in the banking system, in many countries, the banks themselves cease to want them. Jaime Dimon, the chairman of JP Morgan Chase, used to complain about this phenomenon, known as 'excess deposits'.

In 2006, the Financial Services Regulatory Relief Act authorized the Federal Reserve to pay interest on mandated and excess reserves parked with the regulator. This made it cheaper for banks to deposit their excess cash with regulators or other financial investments rather than deploy it to the productive economy.

Excess reserves stored with the US regulator soared from an average of US$200 billion per annum in the 2008-2010 period to US$1.6 trillion between 2009-2015, earning US$30 billion in unproductive interest in the period.[141]

Regulators impose a capital charge on deposits as though they constitute a systemic risk and manage the money supply, when the funds sitting outside traditional deposits are massively larger. All the indicators point to the fact that the deposit business has become unbearably expensive for its own sake.

Overall, not only have deposit-taking institutions been losing market share to other intermediaries, they are also decreasing in number themselves. According to Henry Kaufman, the former Federal Reserve and Salomon Brothers economist, there were 23,700 FDIC insured deposit institutions in 1960. In 2021, there were 4,236 in 2021.[142]

In 1990, the 10 largest financial conglomerates controlled only 10% of all financial assets in the US. In 2016, this figure was 75%. Licensing new digital banks does not give them any hope of succeeding in a business that is hugely stacked against them.

There is so much liquidity in the financial markets that it is impossible to formulate any meaningful strategy around deposits. The Swiss resorted to negative interest rates to push away flight to quality investors to the Swiss Franc as a safe haven.

Given that real wealth is being created in entirely new types of investment classes, the bank deposit has become an untenable asset class, especially for the poor. Given how no intermediary will pay customers a premium for deposits, it is cruel that many banks around the world still encourage their poorest customers to hand over their savings for abysmal rates without helping them build real wealth.

---

[141] "Bank reserves, Federal Reserve Bank of St. Louis", via FRED Economic Research (accessed 26 May 2022).

[142] "Number of US FDIC-insured commercial banks", via Statista.com (accessed 24 May 2022).

But before we dump the humble deposit, we should also understand what this would actually mean for the industry. A robust retail deposit base represents many important things to the industry, which would have to be recreated or preserved as the industry develops into the digital age. As US banks like Commerce Bancorp showed in the past, substantial core retail deposits are a source of strong profitability, lowest cost of funds, and sustainability.

They are also an indication of a bank's intimacy with its customers. Banks with a larger deposit base have a stronger brand name than their competitors. The war of acquiring and retaining customers is still one that is won at an emotional level, one that is not explained by technology alone.

The stable depositor is also the best customer to cross-sell other products to, resulting in strong per customer profitability. I have watched very conservative banks with a solid deposit base successfully scale their lending business 30% year on year, thanks to the confidence that their depositor franchise afforded them.

An old traditional bank that has an established and extensive branch network still has, in all likelihood, the lowest cost of funds in that marketplace – unbeatable no matter what the rest of the competition, including the mobile players, do to try and unseat it. Any technological advances have to be built on all the good old-fashioned benefits that the deposit business used to mean to the industry.

But perhaps more importantly, technology alone cannot recreate the strong sense of corporate discipline that comes with having a strong depositor base – something that was not found in wholesale funding and will not be found in technology alone. Banks that lose their way, as Northern Rock did in the UK in 2007, failed to match assets to liabilities, a core tenant of commercial banking.

In the 1970s, investment bankers in the US told unsuspecting community banks that wholesale funding was cheaper and easier to manage than retail funding. This was not the case. The community bank presidents who kept their eye on the ball of core deposits funding as the basis for the discipline of building a strong asset-liability business did much better than those who signed up for the easier way of borrowing cheap funds from the capital market.

Not losing sight of the value of core deposits, while transposing them into all of the new digital alternatives available today, is a transition that traditional banks have to make.

Credit in a capsule

The single most significant transformation of credit happening in the networked world is the definition of the asset itself. What, exactly, are lenders lending against? Traditionally, lending used to be done against a tangible asset like gold or property, but as assets became increasingly ephemeral over time, lending could be done against cash flow, security, a derivative of security, timeshare, and so on.

In the networked world, lending could be done against all sorts of new asset classes that are commensurate with lifestyles and digital activities still being defined today. In such a world, lending would be against a set of inviolable commitments secured on a network of multiple users who validate each other. The actual asset or collateral is secondary to the community.

We see some of this developing in DeFi with 'flash loans'. These are special uncollateralized loans that allow the borrowing of an ephemeral asset, such as a cryptocurrency being mined, that has to be repaid (with an annual interest of about 0.09% at the time of writing) in minutes, before the end of the transaction.

Flash loans were created to fund the period it takes for a cryptocurrency to be accepted by the network. For Bitcoin, this is about 10 minutes; on Ethereum it is 13 seconds. If the transaction itself does not take place, the entire loan is voided, as if no funds were ever borrowed.

This is almost like going back to the days of ancient Assyria, when debts were recorded in a document called the *errubatum*, which also could be traded between individuals itself.[143] The *errubatum* of flash loans is digital,

---

[143] R. Westbrook and R. Jasnow (eds.), *Security for Debt in Ancient Near Eastern Law* (Leiden: Brill, 2001).

based on an algorithm embedded inside an irrefutable contract.

This makes for almost a risk-free transaction if viewed through the traditional lens of finance. Such flash loans arbitrage between assets (without needing to have the full principal amount to execute the arbitrage) to swapping collateral of loan positions.

This phenomenon attracts mainly computer geeks for now. A trader writes a smart contract code to borrow on a flash loan, buys low on one market, sells high in another market, repays the loan, and pockets the profit. All this is done within the same on-chain transaction via a decentralized exchange.

Platforms like Provenance and Anchor carry tokens called Anchor and Hash respectively. These are owned by lenders who also mutually validate each other. Once the credit record is tokenized digitally, it is accurate, specific to the owner, and can be used as collateral for many more types of transactions.

In all of these transactions, credit is product, content, asset, and the identity of the transacting parties all at once. Credit as a product is a loan that anyone can provide, be it a financial institution or from one person to another. Credit as content is a populated data pool on the profiles, use, and conditions under which the credit can be consumed or extinguished – all of which can be monetized. Credit as an asset is, of course, the income-generating value of the loan.

Finally, credit as identity is all the nuanced personal data on borrowers that banks collect today, whether on lifestyles, supply chains, transaction flows, or other usage habits. Credit as identity allows communities of lenders and borrowers who may be anonymous to each other to still interact with each other with certainty. This profile will sit in an irrefutable personal file owned by the originator of the debt.

As credit becomes increasingly personalized, a whole range of ancillary services, from credit profiling to risk mitigation, can be commercialized. A 'capsule' can be traded in a highly personalized market – individuals slicing and dicing tranches of loans in any way they wish, bought and sold at will between friends, business contacts, and other players in a supply chain.

The credit bureau models today industrialize lending by reducing them to their lowest common denominator. Entire economies are destroyed when today's debt, whether mortgages or corporate loans, is grouped into tranches and traded in the market, without anyone taking responsibility for individual loans.

Information regarding debtors' identities, risk profile, the performance of the debt, and so on is not only neither accurate nor current, but also managed at great expense and wastage. When data is repackaged and traded several times, it loses all connection to the original underlying asset. This was how the 2008 US banking crisis started.

Some studies suggest that traditional banks neither originate nor own as much of the lending business as they used to.[144] The rest were originated by non-banks and alternative lending players. On a token, these can be individuals. In many cases, traditional banks would rather participate in the securitization market than originate or hold the actual loans themselves.

Non-performing loans (NPLs) add costs to the overall loan in a traditional bank. When Citibank was pioneering its credit card business in Indonesia in the 1980s, its credit card portfolio had an operating NPL of up to 25%. This was incorporated into the overall cost carried by the *bona fide* borrower, who paid up their loan commitments on time.

It was a necessary cost at a time when consumers in emerging markets did not even have verifiable identities, let alone bank accounts. Citibank took a 'test-and-learn' approach, looking for sustainable customer pools by issuing cards with small credit lines to pockets of civil servants and school teachers whose income could be verified through salary slips and letters from employers. It is amazing how these 'flash loans' worked while bypassing the entire (expensive) process between complete strangers on the internet.

Even today, the NPLs on credit card portfolios of any bank in any emerging market can consistently amount to more than 10% of the total

---

[144] A. Phaneuf, "A look at nonbank loans and the alternative lending industry business model in 2021", *Business Insider*, 15 January 2021.

portfolio in order for the whole business to be viable. But tokenizing credit and originating it on a blockchain network, mutually validated by peers, can almost eliminate this risk and cost of credit.

The technologies being introduced for venture-backed microfinance and consumer lending today in the name of fintech and innovation add, not reduce, layers of costs. At the major banking and fintech conferences, an onslaught of Java C++-based application players line the exposition booths, selling software that originates, slices, dices, chops, packages, repackages, and resells the same old-fashioned bank loan in a hundred different ways in an already crowded market.

Fintech players also claim to make credit cheaper, but this is simply not true. The venture capitalists who fund start-ups are looking to maximize returns. All the evidence on inclusive finance hitherto is that the cost of credit to the poor did not go down. In many countries, they are still a usury 30-40%, compounded per annum.

There is also general rhetoric going around in fintech circles that what poor people need most is access to credit. Today, both old and new players still insist on extending their lending business to the unbanked and underbanked. They call it by a fancy name, 'financial inclusion,' borrowed from platform language.

In China, India, Indonesia, South Africa, Nigeria, Brazil, and a host of large countries, credit is being introduced to large swathes of transient populations who previously did not even have a verifiable identity as they moved from rural to urban areas. Recalling the example in Chapter 5, extending microfinance credit to poverty-stricken customers in India resulted in a rise in suicides in Andhra Pradesh and other provinces.

The Chinese government put a hard brake on peer-to-peer lending because, despite all the impressive technologies being applied to make the loans more directed to supply chain customers and cheaper to deploy through mobile devices, too much of it was going to conspicuous consumption, such as plastic surgery for young women.

In 2021, Xiaomi's XW Bank, a new digital bank that operates in the far western reaches of China, was fined by regulators for charging beyond the legal lending limit for consumer credit. In other countries, unscrupulous banks bypass legislation by compounding debt in other ways.

The poor, like the rich, need homes, bicycles, refrigerators, and the ability to pay for their kids' education. These are income-generating assets. They certainly do not need a loan. New community-based equity models are much better ways for them to own things to build wealth instead of a loan. Community currencies, described in an earlier chapter, are one such model.

A loan with transactional data of the asset it is lent against, whether it is a car or a house, can be a lease. It can even generate income for the borrower, something totally imaginable given all the new data points that can be added to the product. For all the above reasons, it is the product itself that has to change. We need to reimagine what a loan product becomes when we add speed, convenience, and additional data into the capsule.

Rewriting the P2P playbook

Although the P2P and crowd-sourced lending and investing industries are genuine creations of the internet age, their original iterations were based on technology that had not fully developed. Many failed in trying to replicate traditional lending in the networked world instead of imagining new products.

The real product in P2P investing or lending was always the community. This will become clearer as blockchain-based APIs, artificial intelligence, and greater bandwidth are added, and their focus changes to generating more complete interactions instead of merely matching lenders with borrowers.

The crowdfunding industry has been gaining momentum, with everything from electronic gadgets to blockbuster movies being funded on the back of a good story. The crowdfunding market globally was estimated at US$12.3 billion in 2019 and is predicted to be as large as US$25.8 billion by 2026.

According to one of many estimates, China accounts for 37% of the crowdfunding marketplace,[145] followed by the US at 32% and Europe at 17%, reflecting the stronger sense of community in China on the back of which this industry operates.

A report by Fundera, a research company, breaks down the secrets behind a successful crowdfunding campaign. Adding personal information to a crowdfunding campaign gets 79% more backers. Updating followers regularly increases success rates by 126%, and campaigns with videos earn 105% more than those with just text or images.[146] Rather than being community-centric, most iterations of P2P in the developed world today are designed as lending platforms, just like traditional banks.

When they compete on the same platforms, P2P players invariably have the same cost structures as traditional banks. In fact, in most countries, P2P players go after the same customer pools as banks. However, being unable to compete with the main street players, the P2P platforms end up turning into subprime lenders. In Europe, P2P lenders have to be even more niche, to the extent of focusing on used cars just to stay afloat.

The same cost structures as the traditional banks make it difficult for many disruptors to compete, especially in markets where the banking industry is fully developed. In many cases, P2P players eventually get relegated into originators for the local banks. It is no surprise, then, that many P2P players resort to seeking a banking license themselves.

In China, India, South Africa, Brazil, and other large emerging economies, P2P platforms originally had the advantage of blazing new paths in reaching customer segments that previously did not have access to credit.

In China alone, more than 4,000 P2P lenders set up sites within a year of the technology becoming available in the mid-2010s. The platform software to run a P2P lending business was easily available on merchant sites like Taobao, a platform that is part eBay, part iTunes. In the absence of verifiable data, they used supply chains for small businesses and new data models to credit-score and onboard previously unbanked retail customers.

---

[145] "Global Crowdfunding Market Size Status and Forecast 2021 to 2027", via Valuates.
[146] "Crowdfunding statistics (2021): Market size and growth", via Fundera.

One of the more established P2P players, Shanghai Lujiazui International Financial Asset Exchange (Lufax), grew from nothing in 2011 to having over 33 million registered users on its platform and US$44.3 billion (288 billion RMB) of loans under management by the end of 2017.[147]

But industrial-sized platforms also meant industrial-sized fraud. By February 2016, another platform called Ezubao was able to raise over 50 billion RMB (US$7.6 billion) from 900,000 customers within two short years, promising 14% returns in a market where bank deposits were offering just 3%.[148] It turned out to be nothing more than a huge Ponzi scheme, plain and simple.

In a report in November 2015, the China Banking Regulatory Commission (CBRC, now called the CBIRC) said that there were over 3,600 P2P platforms in the country that had raised more than 400 billion RMB (US$62 billion). Of these, more than 1,000 turned out to be problematic and were closed down.

The CBIRC subsequently published new guidelines on P2P lending, resulting in massive closures. But that still left 2,600 players, some of them still cutting-edge examples of innovation in onboarding and managing small business risk. No other country has these numbers.

The other problem with the earlier iterations of P2P players was that their pioneers were mostly ex-bankers. One name that comes to mind is Ron Suber, a self-styled industry evangelist who was at one point president of Prosper, a leading P2P lending platform in the US.

In multiple speeches, Suber explained how banks should not consider P2P lenders as competitors but as potential partners. A bond salesman in his previous career, Suber was thinking about how P2P players could generate loan books very quickly and then securitize them to the marketplace.

Suber's message was replicated by many others in the industry,

---

[147] "Annual Report 2017", Ping An Bank. Available at https://resources.pingan.com/app_upload/file/bank/7874b206d95048c3b39e8d0bc6d1874d.pdf.

[148] M. Miller and S. Zhang, "China's $7.6 billion Ponzi scam highlights growing online risks", *Reuters*, 3 February 2016. Available at https://www.reuters.com/article/us-china-fraud-idUSKCN0VB2O1.

superimposing the P2P model on the traditional banking business – from originating loans to the collection, trust and custodian, escrow, liquidity, payments, securitization, and other services of traditional banks. It should therefore come as no surprise that the industry eventually degenerated into an origination platform for traditional banks.

The P2P industry would have looked very different if it did not see itself as a platform for selling loans or investing, but simply creating a marketplace for ideas. When Jeff Bezos launched Amazon, the quantifiable goal he set for his business – and the one he communicated to shareholders – was simply "customer satisfaction". Not a product: just customer satisfaction.

The idea may have sounded shallow at the time, but his real focus was not on the actual products being sold at all. Instead of looking mainly at inventory or trying to guess the products that would sell best, he did exactly the opposite: gathering tons of data on users and using it to build a community that felt comfortable with each other on the platform.

Today, Amazon claims to have over 350 million active users. The company processes 1.5 billion items for 2.5 million sellers through its 175 fulfilment centers, which employ 1 million employees worldwide today. Their online catalogue of products receives more than 50 million updates a week, and every 30 minutes, all data received is crunched and reported back to the different warehouses.[149] Despite all these, products were never truly Amazon's focus.

There is a lesson here from the failures in the early days of the dot-com bubble. The experience of Webvan, the predecessor to Amazon and Alibaba, suggests that there is a very important difference between expanding a product base and building a network effect.

None of the reports emanating from Amazon make any talk of 'bundling' or 'rebundling' products or services, something that the financial services industry appears to be particularly fond of, especially in digital finance.

Amazon Web Services (AWS) is a second-level iteration of that

---

[149] "Our Facilities", via Amazon corporate website, www.aboutamazon.com (accessed 13 February 2022).

community, where users can collaborate and find synergies with each other independent of the platform itself. Again, the focus is not on selling products. The community *is* the product, as members interact with each other and generate value organically.

Many P2P players rely solely on social media. I remember a conversation I had with the chairman of a UK P2P lending company, who said that the social media profile of customers was far too fleeting to give enough data to support used car loans for periods of 3–5 years. He never corrected that mismatch.

As such, the first iteration of P2P lenders in the West went back to using the same good old-fashioned credit scores that traditional financial institutions relied on, instead of increasing their profiles and conversations with their customers to come up with an other-world score. This further exacerbated the decline into bank-type lending.

At a conference, the founder of WeLab, a China-based, new-age credit bureau that draws its behavioral data from customers' lifestyles, claimed that his delinquency records are a good 30% lower than that of the traditional industrialized credit bureau modelled on FICO scores used by the banks in Hong Kong.

In the case of migrant workers, the source data used to score them had to be created from scratch, based on mobile phone usage, utility bill payment records, and other data points derived from their daily routines. Traditional data scores have 20-30 data points, while in the digital world, it is possible to have thousands of data points beyond the standard set collected by financial institutions.

Delinquency profiles also take on a whole new dimension. Categories are no longer just about 30-, 60-, and 90-day delinquencies, but also 'willing and able', 'willing and unable', 'unwilling but able', 'unwilling and unable', and a string of other combinations.

Each of these profiles then requires different motivations to help ensure successful delinquency management; the user keeps their credit scores.

Platforms like Ant Financial take things even further by engineering 'social credit' profiles of their users.

For example, when customers had a good track record of paying their bills on time, they were rewarded with practical benefits like being exempted from paying a deposit when checking into a hotel. Customers go a long way to keep their profiles in high standing. This was, however, criticized in the West as the "gamification" of credit, when in actual fact, credit cards and BNPL platforms use much worse addiction-creating algorithms.

Most financial institutions are product-focused, senselessly manufactured at one end of a pipeline and delivered at the other with no regard for the customer. At one point, Bezos was scathing about the way banks advertised their predatory lending products. These encouraged people to take out overdrafts for lifestyle consumption like holidays by, say, mortgaging their house, something that nobody in their right mind should do. He reckoned that institutions clearly did not have their customers in mind.

Technology is getting to the point where borrowers and lenders can find each other through Bluetooth and other device connectors, validate each other, and decide if they want to lend or borrow instantly. Gamified scores and multiple API partners coding new interfaces to other applications are among the applications that will breathe new life into the P2P industry, with additional speed and bandwidth from 5G and quantum computing. All these require new-age financial institutions that are able to reimagine their products, ones which can be embedded into the lifestyle and supply chains of daily life and commerce.

CHAPTER 9

The great transitions

"The stone age didn't end for lack of stones, and the oil age will end long before the world runs out of oil."
Ahmed Zaki Yamani

"We dance round in a ring and suppose, but the Secret sits in the middle and knows."
Robert Frost

As I write these lines in February 2022, the Russian invasion of Ukraine is under way. It lends itself as a grim but appropriate setting to describe the transitions to come. The war will affect the finance industry at all levels, in profound ways that no previous trauma of the same magnitude has ever done before. The effects of this will reverberate for years.

At one level, Russia's invasion can be best described as the first war to take place in a networked world. In the past, wars were a zero-sum game where there were clear winners and losers, a sense of right and wrong, and an ability to ring-fence both the perpetrators and the problems created.

But from the outset, this war demonstrated just how interconnected and interdependent finance, trade, logistics, economies, and countries have become. The financial sanctions imposed to date have already exposed interdependencies at so many levels that their consequences will precipitate a whole new way of looking at the industry well into the future.

Firstly, the effect on payments and supply chains. Governments and oligarchs alike will now actively push back on any globally regulated financial system that could hold entire states to ransom. The unraveling of the shared global financial infrastructure will happen slowly, aided by technology.

The roles of a Bank for International Settlement, or a SWIFT for payments, will likely devolve into multiple systems representing different ideologies and made possible by different overlapping technologies. Many countries today are afraid of a world dominated by any one system whose ideology they don't share.

Secondly, the notion of sovereign assets as reserves will also evolve to be secured by multiple asset types and classes, including cryptocurrencies, in a world where no one player dominates. Such trends will intensify the network effect to make financial systems interoperable.

At a geopolitical level, we see the war as a clash between nation-states and ideologies. There is good and bad, right and wrong. But at the functional level, nation-states, institutions, and individuals alike are faced with the same underlying challenges of navigating alliances in a networked world.

The Covid-19 pandemic that preceded the invasion already saw an increasing awareness of personal rights and freedoms irrespective of political, religious, or social persuasions, whether liberal or conservative. At one level, the pandemic pitted societies that were better organized at containing and managing its effects against the more 'dysfunctional' ones that were ravaged by it. But as it tarried, the countries that had more liberal values appear to have learnt to live with the ever-changing nature of pandemics better.

In a number of countries, there were street protests against compulsory vaccination, primarily to protect personal liberty and to push back against intrusions into this by the state. Nowhere did the dichotomy play out more fiercely than in the US. But eventually, even in China, the state could go only so far in taking a paternalistic approach to social safety.

The US looked decidedly dysfunctional, with turmoil between those who wanted to retain their personal freedoms and those who valued the ability to come together to combat the ravages of the virus as it morphed from one form to the next. Still, the US is the first-born child of the networked age. It is the forebearer of the dichotomies that all societies will eventually have to deal with one way or another.

Throughout its history, the most enduring features of the US as a society were rarely achieved through a congenial process devoid of angst. The notions of diversity and racial equality that the US exports to other countries today through its global corporations were not born out of enlightenment, but bitter domestic conflict.

This ability to play out its contradictions so openly is a price that almost no other country is able to pay, because doing so tears at the very fiber of society. But the US has, over the past 200 years, created the most inspiring responses to its own failings that other countries eventually emulate.

Individualism is exercised at the street level in everyday life, but it is also found in the corridors of power. The US is the country where individuals, be they industrialists, hedge fund managers, or entrepreneurs, have been able to amass as much personal financial and social capital as its largest corporations and play a role as large as the state in society.

And so it is that individuals, corporations, and the state all weigh in on the debates on decentralized finance. The outcome is always one that preserves personal liberties, where all actors are able to assert influence on the process. In other countries, a lot of the policymaking which aims to contain the transformational changes taking place in finance today is dominated either by the state or big business. They are mostly couched to reinforce the existing world order and preserve the interests of the incumbents.

But these are just buying time. Over time, more countries will be faced with the same distressing social disorder that comes with embracing the technologies that increase personalization. It is with this big picture perspective that we must attend to these transitions. In the sections below, I have outlined how they will play out in finance and tried to distinguish the signal from the noise.

From tribes to networks

In 1996, David Ronfeldt, a senior social scientist at RAND Corporation, published a thesis that I still find prescient today.[150] Ronfeldt postulated that there are four basic forms of organization, Tribal (T), Institutional (I), Markets (M), and Networks (N), and that human society transitions from one into the next.

I have applied his thesis to the transitions I have seen in finance. I reference Ronfeldt's work here for readers who wish to study his original ideas in greater detail, which it amply deserves.

I use his theory to assert that the financial services industry has moved from its own 'tribal' phase into its 'institutional' and 'markets' ones, and will further evolve into the 'networks' phase in which the personalization of finance will dominate. There are some significant and useful insights that the industry stands to gain by looking at itself this way.

I have added my own annotations to describe how Ronfeldt's four types of organizations apply to finance:

   i.   The Tribal (T) Phase = T. Here, organizations are tribal, denoted by groups like extended families, clans, homogenous communities, and modern big-city gangs. I would postulate that several significant phases in banking also had tribal origins, especially the old boys-school neck-tie bonds of the British guilds, associations, and industries.

   ii. The Institutional (I) Phase = T+I. Institutions are exemplified by the military, religious institutions, the bureaucratic state, and impersonal organizations. But because the institutional phase carries the legacy of its tribal origins, it is epitomized by states that reinforce tribes with institutions. Ethnically homogenous countries like China, Japan, or religious groups like the Ethiopian or Greek

---

[150] D. Ronfeldt, "Tribes, Institutions, Markets, Networks: A framework about societal evolution", RAND Corporation paper, 1996. Available at https://www.rand.org/content/dam/rand/pubs/papers/2005/P7967.p

Orthodox churches have institutionalized their tribal origins. Looking to finance, it can be argued that an institution like HSBC, in its heyday, was run by a tribal collegiate of close-knit, white, male expatriates representing just one country.

The social philosopher Max Weber pointed out that the institutional form was authoritative and involved, among other things, administrative specialization and differentiation. It also developed sanctions that demanded conformity and phased out the egalitarian nature of the tribal form.

Supposing we place regulators and central bankers on Ronfeldt's tribes-to-markets continuum, we can argue that the Securities and Exchange Commission (SEC) is an independent institution with tribal origins. President Roosevelt appointed Joseph Kennedy as its first chairman in 1934 precisely because of his 'insider' role, which enabled him to clean up collegiate behavior in the finance industry at the time.[151]

iii. The Markets (M) Phase = T+I+M. The 'marketplace' as we know it today arose in the 18th century, on the eve of the Industrial Revolution, when the writings of Scotland's Adam Smith and the French Physiocrats described a market economy that functions as a self-regulating system independent of the state.

It also released previously fixed assets, such as land, to be traded independent of tribal or institutional affiliations. Capitalism is a market phenomenon that enabled the state and commerce to operate quite independent of each other in the 1700s. The market economy helped trade, commerce, and investment blossom.

The ideal system in the institutional phase was hierarchical. By contrast, the ideal system in a markets phase is a competitive interaction of independent actors, processing complex transactions

---

[151] D. Nasaw, *The Patriarch: The Remarkable Life and Turbulent Times of Joseph P Kennedy* (New York: Penguin, 2013).

better than they would have in a tribal or purely institutional system.

Assets like property, products, services, and even knowledge could be traded across great distances at terms and prices that represent a wide variety of profit opportunities and very specific individual interests. Symmetry of information, where all parties have access to the same information at the same time, is the core operating principle in a market ecosystem.

The development of the London market for 'trading in risk' that began in the Lloyd's Coffee House, opened by Edward Lloyd around 1688 on Tower Street, is instructional. The coffee house could be best described as tribal, an ideal place for gentlemen who were known to each other to obtain marine news. The insurance industry developed from there.

Nearly 200 years later, in 1871, the Lloyd's Act was passed. It institutionalized the business so that membership could be opened more widely. When the exchange entered its 'markets' phase, the idea of a self-regulating community disintegrated. It engendered, to use Ronfeldt's words, exploitation of customers' money by market participants for excessive profit.

As there are always winners and losers in a market economy, the need for regulation by an external party arose. In this we have a transition that was not adequately understood as such – that is, from self-regulation to an independent regulator. The 1990s and the 2000s saw the widespread demutualization of stock exchanges worldwide, driven by increasing efficiency and symmetry of trading information between participants.

The Stockholm Stock Exchange was the first to be demutualized in 1993. The New York Stock Exchange (NYSE) was finally demutualized in 2006 through its merger with Archipelago, a publicly listed electronic exchange.

Over time, markets became more powerful than institutions

because they expanded an economy's overall capacity. But strong markets also strengthened states that knew how to extract rent through taxation and licences.

In the markets phase, regulators increased capital requirements and imposed fines on institutions, sparing managers but punishing shareholders. In one episode, when the SEC instituted hefty fines for market conduct violations, Paul Atkins, a Republican former member of the SEC from 2002-2008, argued vociferously against the SEC using such fines to punish shareholders rather than managers. Atkins dissented when the company Qwest was fined US$250 million in 2004. What he was really fighting against was the ability of the state to extract rent from the markets.

Later, the state also routinely encouraged moral hazard by allowing shareholders to profit when banks did well and socialize the losses from market conduct when they failed, ostensibly to protect depositors.

Increasing overreach of the state has become more full-blown in recent years. The leaking of the mammoth US$14 billion fine proposed by the New York State Financial Regulator for Deutsche Bank in 2016 before it was rescinded was the high watermark of this power. Nonetheless, there is a ceiling to this power because the state is now in a parasitic relationship, feeding off the very institutions that they regulate.

iv. The Networked (N) Phase = T+I+M+N. This is the phase that the world is clearly entering into today, and we will do well to explore it fully.

Even at the time of his writing in the 1990s, Ronfeldt was able to foresee that we were on the cusp of the emergence of a T+I+M+N society. Adam Smith articulated the primacy of the market as the most efficient model in 1776, but he had not seen enough to postulate the networked economy in his time.

Ronfeldt thought that the best demonstration of the networked form was the 'civil society', where communities rally to pursue an interest for common good. Civil societies are organized in many different ways in different countries, from the informal getting-together of people with shared interests to more formal cooperatives. With the benefit of hindsight, we can now see how the civil society he envisioned could exist entirely in a digital form with no physical or institutional borders to define it.

He also envisioned what would be called a 'social commons' today. One example – which has generated considerable debate – being the 'social commons' that exists entirely on social media platforms.

US regulators insisted that the 2008 banking crisis developed because derivative trades were mostly done over-the-counter (OTC) and not on central counterparties (CCPs). But despite many attempts to phase it out, the over-the-counter (OTC) market never went away. The OTC market has a multiplier effect not found in exchanges. It appears to be the natural parent of the networked world to come.

Technically, this makes the OTC market a brilliant candidate to be 'block-chained' into a thousand blooming cottage exchanges. In fact, 'atomic swap' technology now does exactly that, operating as an escrow 'cross-chain' account without the need for intermediaries. It is an open protocol to move assets without actually moving them – making trades without an exchange.

New-age exchanges are sprouting up for new asset classes, such as AirCarbon for trading carbon tokens, that take advantage of the network effect that blockchain affords. Anyone who can provide the required liquidity can start an exchange.

In the meantime, traditional financial institutions are still struggling with interoperability, clinging to language they are familiar with like 'delivery

Table 3: Ronfeldt's Tribal to Networks Transition Table

	Tribal	Institutional	Markets	Networked
Key realm	Family/ Culture	State/ Government	The Economy	The Shared Society
Key purpose	Identity	Power	Wealth	Data/ Knowledge
Key values	Belonging	Order	Trade	Self-Interest
Idealization	Solidarity	Sovereignty	Competition	Cooperation
Products	Household goods	Public goods	Personal Property	Shared Assets
Products	As needed	As produced	As traded	As shared
Key risk	Nepotism	Corruption	Exploitation	Deception
Motivation	Family survival	Higher authority	Self-interest	Empowerment
Structure	Acephalous (headless)	Hierarchical	Atomized	Webbed
Time Sense	Mythical	Past	Present	Future
Action	Solidarity	Command/ Control	Exchange/ Trade	Consultative/ Coordination
Ties	Tightly bound			Loosely Coupled
External boundaries	Solid closed			Fluid open
Architect	Labyrinth/ Circle	Pyramid	Billiard Balls	Geodesic dome
Biological analogy	Skin color	Skeletal	Circulatory	Sensory
Information technology	Symbols	Publishing	Telecom -munications	Networks

Source: David Ronfeldt, RAND Corporation

versus payment' and looking for "liquidity" providers. These problems have already been solved.

We can argue that organizations like the International Organization of Securities Commissions (IOSCO) still operate with a pre-2008 markets mindset, reinforcing intermediation based on the gospel of regulated exchanges and resisting the impact that a network effect would have on the infrastructure they promote.

Ronfeldt advises that to do well in the 21st century, all four forms must function well together despite their contradictions. He also points out that the impact of technology has a feedback effect that may alter, even strengthen, the older phases. We see this today in the way that the network effect accentuates rather than ameliorates tribal biases.

Ronfeldt's thesis applies not just to technological phenomena, but the mechanics of all forms of social transition. In my opinion, the most valuable iteration of his theory is his table outlining the characteristics of society in each phase.

The elements in Table 3 outline the characteristics of the networked world that its participants will have to subscribe to – a realm built on shared assets, by parties seeking data and motivated by empowerment, with loose ties and grappling with deception as the operating evil. I would go so far as to suggest that the same principles apply regardless if the body in question is an individual, organization, society, or a nation-state.

The TIMN framework can be read together with observations of other social scientists like Peter Drucker and Jeremy Rifkin that a new social order is emerging. As early as the 1990s, Drucker and Rifkin envisioned that society would develop a third pillar that Drucker called "the autonomous community organization" as a "new center of meaningful citizenship," alongside the private sector of business and the public sector of government.[152]

Ronfeldt's ideas were developed in the days before the rise of AI and augmented reality, which turbo-charged closed communities by reinforcing

---

[152] P F Drucker, "The new society of organizations", *Harvard Business Review*, September 1992. Available at https://hbr.org/1992/09/the-new-society-of-organizations.

and even expanding their tribal identities using the network effect. The fact that tribal societies can still exist within their own realities while using technology raises social issues that will need to be resolved in the future.

It is also for these reasons that I have suggested that the Russian invasion of Ukraine in 2022 was the world's first war in the networked age. All the parties have extensive trade and people-to-people exchanges between them such that there will be no winner or loser in the traditional sense. The best resolution of this war would be to reinforce the networks between parties, an idea that will be strengthened over time.

LIBOR, again and again

Some readers are going to be unhappy with me when I say that the LIBOR (London Interbank Offered Rate) crisis was not a morality tale at all, but a symptom of an industry in transition. Moreover, it is a phenomenon that will be repeatedly played out every time an industry moves from one phase into the next.

Unfortunately, society has not been kind enough to see this episode as a transitional issue. Instead, the LIBOR crisis was framed as a fraud on society, the Gramm-Leach-Bliley legislation as a mistake that allowed that fraud, and so on.

In general, regardless of culture, employees do not go to work every morning to defraud their employers or customers. Most are taught to understand what is required of them, how to keep to the rules, and do a good day's work. Almost everyone learns these rules as hand-me-downs from their peers, via formal training, or habit.

Employees are also victims in a changing world. When culture and expectations change around them, without proper training and instruction, employees are unable to adapt to these proactively. In this way, habits that started in the tribal phase get carried into the institutional and subsequent phases without being the fault of any one person.

My argument goes like this: everyone agrees that LIBOR was never intended as an index for the markets, but as a reference borrowing rate between institutions in the UK's banking system. But the rise of the markets in the 1990s quickly made it an essential index, and the media-driven description of the role of LIBOR focused on the index while forgetting its original purpose.

When the LIBOR fines hit in 2010, and the UK's regulators were starting to prosecute its banks, TV anchors would call LIBOR "a US$5 trillion industry". But LIBOR was never a US$5 trillion industry; the financial derivatives market was. The US$5 trillion financial derivatives markets used LIBOR as one of several indices to trade on.

Until the issue was forced upon them, the regulators were themselves oblivious to this nuance. No less than the then-governor of the Bank of England, Mervyn King himself, was dismissive about the collusion when it was first brought up to him. He was quoted in *The Wall Street Journal* in 2008 as saying in an email to Timothy Geithner, the US Secretary of the Treasury, "We will ask the BBA (the British Bankers' Association) to include in their consultation document the ideas contained in your note". His aides reported that he was "not interested" in thinking of the LIBOR phenomenon as an issue.[153]

The Bank of England had officially dismissed it as a minor issue by stating that "despite not having any regulatory responsibilities in this area", it was concerned that the review should be "as comprehensive as possible." The head of the BBA had said that while they would take the Fed's recommendations in its consultation document on LIBOR into account, "There is no show stopper as far as we can see."[154]

At the time, LIBOR was described as having started about 30 years

---

[153] M. Hasan, "Mervyn King 'Not Interested' In 2008 Libor Rate Warnings, Say Ex-BoE Colleagues", *Huffington Post*, 16 July 2012. Available at https://www.huffingtonpost.co.uk/2012/07/16/mervyn-king-not-interested-in-2008-libor-rate-warnings_n_1676468.html.

[154] "BoE emails show Sir Mervyn King was aware of Libor 'misreporting' fears in 2008", *The Telegraph*, 13 July 2012. Available at https://www.telegraph.co.uk/finance/newsbysector/banksandfinance/9398177/BoE-emails-show-Sir-Mervyn-King-was-aware-of-Libor-misreporting-fears-in-2008.html.

earlier by averaging the daily estimates of short-term interbank borrowing rates, based on the tradition of a collective approach. It was eventually 'borrowed', in a manner of speaking, by the traders looking for indicators to trade on (as were other indices).

To borrow from Ronfeldt's terminology, the rate-setters clearly did not realize the transition afoot – that things were going from their 'institutional' to their 'markets' phase, without someone formally establishing who owed a duty of care to whom. A rate-setter working in a bank in the 2000s also carried some of the 'tribal' informality between themselves in what was eventually described as collusion.

The compromise started when the LIBOR rate-setters started interacting openly with market traders within the same institutions and the roles became fungible. Eventually, in 2016, the English courts did establish that there was indeed a duty of care by choosing to point out that both the traders and the rate-setters, working within the same organizations, knew that LIBOR was now serving a much larger purpose than it was originally intended to.

It was still technically challenging to secure the convictions of the rate-setters and the traders. Five defendants were acquitted on 10 January 2015. In January 2022, ex-Deutsche Bank traders, Matthew Connolly and Gavin Black, had their convictions overturned in the US Federal Court of Appeals for failing to "show that any of the trader-influenced submissions were false, fraudulent or misleading."[155]

In the end, only Tom Hayes, a broker, was ever convicted in the UK. Even so, this was solely on the basis of a statement he previously made on record to the Serious Fraud Office (SFO), rather than on the legality of the nature of the relationship between broker and rate submitters. This was always assumed but never established,[156] despite the SFO spending over £65

---

[155] J. Rennison and J. Dye, "Ex-Deutsche Bank traders have Libor-rigging convictions overturned", *Financial Times*, 27 January 2022. Available at https://www.ft.com/content/2bba9f8d-12f7-4f7a-ba59-f49555f7f01d.

[156] Enrich, D. (2015, September 15). The Unravelling of Tom Hayes. *Wall Street Journal*, pp. http://graphics.wsj.com/libor-unraveling-tom-hayes/3.

million to establish its case.[157]

Like all the others charged with this fraud, Hayes' pleas that he was working under instruction and that his bosses were cognizant of the common practice were not accepted by the courts, whether as evidence or in mitigation.

Ronfeldt says that there will be such "guaranteed conflicts" in societies dealing with similar transitions in the TIMN progression. Futurists like Alvin and Heidi Toffler have made the same point about conflicts between actors who represent different waves of development.

None of the major financial centers in the Asia-Pacific region, which also saw similar practices of collusion in setting their own domestic interbank offered rates, took the prosecution route. The major ones issued new guidelines that formalized the duty of care between the rate-setters and the markets – and saved millions of dollars in pursuing a sideshow that would have benefited only the media and lawyers.

The Asian regulators were, however, less forgiving about the FX rate scandal that happened later in 2013, because the collusion there was directly related to the trade itself with specific intent to defraud.

The difference between the FX fraud of 2013 and the LIBOR scandal set them in clear relief to each other. In the LIBOR episode, none of the actors thought they were harming someone else, even if they were undermining institutional and market rules. In the FX scandal, real collusion was far more conscious and intentional.

A 2012 review of LIBOR described it as "not fit for purpose," – in other words, that it was not being used for the purpose it was originally intended. In fact, the Chicago Board Options Exchange's (CBOE) Volatility Index, or VIX, which was developed by Robert Whaley in 1992 and tracks market volatility, was a far more appropriate index for the markets than LIBOR ever was.

---

[157] Tim Wallace, "Five of six Libor traders found not guilty". *The Telegraph*, 27 January 2016. Available at https://www.telegraph.co.uk/finance/financial-crime/12125430/Five-of-six-Libor-traders-found-not-guilty.html.

The subsequent administration of LIBOR under Intercontinental Exchange (ICE) brought the practice into a proper 'institutionalized' setting as opposed to a college of rate-setters. This would arguably have kept it in a 'tribal' format between peers who knew each other. The ICE model used actual transactions that included both bank-to-bank lending, as well as short-term rates from central banks, companies, non-bank financial institutions, and other counterparties.

ICE had hoped to develop a computer process that could calculate LIBOR without human estimates.[158] Perhaps more importantly, ICE consciously built its model as an index for traders, not bankers.

The Bank of England eventually announced a Sterling Overnight Index Average (SONIA), using actual lending rates but building them into an index. In the US, the Federal Reserve's Alternative Reference Rates Committee (ARRC) selected the Secured Overnight Financing Rate (SOFR) based on overnight transactions in the USD Treasury repurchase, or repo, market.

Ronfeldt describes the operating risk in the 'tribal' phase as nepotism, as corruption in the 'institutional' phase, and as exploitation in the 'markets' phase. This observation maps neatly onto how the LIBOR crisis could have been labeled as it moved from one phase to the next.

As it became institutionalized, nepotism between the rate-setters turned into corruption, and in the 'markets' phase, traders exploited the index for profit. The plot played almost to a script, if you base it on Ronfeldt's model. In the 'markets' world, there is a winner and a loser, an idea that was alien to the institutional nature of the clueless rate-setters.

The point to be made here is that the 'networked' phase of human development will feature similar transitional issues as the LIBOR episode, as more financialized assets being traded on digital platforms will look for indices to leverage on and to guide them.

In the absence of clarity, narcissism – where all participants act in their own self-interest – may well be a natural form of motivation in the industry.

---

[158] T. Hale, "ICE shakes up scandal hit Libor", *Financial Times*, 17 March 2016. Available at https://www.ft.com/content/f9853db6-ec4f-11e5-888e-2eadd5fbc4a4.

Things will play out in a far more adversarial manner than the LIBOR and other episodes did in the past.

The question that arises now is how regulation will evolve in the networked phase. In the networked age, regulators will no longer be regulating actual institutions, but rather the protocols or algorithms that process tons of external data being fed into decision-making.

Every protocol has its inherent biases, depending on what algorithms that drive the decisioning processes are trained to look for. Algorithms are already used in a wide range of daily decisions, including selecting candidates for job interviews, determining Medicaid eligibility, and self-driving cars. Within the judicial system, algorithms have been known to accentuate biases by making jurists likely to impose more punitive sentences on black defendants than on white ones.

The International Organization for Standardization (ISO) is still studying the elements that must exist in data protocols that are already driving AI. The focus appears to be establishing accountability, transparency, and recourse in any protocols that process data, which is a very different set of priorities from the days of regulating markets, institutions, and tribes. But even here, we will be faced with unintended consequences.

The next financial crisis...

Let me now apply all the areas I have covered in this book into a 'thought bubble' that can help us capture the transitions to come in finance: what will the next financial crisis look like?

In essence, the next financial crisis will be more 'asset-lite' than previous ones. It will also be caused by more factors affecting each other in a networked way, just like the Russian invasion of Ukraine, such that it will be harder to resolve in an isolated cause-and-effect manner, as we were able to with previous ones.

In economics, the phrase "not since the Great Depression" is actually a euphemism borrowed from the vocabulary of American sports. Declarations like "the 1898 Cleveland owns the worst single-season record of all time" or "the best Super Bowl comeback since the New England Patriots in 2017" are always about the best thing since the previous best thing.

Instead of looking for the first principles of a current trend, economics writers, academics, and consultants look for analogies from the past. Editors briefing their inexperienced junior reporters on a story throw in past references that completely obfuscate the issues in front of them.

Similarly, it is popular to draw parallels to the 'tulip bubble of 1637', even though there was *no* tulip bubble. The historian Anne Goldgar has pointed out that it is hard to find anyone who went bankrupt due to the collapse of the very short-lived tulip mania.[159]

When we line up all the financial crises since the end of Bretton Woods in 1971 and the Basel regimes that were promulgated to deal with them in each aftermath, a pattern can be discerned, which I have outlined in Table 4: with every subsequent crisis, the assets in question were increasingly intangible. (By the Basel regime, I mean the rules that were promulgated by the Bank for International Settlement (BIS) based in Basel, Switzerland, which brought together the banking regulators of all the major economies to respond to major banking crises.)

The first rules promulgated by the Basel regime in the aftermath of the 1984 US housing loan crisis were nicknamed Basel I. We have since had Basel II in 2004 and Basel III in 2010. In Table 4, I outline the nature of each crisis, the composition of the assets involved, and extrapolate the Basel regulation that would need to be developed to deal with crises in the personalization phase, based on the trends we can observe from previous ones.

In the first Basel I accord in 1988, the BIS implemented a so-called Capital Adequacy Ratio (CAR), designed to prevent systemic risk on account of loan defaults on actual mortgage assets and deposit runs originating in main-street American banks.

In that first accord, the BIS also shifted its focus from 'reserve

---

[159] A. Goldgar, *Tulipmania: Money, Honor, and Knowledge in the Dutch Golden Age* (Chicago: University of Chicago Press, 2007).

Table 4: Extrapolating the evolution of the Basel regime

	Asset Phase	Institutional Phase	Markets Phase	Networked Phase	Personalization Phase
The trigger	The savings and loans crisis - mortgages	The Asian financial crisis, the dot-com Bubble – institutional stability	The US banking crisis – derivatives and markets	A financialized networked economy?	Malicious narcissism?
The asset	Actual mortgage loans secured against actual properties	Securities	Derivatives	Data Networks	Intentions
Evolution of Basel regime	Basel 1 - 1988 Capital Adequacy Ratio	Basel II – 2004 Three pillars: Capital Adequacy Ratio, Market Risk, Operational Risk, Advanced Internal Ratings	Basel III – 2010 Liquidity risk Counterparty risk	Basel IV – 2030? Network Risks? Symmetry of deception	Basel V – In the distant future Externalized token risks?

Source: Emmanuel Daniel

requirements' to 'capital adequacy', reflecting a desire by regulators at that time to see shareholders of banks holding ultimate responsibility for a business. In reality, in subsequent years, shareholders were bailed out by taxpayers during every economic crisis.

Even before the first Basel accord was signed, a new shift was fermenting during the stock market bubble of October 1987, this time from mortgages to the valuation of income-generating companies that sat on the stock exchange.

Shares can be argued to be hard assets because they involve real companies generating real income, though a little less so than mortgages, which are invested in physical properties. The value of stocks during the dot-com bubble of 2000 was even more intangible because these were companies whose stocks were no longer valued against any fundamentals anymore.

It was during this time that the Commodity Futures Modernization Act of 2000 (CFMA) allowed for financialized assets that do not trade on regulated exchanges, such as derivatives and futures, to *not* be defined as 'securities' or 'futures'.

This allowed the market for financialized assets to take on a life of its own. The Enron scandal of 2001 followed soon after. The markets developed their own myriad of sophisticated practices, including those involving credit default swaps (CDS).

Over time, the Basel regime recognized that the composition of banks' balance sheets was changing. They incorporated securities that were not based on any fundamental value, which presented increasing difficulty for measuring and calibrating them, when this could be done against a number that could mean whatever you wanted it to.

The second iteration of the Basel regime in 2004 increased the complexity of the kind of data that banks had to look at, including asset types, quality, and liquidity. In Ronfeldt's timeline, the banking industry was trying to internalize the impact of markets on the valuation of its assets on the institution as a whole.

Today, risk managers shake their heads in disbelief that the Basel II regime required banks to calculate their probability of defaults by storing

7-8 years of historical data. Many banks spent the same length of time just getting their databases scrubbed and cleaned, albeit to no effect, as the valuations were a constantly moving target.

In keeping with the spirit of the time, which believed in market discipline and less government, the BIS regime also allowed banks to develop their own risk assessment called the Advanced Internal Rating-based Approach, or AIRB, subject to the local regulator's approval. Each bank was allowed to opt to calibrate its own credit and market risks.

But true to Ronfeldt's prediction, by 2010, the leading Western banks, which were presumed to be run by far more professional risk managers than banks in developing countries, were consciously under-declaring their risk-weighted assets, weaponizing the AIRB approach.

Global banks like Citibank and Deutsche Bank were declaring that their risk-weighted capital was up to 20 times smaller than their total assets so as to attract less risk-weighted capital charge. It did not help that when the global financial crisis arrived in 2008, their capital was anything but adequate. This practice should have been far more criminal than LIBOR, but the media did not catch on to it.

In Ronfeldt's TIMN paradigm, the AIRB approach can be best described as wanting to engender a 'tribal' response, where compliance was assumed for fear of censure. What really transpired, however, was a 'markets' response of individual banks pursuing self-interest and exploitation.

A marketplace, according to Ronfeldt's assessment, does not engender self-regulation, but rather competition, exploitation, and self-interest. The winner takes all. The Basel regime took us from the asset regime to the world of the markets and left us there.

Things got worse when Basel III was implemented, with even more complicated rules governing leverage (directed at an institution's assets) and liquidity (directed at its participation in the markets, as well as on counterparties).

We have now come a long way from the days of Basel I, of tangible deposits, securities, and gold. The sheer size of the financial liquidity (or money circulating) outside of the institution, in the marketplace, and the increase in the range of asset classes is distorting the dynamics between macroeconomic indicators, including inflation, liquidity, and asset valuations.

In addition, new classes of digitalized assets such as fungible and non-fungible crypto assets are as large as traditional assets like gold today. These have not taken root in the balance sheets of financial institutions yet, but they will, firstly through corporations and later via individuals who hold them. Even if banks do not hold these assets directly, they will be affected by how these assets perform in a multifaceted and networked world.

Several of the more credible economic forecasters of our time – some of whom predicted the 2008 crisis, including Gerald Celente from the Trends Research Institute, Peter Schiff, the president of Euro Pacific Capital, and Nobel Laureate Vernon Smith – all agree that the next economic crisis will be triggered by government debt.

The result of runaway government debt is a highly financialized economy, as we discussed in previous chapters. This puts enormous strain on the role of central banks. The more liquidity they pump in to fund government debt, the more money is created for investing in a whole range of ephemeral asset classes.

As we extrapolate these further, it is not impossible to imagine that under Basel IV, the composition of assets will be more financialized than in 2008, simply because the economy itself is so financialized. There is every likelihood that Basel IV will start de-emphasizing assets and start adding elements of data and the network effect to systemic risks.

The 'network' in the global financial crisis of 2008 was counterparty risks and applied mostly to the relationships that banks had with each other. That crisis also involved large corporations with highly financialized assets.

The 'network' in the next crisis, when fully formed, will include the networked effect of the interactions between different classes of digital assets. The traditional markets we know today will devolve into one of the network nodes, interacting with new digital markets that are already highly networked themselves. Financial institutions or exchanges will become just two of many players in the node.

At the moment, players will find it difficult to fathom how, in a highly networked crisis, the risks they will have to deal with will be entirely external to any one institution. Moreover, these risks will be more significant than the risks within any one institution, as discussed in Chapter 7.

By that time, we will be living in a very different world, one that does not distinguish between individuals or institutions. Exchanges and intermediaries would have been reduced to algorithms, which will present their own risks. These risks will lie in the information that is traded between players in the nodes and not in the institutions that make the networks, as they do today.

This externalization of risks will accentuate the ability of individuals to operate as players in the nodes. There will be more Navinder Singh Saraos in 2030 than there were in 2010. We are inching towards the personalization of society, even if it is still an idea in the making, with a long road ahead.

New technologies such as blockchain and virtual and augmented reality facilitate individuals' ability to create and propagate such societies more than ever before. Vitalik Buterin invoked the concept of a decentralized autonomous organization (DAO) on the Ethereum blockchain platform in 2015, when he was only 19 years old. Nobody taught him why this was even important. Today there are already hundreds of platforms, from financial exchanges to supply chains, that run on the DAO principle.

The question that naturally arises in finance today is whether this development can be regulated and curated. Not a few 'futurists' have pointed out that the transformations that we are going to be seeing in engineering technology, computing power, pharmaceuticals, genetics, and many other fields in the next 50 years will be exponentially greater and faster than those in the last 200 years combined.

It will also take on a diametrically non-linear projection. In a device-independent world, cryptocurrencies may well become the currency for machines to communicate with each other, with nothing to do with payments between institutions (as is the case today).

Any regulator, policymaker, or banker who imagines that they will be able to organize the process logically is talking gibberish. They would do well instead to track the forces that enable individuals in society to associate and create meaning organically.

The idea that individuals have the ability to organize without the need for institutions, be they state, religious, or commercial ones, appears too radical today, but the idea already exists in so many segments of society that one might say it is hidden in plain sight.

In the Latin dancing community worldwide, a 'cross-body lead' movement is understood and executed in the same way in Havana as it is in Los Angeles, Johannesburg, Dubai, Tokyo, Beijing, Singapore, Sydney, or wherever you find groups of Latin dancers.

There is not a trace of evidence that this shared understanding has been brought about by a ruling council sitting somewhere, which has dictated some standards or conventions for how the movement is performed. Millions of dancers around the world simply know exactly what to do when they take to the dance floor. The same can be said to be true in almost all dance forms, including tango, lindy hop, ballroom, or Bollywood, or in other creative forms, like Impressionist art, or reggae, jazz, and rap in music.

These creative fraternities also keep evolving by introducing new fads and movements that define periods in time, with no single party dictating the terms. Between this at one end, and totalitarian control at the other, society has more organizational forms than are obvious to those who look to governments or institutions to set the rules. In fact, a formally organized society is the poor cousin of one that is organized intuitively, like a living, breathing organism.

Full personalization will introduce new dimensions into all aspects of humanity, with implications far beyond the finance industry. Some of these effects might be positive. We might become increasingly acquisitive about the intangible things we value, like time, opportunity, scarcity, beauty, and self-gratification – though not money, because in an increasingly personalized world, we will not be subject to the vagaries of asset inflation in a global economy.

Some of the effects will also be clearly negative. Personalization increases narcissism, which we already see in today's platform world. But just as CFCs were eventually found to be toxic and damaging to the Earth's atmosphere and were replaced by hydrofluorocarbons, personalization will also create problems that will need to be addressed. It will need to be augmented with other forms of association for human civilization to progress. But that is a subject for another day.

Glossary for the General Reader

This glossary contains only the few annoying words and phrases that stand in the way of the general reader enjoying the book. Some are simple terms which are understood in a very specific or technical way within the financial community. I have explained these below to reassure the general reader of their ordinary meaning. There are many technical words, especially those used in other industries, that are not covered in this glossary, the meanings of which the reader can easily search for on the internet.

Central bank digital currency (CBDC)

Currency in a digital format, instead of the physical cash we are familiar with, issued by central banks. Some central banks around the world have either started issuing one, are experimenting with issuing one, or still thinking about it.

CBDCs will have unintended repercussions for the existing financial systems if this experiment succeeds; we will not need banks. On the other hand, there is the possibility that some cryptocurrencies, especially stablecoins (see below), issued by a well-regulated party, could be a potential alternative to CBDCs.

Core banking systems

A technical-sounding term, which simply refers to where core accounting data on the customer is located. In the early days of banking technology, this used to be in huge and cumbersome software and machines called 'mainframes', which required years of programming just to keep them updated. Today, the same volume and speed of data transactions is conducted with far more nimble software and on smaller machines, even laptops, which enables banks to compete with each other more vigorously. Some of the software in use today is even 'open-source', developed communities in a collaborative manner (as discussed in the book).

Customer relationship management (CRM)

The use of massive amounts of data on customers and the organization's interactions with them to identify patterns for acquiring, serving, and retaining customers. In a typical corporation (including banks), where this data sits in the organization's IT infrastructure is a matter of great complexity.

Crowd-lending/ Crowd-investing
(see also: Intermediation/Disintermediation, Peer-to-peer (P2P))

Platforms where individuals are able to come together to raise funds to lend or invest in a stated cause. Parties all take personal responsibility for their involvement. The platform provider only provides the information necessary for the parties to come together.

This phenomenon started in a promising manner and threatened to 'disintermediate' banks and other financial institutions, which used to do the lending or investing on behalf of their clients. However, increasing regulation has slowed down this industry. It is the thesis of this book that this field will continue developing, particularly as improvements in technology increase the network effect, giving participants information on transactions that even banks do not currently have.

Decentralized finance (DeFi)
(See also: Peer-to-peer (P2P))

When we say that the finance industry has always been centralized, we mean that an intermediary has always been involved, be it a bank, a fund manager, or insurance company and so on. This role was always important, both for practical reasons and because intermediaries had to be licensed to deal with people's money. Technology is now enabling people to deal directly with each other, so they no longer need a central intermediary. In decentralized finance, we also say that the institution in the middle is being 'disintermediated'.

Device-independent

Everything we do today is device-specific. There are things we do on mobile phones that we cannot do on a laptop computer (or, say, a programmable refrigerator). In the future, data and instructions can be sent to or carried on any equipment, such as an automobile, as easily as on a mobile phone.

Disruptor

Any business model that disrupts the role of traditional financial institutions and the way finance is delivered today.

Dodd-Frank Act

The Dodd-Frank Act, more formally called The Dodd-Frank Wall Street Reform and Consumer Protection Act 2010, is the most important and comprehensive financial legislation in operation in the United States today that arose from the financial crisis of 2008. It carries the names of the bipartisan senator and congressman who sponsored it through the US legislature and inspired other similar legislations in other countries around the world.

Externalized

In today's financial institutions, the focus is on data, information, and monetary value that is held inside institutions, by institutions. Externalized data refers to the need for institutions to use the data, information, and monetary value that exists outside them in order to serve their customers.

Financial crisis

There have been many financial crises throughout history, some which were specific to certain countries and others which were global in nature. Often, these were precipitated by excesses in spending, lending, or trading that took place in good times, or failure to correct inflationary or deflationary forces in the economy. Financial crises affect financial institutions badly. Remedying this has often relied on taxpayers' money.

Financialization

Financialization refers to monetary value that is tied to an underlying asset, which might itself be a financialization of another underlying asset and so on. A very financialized asset is one that is not tied to any hard asset anymore.

A mortgage is a financialization of a property. A derivative can be a financialization of a mortgage. A futures contract can be the financialization of a derivative, which is now two steps removed from the original underlying property. In this way, the financialized asset becomes increasingly more important than the underlying asset. The more financialized an economy becomes, the more detached it becomes from the real economy.

Fintech

A fashionable shorthand for 'financial technology' companies. Fintechs were originally supposed to be technology-driven players 'challenging' traditional banks and 'disrupting' their operations. This book argues that over time, increased regulation reduced many to old-fashioned traditional IT companies that sell software to banks, except that these were now funded by venture capitalists (VCs).

Float

Money that earns income (usually interest) when it is in the possession of a bank or a corporation while in transit from one person to another. When a person gives another person a check, there is a day when the money is under the ownership of the bank while it is in transit from the issuer to the receiver. For this reason, traditionally, it was not in a bank's interest to complete a transaction quickly, usually sitting on the payment for a day or more before the recipient received it. Digital banking has made it possible to transmit money almost instantaneously, causing banks to lose this source of income.

LIBOR

The London Interbank Offered Rate is a number that several high street bankers in London used to put together daily by sharing their respective lending rates with each other. At first, it was designed to help banks in the UK have a reference rate between themselves, but over time, the number was used by bankers around the world to price their own loans. More importantly, it came to be used by traders to lay bets on. In the mid-2010s, a scandal erupted when it was found that there was a lot of collusion between the traders and the rate-setters.

Legacy

Refers to pre-existing technology, business processes, or ways of doing things from the past. In most cases, legacy systems, products, or cultures can be blamed for the inability of organizations to innovate or incorporate new technology.

Liquidity

Any business, be it a bank, a corporation, or a country's economy, might have sufficient money on its balance sheet but not in reality when its commitments do not match the actual cash it has in hand. Corporations need to pull together as much information on where their money is located in order to fulfil its commitments at any given moment. With good liquidity, businesses can transact more with each other.

In the past, such information was found inside institutions. It is the thesis of this book that increasingly, corporations, including financial institutions and governments, are able to pull in more liquidity from *outside* institutions, including from how their customers transact, in supply chains, and in transactions with counterparties like other banks, suppliers, and corporations. The same concept applies to liquidity in currencies. If there are enough US dollars in the global markets, it becomes easier for corporations and governments that have commitments to each other to find dollars.

Intermediation / disintermediation

Banks, insurance companies, asset management companies, stock exchanges, and financial institutions are also called financial 'intermediaries'. They perform the role of a middleman in moving money between people, businesses, and governments. This intermediation function is where they generate their income. Governments, central banks, and regulators use this function to guide the flow of money and calibrate the economy.

This intermediation function is under threat because digital technologies enable parties to increasingly 'disintermediate', bypassing the need for intermediaries. Rules can be put in place to either protect intermediation or facilitate the transition.

Personalization

Personalization refers to the increasing ability of individuals to control their own data, identity, and how they choose to transact. This book argues that personalization will have a profound effect on how institutions that generate profit from aggregating people's data on public platforms will survive in the future. It also has massive implications for how society as a whole will be organized.

Platforms

In technology, platforms refer to applications that onboard users who go on to generate their own content and transactions. These include social media platforms like Facebook as well as ones like Google, Uber, and TripAdvisor.

Financial platforms refer to financial institutions that try to do this. This book argues that the negative effects of platforms and the advent of blockchain technology are moving users towards greater personalization, where individuals have greater control over their data and how it is used.

Peer-to-peer (P2P)

Transactions that take place directly between parties without the involvement of an intermediary. Parties to a financial transaction can do so without the need for a financial institution of any kind to process the transaction between them.

In crowd-lending or crowd-investing, an 'intermediary' might provide the platform for parties to meet and transact with each other, but does not take ownership of the transaction or carry the asset or risk on its own balance sheet.

Protocols

In most cases in this book, protocols refer to the design of blockchains, how they operate and what they are designed to achieve in their transactions. Mostly, these are embedded in the algorithms that dictate how these blockchains operate, and carried in the cryptocurrencies or tokens that carry them.

Ring-fencing

A typical bank has the full range of business operations, which in any other industry would be identified as ranging from wholesale to retail. Because of the 2008 financial crisis, governments in several countries put in place regulations to 'ring-fence' or separate the wholesale and other businesses from adversely affecting the retail side, which is especially sensitive because it affects the ordinary, defenseless customers of the bank. This book suggests that this has not worked very well.

Transition

In this book, it refers mostly to the idea that the world is moving from the 'platform' industry or economy of today to a more personalized one, where the individual has greater control over their own transactions.

Notes

Preface

1. R. O. Cummings, *The American Ice Harvests: A Historical Study in Technology, 1800–1918* (Berkeley: California University Press, 1949).
2. F. Fukuyama, *The End of History and The Last Man* (New York: Free Press, 2006).

Chapter 1: From platforms to personalization

3. "UnionPay network processed transactions worth 53.9 trillion Yuan in 2015", Unionpay International News Center, 22 January 2016. Available at https://www.unionpayintl.com/en/mediaCenter/newsCenter/companyNews/3009190.shtml.
4. "Visa, China UnionPay in Dispute on International Transactions", *Bloomberg News*, 4 June 2010. Available at https://www.bloomberg.com/news/articles/2010-06-04/visa-hong-kong-says-there-is-no-change-to-how-it-s-handling-transactions?sref=7pLQsG4l.
5. Number of users of Robinhood from 2014 to 2022, via Statista.com.
6. D. Curry, "Robinhood Revenue and Usage Statistics (2022)", via BusinessofApps, 9 May 2022. Available at https://www.businessofapps.com/data/robinhood-statistics/.
7. K. F. Lee, *AI Superpowers: China, Silicon Valley and the New World Order* (New York: Houghton Mifflin Harcourt, 2018).
8. E. Huet, "Uber Continues To Finance Its Drivers With New Gas Credit Card", *Forbes*, 9 June 2015. Available at https://www.forbes.com/sites/ellenhuet/2015/06/09/uber-driver-gas-credit-card-fuel-mastercard/#2c3e9b36ca2c.
9. Alipay, via Chinainternetwatch.com (accessed 12 February 2022).
10. "China Third Party Payment Report 2017 Q4", AnalysysMason report.
11. "Alibaba Group Announces March Quarter and Full Fiscal Year 2021 Results", *Businesswire*, 13 May 2022. Available at https://www.businesswire.com/news/home/20210513005533/en/Alibaba-Group-Announces-March-Quarter-and-Full-Fiscal-Year-2021-Results
12. J. Horwitz, "Alibaba Singles Day sales hit $13 billion in the first hour - up 32% from 2018", *Business Insider*, 11 November 2019. Available at https://www.businessinsider.com/alibaba-says-singles-day-sales-hit-912-billion-yuan-in-first-hour-2019-11.
13. "Alibaba Group Announces March Quarter and Full Fiscal Year 2021 Results", above, at 11.
14. F. Holmes, "No, Really, It's Good That Black Friday And Cyber Monday Sales Declined This Year", *Forbes*, 2 December 2021. Available at https://www.forbes.com/sites/greatspeculations/2021/12/02/no-really-its-good-that-black-friday-and-cyber-monday-sales-declined-this-year/?sh=17267ef9726e.

15. F. Ali, "Amazon's Prime Day 2021 sales total $11.19 billion", *Digital Commerce 360*, 23 June 2021. Available at https://www.digitalcommerce360.com/2021/06/23/amazons-prime-day-2021-sales-total-11-19-billion/

16. eBay: total active buyers worldwide 2010-2021, via Statista.com (accessed 19 August 2021).

17. Alibaba recorded 863 million annual buyers in China retail marketplace in Q3 2021, via Chinainternetwatch.com (accessed 20 November 2021).

18. S. Chan, "Tiktok becomes the first non-Facebook Mobile App to reach 3 billion downloads globally", *SensorTower* blog, July 2021. Available at https://sensortower.com/blog/tiktok-downloads-3-billion.

19. "Web 1.0 vs Web 2.0 vs Web 3.0 vs Web 4.0 vs Web 5.0 – A bird's eye on the evolution and definition", *FlatWorldBusiness* blog, 2011. Available at https://flatworldbusiness.wordpress.com/flat-education/previously/web-1-0-vs-web-2-0-vs-web-3-0-a-bird-eye-on-the-definition/.

20. P. A. Bernal, Web 2.5: the symbiotic web, *International Review of Law, Computers & Technology* 24 (1) pp. 25-37 (2018). DOI: 10.1080/13600860903570145.

21. D. Weinberger, "How the father of the World Wide Web plans to reclaim it from Facebook and Google" *Digital Trends*, 8 October 2016. Available at https://www.digitaltrends.com/web/ways-to-decentralize-the-web/.

Chapter 2: The personalization of finance

22. J. M Bessette and J. J Pitney Jr., *American Government and Politics: Deliberation, Democracy and Citizenship* (Boston: Cengage Learning, 2010).

23. A. Monnappa, "How Facebook is Using Big Data - The Good, the Bad, and the Ugly", *Simplilearn*, 16 March 2022. Available at https://www.simplilearn.com/how-facebook-is-using-big-data-article

24. M. Ali, R. Shea, J. Nelson, and M. J. Freedman, Blockstack Technical Whitepaper version 1.1, 12 October 2017. Available at https://pdos.csail.mit.edu/6.824/papers/blockstack-2017.pdf

25. D. Kariuki, "10 Projects in Blockchain-based Identity Management", *Cryptomorrow*, 28 August 2019. Available at http://www.cryptomorrow.com/2018/01/17/10-projects-in-blockchain-based-identity-management/.

26. "South Korea's Busan city launches decentralized identity platform for public services", *Ledger Insights*, 9 June 2019. Available at https://www.ledgerinsights.com/south-korea-busan-city-decentralized-identity-public-services/.

27. N. Reiff, "What is ERC-20 and What Does it Mean for Ethereum?", *Investopedia* blog, 20 June 2017. Available at https://www.investopedia.com/news/what-erc20-and-what-does-it-mean-ethereum/.

28. R. Hackett, "Why Blockchain and Identity Go Together", *Fortune*, 20 January 2018. Available at http://fortune.com/2018/01/20/blockchain-identity-civic-silicon-slopes/.

29. E. Maroutian, *Thirty: A collection of personal quotes, advice, and lessons* (Los Angeles: Maroutian Entertainment, 2018).

30. K. Wu, Y. Ma. G. Huang, and X. Liu, A first look at blockchain-based decentralized applications. *Journal of Software: Practice and Experience* 51(10) pp. 2033-2050 (2019). DOI:10.1002/spe.2751.

31. "CryptoKitties craze slows down transactions on Ethereum", *BBC News*, 5 December 2017. Available at https://www.bbc.com/news/technology-42237162.

32. L. Beckett, "MIT to investigate research lab's ties to Epstein as director resigns", *The Guardian*, 7 September 2019. Available at https://www.theguardian.com/education/2019/sep/07/jeffrey-epstein-mit-media-lab-joi-ito-resigns-reports

33. H. Sheffield, "Do community currencies really work?", *Milken Institute Review* blog, 23 September 2019. Available at https://www.milkenreview.org/articles/do-community-currencies-really-work.

34. M. Waters, "Why a small town in Washington is printing its own currency during the pandemic", *The Hustle*, 12 June 2020. Available at https://thehustle.co/covid19-local-currency-tenino-washington/.

35. S. Hargrave, "From Brixton to Totnes, the UK's dream of local currencies is over", *Wired*, 2 March 2020. Available at https://www.wired.co.uk/article/local-currencies-dead.

36. See Sarafu.Network, via Grassroots Economics. Available at https://www.grassrootseconomics.org/pages/sarafu-network.html

37. J. Rifkin, *The Zero Marginal Cost Society: The Internet of Things, The Collaborative Commons and the Eclipse of Capitalism* (New York: St Martin's Press, 2014).

38. N. Jones, "How scientists are embracing NFTs", *Nature*, 18 June 2021. Available at https://www.nature.com/articles/d41586-021-01642-3

39. See Digihealth Informer, Digital Health Maven. Available at http://digitalhealthmaven.com/digihealth_informer/

40. M. Brunnermeier, H. James, J. Landau, The Euro and the Battle of Ideas, Princeton University Press , 2017.

41. T. Wijman, "The Games Market and Beyond in 2021: The Year in Numbers" *Newzoo Insights* blog, 12 December 2021. Available at https://newzoo.com/insights/articles/the-games-market-in-2021-the-year-in-numbers-esports-cloud-gaming#:~:text=The%20games%20market%20in%202021,%2B1.4%25%20over%20last%202020.

42. S. E. Kohan, "Walmart revenue hits $559b for fiscal year 2020", Forbes, 18 February 2021. Available at https://www.forbes.com/sites/shelleykohan/2021/02/18/walmart-revenue-hits-559-billion-for-fiscal-year-2020/?sh=797882c13358

43. J. Harty, "Newzoo's Games Trends to Watch in 2022", Newzoo Insights blog, 13 January 2022. Available at https://newzoo.com/insights/articles/newzoos-games-trends-to-watch-in-2022-metaverse-game-ip-vr

44. K. T. Smith, "StockX's Move Into NFTS has major implications for the retail industry", *Highsnobiety*, 10 February 2022. Available at https://www.highsnobiety.com/p/stockx-nft/.

45. L. Callon-Butler, "The NFT Game That Makes Cents for Filipinos During Covid", *CoinDesk*, 26 August 2020. Available at https://www.coindesk.com/markets/2020/08/26/the-nft-game-that-makes-cents-for-filipinos-during-covid/

Chapter 3: The financialization of everything

46. H. McCracken, "How the Bloomberg Terminal made history — and stays ever relevant", *Fast Company*, 6 October 2015. Available at https://www.fastcompany.com/3051883/the-bloomberg-terminal.

47. J. Fox, "Mutual Funds Ate the Stock Market. Now ETFs Are Doing It", *Bloomberg View*, 16 May 2017. Available at https://www.bloomberg.com/opinion/articles/2017-05-16/mutual-funds-ate-the-stock-market-now-etfs-are-doing-it

48. "Statistical Release: OTC derivatives statistics at end June 2019", Bank for International Settlement report (2019).

49. A. Rappeport, "The U.S. budget deficit hit a record $1.7 trillion in the first half of the fiscal year.", *The New York Times*, 12 April 2021. Available at https://www.nytimes.com/2021/04/12/business/united-states-budget-deficit.html.

50. R. Foroohar, *Makers and Takers: The rise of finance and the fall of American business* (New York: Penguin Random House, 2016).

51. B. Noverini, "Plan to Shrink GE Capital a Needed Shot in Arm for GE", *Morning Star*, 10 April 2015. Available at https://www.morningstar.com/articles/692310/plan-to-shrink-ge-capital-a-needed-shot-in-the-arm-for-ge.

52. W. Feuer, "Apple now has $207.06 billion in cash on hand, up slightly from last quarter", *CNBC Tech*, 20 Jan 2020. Available at https://www.cnbc.com/2020/01/28/apple-q1-2019-cash-hoard-heres-how-much-cash-apple-has-on-hand.html

53. S. Goldman, "Harvard's endowment gains are not something to be celebrated", *The Harvard Crimson*, 25 October 2021. Available at https://www.thecrimson.com/article/2021/10/25/goldman-harvard-endowment/.

54. S. D Solomon, "Dole case illustrates problems in shareholder system", *The New York Times*, 21 March 2017. Available at https://www.nytimes.com/2017/03/21/business/dealbook/dole-case-illustrates-problems-in-shareholder-system.html

55. H. Clancy, "How GE generates $1b from data", *Fortune*, 10 October 2014. Available at https://fortune.com/2014/10/10/ge-data-robotics-sensors/.

56. G. Paolini, "Tesla, the data company", *CIO*, 28 August 2019. Available at https://www.cio.com/article/3433931/tesla-the-data-company.html.

57. H. Jin and N. Balu, "Musk's bets on Tesla: human-like robots and self-driving cars", *Reuters*, 27 January 2022. Available at https://www.reuters.com/article/tesla-robots-idCAKBN2K11O.

58. J. Diamond, *Guns, Germs and Steel, The Fate of Human Societies* (New York: W. W. Norton, 1997).

59. O. Kaplan, "Mobile gaming is a $65 billion global business, and investors are buying in", *Techcrunch*, 22 August 2019. Available at https://techcrunch.com/2019/08/22/mobile-gaming-mints-money/.

60. "2022 Global Macro Outlook: Growth Despite Inflation", report by Morgan Stanley (accessed December 2021). Available at https://www.morganstanley.com/ideas/global-macro-economy-outlook-2022.

61. D. J. Fixler, R. Greenaway-McGrevy, and B. Grimm, "The Revisions to GDP, GDI, and Their Major Components", US Bureau of Economic Analysis report, 20 August 2014. Available at https://apps.bea.gov/scb/pdf/2014/08%20August/0814_revisions_to_gdp_gdi_and_their_major_components.pdf.

62. J. Haskel and S. Westlake, *Capitalism without capital: The rise of the intangible economy* (Princeton, New Jersey: Princeton University Press, 2018).

63. P. Cohen, "The Economic Growth That Experts Can't Count", *The New York Times*, 6 February 2017. Available at https://www.nytimes.com/2017/02/06/business/economy/what-is-gdp-economy-alternative-measure.html.

64. M. Fox, "Tesla just surpassed Walmart in market value. Here are the 8 remaining S&P 500 companies worth more than Tesla", *Business Insider*, 21 August 2020. Available at https://markets.businessinsider.com/news/stocks/tesla-surpasses-walmart-market-value-most-valued-sp500-us-companies-2020-8-1029524035#.
65. P. Villegas, "Cristiano Ronaldo snubbed Coca-Cola. The company's market value fell $4 billion.", *The Washington Post*, 16 June 2021. Available at https://www.washingtonpost.com/sports/2021/06/16/cristiano-ronaldo-coca-cola/.

Chapter 4: Rise of the rebels

66. "Staff Report on Equity and Options Market Structure Conditions in Early 2021", US Securities and Exchange Commission report, 14 October 2021. Available at https://www.sec.gov/files/staff-report-equity-options-market-struction-conditions-early-2021.pdf
67. S. Brush and L. Fortado, "How a Mystery Trader With an Algorithm May Have Caused the Flash Crash", *Bloomberg*, 22 April 2015. Available at https://www.bloomberg.com/news/articles/2015-04-22/mystery-trader-armed-with-algorithms-rewrites-flash-crash-story.
68. A. I Weinberg, "Should You Fear the ETF?", *The Wall Street Journal*, 6 April 2015. Available at https://www.wsj.com/articles/should-you-fear-the-etf-1449457201.
69. R. Cooper, "US has itself to blame for flash crash trading", letter published in *The Guardian*, 24 April 2015. Available at https://www.theguardian.com/business/2015/apr/24/us-has-itself-to-blame-for-flash-crash-trading.
70. C. Shirky, *Here Comes Everybody: The Power of Organizing Without Organizations* (New York: Penguin Press, 2008).
71. G. Bhalla, *Collaboration and Co-Creation: New Platforms for Marketing and Innovation* (New York: Springer, 2011).
72. Y. Benkler, *The Wealth of Networks: How Social Production Transforms Markets and Freedom* (New Haven, Connecticut: Yale University Press, 2006).
73. A. Tapscott and D. Tapscott, *The Blockchain Revolution: How the Technology Behind Bitcoin is Changing Money, Business, and the World* (Toronto: Penguin, 2016).
74. S. Chacon and B. Straub, *Pro Git, 2nd Edition* (Apress, under Creative Commons license, 2014). Available at https://git-scm.com/book/en/v2.
75. L. Wiener, L. Kelman, S. Fisher, and M. Abraham, "The $100 Billion Media Opportunity for Retailers", Boston Consulting Group blog, 19 May 2021. Available at https://www.bcg.com/publications/2021/how-to-compete-in-retail-media.
76. B. Iyer and M. Subramaniam, "The Strategic Value of APIs", *Harvard Business Review*, 7 January 2015. Available at https://hbr.org/2015/01/the-strategic-value-of-apis.
77. J. Koetsier, "With Billions of People and Millions of Apps, Can Unity Create The Metaverse?", *Forbes*, 7 December 2021. Available at https://www.forbes.com/sites/johnkoetsier/2021/12/07/with-billions-of-people-and-millions-of-apps-can-unity-create-the-metaverse/?sh=4459fdbc6b8c.
78. C. Shumba, "Cardano founder Charles Hoskinson says crypto world needs 'that wifi moment' - where users can work with any blockchain seamlessly - more than it needs a dominant network", *Business Insider*, 14 September 2021. Available at https://news.yahoo.com/cardano-founder-charles-hoskinson-says-070725626.html?fr=sycsrp_catchall.

Chapter 5: The agents of change

79. J. Sommer, "Vanguard's Jack Bogle Wasn't a Billionaire. He Was Proud of That", *The New York Times*, 16 January 2019. Available at https://www.nytimes.com/2019/01/16/business/vanguard-jack-bogle-death.html?.

80. W. B. Crawford Jr, "Pioneer Still Trying to Change the World With Futures", *Chicago Tribune*, 2 October 1993. Available at https://www.chicagotribune.com/news/ct-xpm-1993-10-03-9310030118-story.html.

81. N. Acharya, "Why microfinance crisis is still not over even 10 years after the clampdown" *Business Standard*, 14 March 2020. Available at https://www.business-standard.com/article/finance/why-microfinance-crisis-is-still-not-over-even-10-years-after-the-clampdown-120031401057_1.html.

82. I. Guerin, M. Labie, and J. M. Servet (eds.), *The Crises of Microcredit* (London: Zed Books, 2015).

83. G. Goodman, *Paper Money* (London: MacDonald and Company, 1983).

84. "United States - public debt by month, 2020/2021", via Statista.com (accessed 7 January 2022).

85. M. Phillips, "The Long Story of US Debt, from 1790 to 2011, in 1 Little Chart", *The Atlantic*, 13 November 2012. Available at https://www.theatlantic.com/business/archive/2012/11/the-long-story-of-us-debt-from-1790-to-2011-in-1-little-chart/265185/

86. "Major Foreign Holders of Treasury Securities", US Department of the Treasury. Available at https://ticdata.treasury.gov/Publish/mfh.txt.

87. "China's debt ratio is growing as its economy loses steam", *Bloomberg News*, 16 July 2019. Available at https://www.bloomberg.com/news/articles/2019-07-16/china-s-debt-growth-keeps-marching-on-as-economy-loses-pace.

88. R. Sharma, "There is no easy escape from the global debt trap", *Financial Times*, 21 November 2021. Available at https://www.ft.com/content/c9e0c2c1-55af-4258-9c92-92faa111f41e.

89. S. Legge, "What Adam Smith said on inflation and the debt trap", letter published in the *Financial Times*, 17 January 2022. Available at https://www.ft.com/content/27c76498-937f-41b4-a552-338b105235b4.

90. "China Third Party Payment Report 2017 Q4", AnalysysMason report.

91. "Eastern Caribbean launches central bank digital currency pilot DCash", *Ledger Insights*, 1 April 2021. Available at https://ledgerinsights.com/eastern-caribbean-launches-central-bank-digital-currency-cbdc-pilot-dcash/.

92. K. Webb, "Facebook's new payment service will let you send money without fees across Facebook, Instagram, WhatsApp and Messenger", *Business Insider*, 13 November 2019. Available at https://www.businessinsider.com/facebook-pay-payments-instagram-whatsapp-messenger-send-money-2019-11.

93. A. Rolfe, "Facebook digital wallet Novi ready for market launch", *Payments Cards and Mobile*, 19 August 2021. Available at https://www.paymentscardsandmobile.com/facebook-digital-wallet-novi-ready-for-market-launch/.

94. "Fed Vice Chair: Stablecoins could make CBDC efforts superfluous", *Ledger Insights*, 29 June 2021. Available at https://www.ledgerinsights.com/fed-vice-chair-stablecoins-could-make-cbdc-efforts-superfluous-digital-dollar/.

95. O. Adejumo, "Boston Fed and MIT See Promising Results in CBDC Code Testing", *Be In Crypto*, 5 February 2022. Available at https://beincrypto.com/boston-fed-and-mit-see-promising-results-in-cbdc-code-testing/.

96. J. Haworth, "How many people own bitcoin?95 Blockchain Statistics (2022)", *Exploding Topics* blog, 18 March 2022. Available at https://explodingtopics.com/blog/blockchain-stats.

97. F. Klauder, "How many people use DeFi?", *DeFi Times* newsletter, 7 June 2021. Available at https://newsletter.defitimes.io/p/how-many-people-use-defi.

98. "DeFi TVL in the Ethereum blockchain", via Statista.com (accessed 12 January 2022).

99. M. Trajcevski, "DeFi surges by 1,2000% in 2021, $240 billion Total Value Locked in Defi", *Dailycoin*, 31 December 2021. Available at https://www.investing.com/news/cryptocurrency-news/defi-surges-by-1200-in-2021-240-billion-total-value-locked-in-defi-2728005.

100. S. Aramonte, W. Huang, and A. Schrimpf, "DeFi risks and the decentralization illusion", *BIS Quarterly Review*, 6 December 2021. Available at https://www.bis.org/publ/qtrpdf/r_qt2112b.htm.

101. A. Berwick and E. Howcrot, "From Crypto to Christie's: how an Indian metaverse king made his fortune", *Reuters*, 17 November 2021. Available at https://www.reuters.com/investigates/special-report/finance-crypto-sundaresan/.

102. S. Kirsner, "Venture capital's grandfather", *The Boston Globe*, 6 April 2008. Available at https://www.boston.com/business/articles/2008/04/06/venture_capitals_grandfather/.

103. S. O'Sullivan, C. Ebersweiler, and B. Joffe, "70 years of VC innovation", *TechCrunch*, 9 November 2017. Available at https://techcrunch.com/2017/11/09/70-years-of-vc-innovation/.

104. Fintech Innovation (ARKF) Holdings, portfolio details by ARK Holdings, 17 August 2021. Available at https://ark-funds.com/wp-content/uploads/2021/08/ARK_FINTECH_INNOVATION_ETF_ARKF_HOLDINGS.pdf.

105. "Annual Report 2017", Visa. Available at https://s1.q4cdn.com/050606653/files/doc_financials/annual/2017/Visa-2017-Annual-Report.pdf.

106. A. Lo, *Adaptive Markets: Financial Evolution at the Speed of Thought* (Princeton: Princeton University Press, 2017).

107. A. G. Martinez, *Chaos Monkeys: Inside the Silicon Valley Money Machine* (London: Ebury Press, 2016).

Chapter 6: The anatomy of innovation

108. "NYSE mobile phone options now available to traders", *Mobile Commerce Press*, 30 June 2016. Available at http://www.mobilecommercepress.com/nyse-mobile-phone-options-now-available-traders/8522622/.

109. J. Rickards, *Currency Wars: The Making of the Next Global Crisis* (New York: Portfolio/Penguin, 2011).

110. "The Firm's Cash Management Account is Dazzling a Lot of Well-Heeled Customers - And Scaring the Competition. *Fortune*, October 1980, pp. 135-144, cited in E. K Clemons and M. C. Row, "The Merrill Lynch cash management account financial service: a case study in strategic information systems", Proceedings of the Twenty-First Annual Hawaii International Conference on System Sciences (1988), Vol.IV, Applications Track. Available at https://ieeexplore.ieee.org/document/11972.

111. J. Rickards, *Currency Wars: The Making of the Next Global Crisis,* above at 108.

112. B. Jovanovic and P. Rousseau, "General Purpose Technologies", chapter in *Handbook of Economic Growth*, vol. 1, part B, pp. 1181-1224. Available at https://econpapers.repec.org/bookchap/eeegrochp/1-18.htm.

113. C. Y. Min, "AI firm Taiger gives clients more bite in slashing costs", *The Business Times*, 6 March 2018. Available at https://www.businesstimes.com.sg/sme/ai-firm-taiger-gives-clients-more-bite-in-slashing-costs.

114. I. Kaminska, "HFT as an insight into where fintech is going", *Financial Times*, 28 March 2017. Available at https://ftalphaville.ft.com/2017/03/28/2186482/hft-as-an-insight-into-where-fintech-is-going/.

115. J. Rennison and J. Dye, "Ex-Deutsche Bank traders have Libor-rigging convictions overturned", *Financial Times*, 27 January 2022. Available at https://www.ft.com/content/2bba9f8d-12f7-4f7a-ba59-f49555f7f01d.

116. S. Brush and L. Fortado, "Panther, Coscia Fined Over High-Frequency Trading Algorithms", *Bloomberg*, 22 July 2013. Available at https://www.bloomberg.com/news/articles/2013-07-22/panther-coscia-fined-over-high-frequency-trading-algorithms-1-.

117. A. Kharpal and R. Browne, "Hackers return nearly half of the $600 million they stole in one of the biggest crypto heists", *CNBC*, 11 August 2021. Available at https://www.cnbc.com/2021/08/11/cryptocurrency-theft-hackers-steal-600-million-in-poly-network-hack.html.

118. S. Lynch, R. Satter, and L. Cohen, "U.S. accuses couple of laundering $4.5 bln in bitcoin tied to 2016 hack", *Reuters*, 10 February 2022. Available at https://www.reuters.com/technology/us-arrests-couple-allegedly-laundering-45-bln-crypto-tied-bitfinex-hack-2022-02-08/.

119. C. Shirky, "A Speculative Post on the Idea of Algorithmic Authority", blogpost on shirky.com, 15 November 2009. Available at http://www.shirky.com/weblog/2009/11/a-speculative-post-on-the-idea-of-algorithmic-authority/

Chapter 7: The institution crumbles

120. J. Franklin, "Morgan Stanley lifts profitability target as it seeks $10tn in client assets", *Financial Times*, 19 January 2022. Available at https://www.ft.com/content/b7c1961f-09c4-4109-8c25-89acb00264b9.

121. R. H. Coase, "The Nature of the Firm", *Economica* vol. 4 pp. 386-405 (2018). DOI: 10.1111/j.1468-0335.1937.tb00002.x

122. U. Fichtner, H. Goos, and M. Hesse, "How a Pillar of German Banking Lost Its Way", *Der Spiegel*, 22 October 2016. Available at https://www.spiegel.de/international/business/the-story-of-the-self-destruction-of-deutsche-bank-a-1118157.html.

123. M. Arnold, "Boost for Staley's as Barclays investment bank outperforms rivals", *Financial Times*, 27 April 2018. Available at https://www.ft.com/content/97250344-491e-11e8-8ee8-cae73aab7ccb.

124. A. Phaneuf, "Largest US Banks by Assets in 2022", *Insider Intelligence*, 2 January 2022. Available at https://www.insiderintelligence.com/insights/largest-banks-us-list.

125. M. Bird, "Understanding Deutsche Bank's $47 Trillion Derivatives Book", *The Wall Street Journal*, 5 October 2016. Available at https://www.wsj.com/articles/does-deutsche-bank-have-a-47-trillion-derivatives-problem-1475689629.

126. J. Choi, Y. Erande, Y. Yu, and C. J. Aquino, " Emerging Challengers and Incumbent Operators Battle for Asia Pacific's Digital Banking Opportunity", Boston Consulting Group report, 7 June 2021. Available at https://web-assets.bcg.com/53/42/92f340e345dab62aa227fd53ccd4/asian-digital-challenger-bank.pdf.

127. A. K. Kashyap, R. Rajan, and J. Stein, "Banks as Liquidity Providers: An Explanation for the Co-Existence of Lending and Deposit-Taking", *Journal of Finance* vol. 57(1) pp. 33-73 (2002). Available at https://scholar.harvard.edu/files/stein/files/liqpro-jf-final.pdf.

128. H. DeAngelo & R. M. Stulz. "Liquid-claim production, risk management, and bank capital structure: Why high leverage is optimal for banks", *Journal of Financial Economics*, 116 (2), pp. 219-236 (2015).

129. D. W. Diamond and P. Dybvig, "Bank Runs, Deposit Insurance, and Liquidity," *Journal of Political Economy* vol. 91(3) pp. 401-419 (1983). Available at http://www.bu.edu/econ/files/2012/01/DD83jpe.pdf.

130. D. W. Diamond and R. Rajan, "Banks and Liquidity", *American Economic Review* 91(2) pp. 422-425 (2001). Available at https://www.aeaweb.org/articles?id=10.1257/aer.91.2.422.

131. "TransferWise's Kaarman: Banks haven't really treated their users transparently", *The Asian Banker*, 13 April 2018. Available at https://live.theasianbanker.com/video/transferwises-kaarmann-banks-havent-really-treated-their-users-transparently.

132. C. Terenzi, "Brad Garlinghouse says Ripple wants to reach $2 trillion XRP liquidity", *Use The Bitcoin*, November 2019. Available at https://usethebitcoin.com/brad-garlinghouse-says-ripple-wants-to-reach-2-trillion-xrp-liquidity/.

133. R. Ungarino, "Here are 9 fascinating facts to know about BlackRock, the world's largest asset manager", *Business Insider*, December 2020. Available at https://www.businessinsider.com/what-to-know-about-blackrock-larry-fink-biden-cabinet-facts-2020-12.

134. J.D. Alois, "Zopa Becomes a Bank. Fintech Announces Approval of Full Bank License as it Moves Beyond Online Lending", *Crowdfund Insider*, 23 June 2020. Available at https://www.crowdfundinsider.com/2020/06/163139-zopa-becomes-a-bank-fintech-announces-approval-of-full-bank-license-as-it-moves-beyond-online-lending/.

Chapter 8: Reimagining the product

135. "United States Total Deposits for June 2021", via CEICData.

136. "Mobile Payment Market Size, Share and Covid-19 Analysis", Fortune Business Insights report, January 2022. Available at https://www.fortunebusinessinsights.com/industry-reports/mobile-payment-market-100336.

137. "*Mobile Wallet Market by Type, Technology, End User and Industry Vertical: Global Opportunity Analysis and Industry Forecast, 2020-2027*", Research and Markets report, April 2020. Available at https://www.researchandmarkets.com/reports/5118741/mobile-wallet-market-by-type-technology-end?utm_source=dynamic&utm_medium=CI&utm_code=9jzr3m&utm_campaign=1408567+-+Global+Mobile+Wallet+Market+(2020+to+2027)+-+by+Type%2c+Technology%2c+End-user+and+Indus.

138. V. Subburaj, "Stablecoins: What are they? And how are they redefining the crypto ecosystem?" *The News Minute*, 30 December 2021. Available at https://www.thenewsminute.com/article/stablecoins-what-are-they-and-how-are-they-redefining-crypto-ecosystem-159324.

139. H. Sender, "Ant Financial extends dominance in Chinese online finance", *Financial Times*, 17 May 2018. Available at https://www.ft.com/content/fde8fe0c-5830-11e8-b8b2-d6ceb45fa9d0.

140. Q. Yue and D. Jia, "China curbs money market funds, amongst them Ant's Yue Bao", *Nikkei Asia*, 17 January 2022. Available at https://asia.nikkei.com/Spotlight/Caixin/China-curbs-money-market-funds-among-them-Ant-s-Yu-e-Bao.

141. "Bank reserves, Federal Reserve Bank of St. Louis", via FRED Economic Research (accessed 26 May 2022).

142. "Number of US FDIC-insured commercial banks", via Statista.com (accessed 24 May 2022).

143. R. Westbrook and R. Jasnow (eds.), *Security for Debt in Ancient Near Eastern Law* (Leiden: Brill, 2001).

144. A. Phaneuf, "A look at nonbank loans and the alternative lending industry business model in 2021", *Business Insider*, 15 January 2021.

145. "Global Crowdfunding Market Size Status and Forecast 2021 to 2027", via Valuates.

146. "Crowdfunding statistics (2021): Market size and growth", via Fundera,

147. "Annual Report 2017", Ping An Bank. Available at https://resources.pingan.com/app_upload/file/bank/7874b206d95048c3b39e8d0bc6d1874d.pdf.

148. M. Miller and S. Zhang, "China's $7.6 billion Ponzi scam highlights growing online risks", *Reuters*, 3 February 2016. Available at https://www.reuters.com/article/us-china-fraud-idUSKCN0VB2O1.

149. "Our Facilities", via Amazon corporate website, www.aboutamazon.com (accessed 13 February 2022).

Chapter 9: The great transitions

150. D. Ronfeldt, "Tribes, Institutions, Markets, Networks: A framework about societal evolution", RAND Corporation paper, 1996. Available at https://www.rand.org/content/dam/rand/pubs/papers/2005/P7967.pdf.

151. D. Nasaw, *The Patriarch: The Remarkable Life and Turbulent Times of Joseph P Kennedy* (New York: Penguin, 2013).

152. P. F Drucker, "The new society of organizations", *Harvard Business Review*, September 1992. Available at https://hbr.org/1992/09/the-new-society-of-organizations.

153. M. Hasan, "Mervyn King 'Not Interested' In 2008 Libor Rate Warnings, Say Ex-BoE Colleagues", *Huffington Post*, 16 July 2012. Available at https://www.huffingtonpost.co.uk/2012/07/16/mervyn-king-not-interested-in-2008-libor-rate-warnings_n_1676468.html.

154. "BoE emails show Sir Mervyn King was aware of Libor 'misreporting' fears in 2008", *The Telegraph*, 13 July 2012. Available at https://www.telegraph.co.uk/finance/newsbysector/banksandfinance/9398177/BoE-emails-show-Sir-Mervyn-King-was-aware-of-Libor-misreporting-fears-in-2008.html.

155. J. Rennison and J. Dye, "Ex-Deutsche Bank traders have Libor-rigging convictions overturned", *Financial Times*, 27 January 2022. Available at https://www.ft.com/content/2bba9f8d-12f7-4f7a-ba59-f49555f7f01d.

156. D. Enrich, "The Unravelling of Tom Hayes", *The Wall Street Journal*, 15 September 2015. Available at http://graphics.wsj.com/libor-unraveling-tom-hayes/3.

157. Tim Wallace, "Five of six Libor traders found not guilty". *The Telegraph*, 27 January 2016. Available at https://www.telegraph.co.uk/finance/financial-crime/12125430/Five-of-six-Libor-traders-found-not-guilty.html.

158. T. Hale, "ICE shakes up scandal hit Libor", *Financial Times*, 17 March 2016. Available at https://www.ft.com/content/f9853db6-ec4f-11e5-888e-2eadd5fbc4a4.
159. A. Goldgar, *Tulipmania: Money, Honor, and Knowledge in the Dutch Golden Age* (Chicago: University of Chicago Press, 2007).

Acknowledgments

I have three categories of people to whom I owe a debt for the eventual birth of this book.

Firstly, Foo Boon Ping and Cindy Yu, my business partners and personal friends. We run TAB Global, the owner of The Asian Banker, Wealth and Society, The Banking Academy, TAB Insights that we built together. Both held the fort on the business while I struggled with this book for so long. They accepted my ever-stretched deadlines without ever questioning if I was ever going to complete this book. They are also my intellectual soulmates on the journey of building a business around the ideas that shape the world of finance.

Some employees also contributed to my understanding of issues. Over the years, these have included Chris Kapfer, Peter Hoflich, Matthew Taylor and Busch Pu, who had refreshing ways of adding their own insights to my ideas. Separately, I owe a personal debt to Sophie Zhang Cheng for having supported me over the many years that I struggled with it.

Secondly, I want to thank my intellectual mentors and sparring partners: Nick Dove, Gordian Gaeta, John Howell, Thomas McMahon, Philippe Paillart, Wilson Chia, Varun Sablok, Mathew Welch, Alex Escucha, D.K Kim and Kelvin Lim. I am a product of the intellectual cauldron in which we interacted with each other over the years, spanning many conferences, seminars, and working groups. Special thanks to Peter Peh Shi Wei for guiding me in all things technical on decentralized finance, and also to Bill Chua and Alex Manson who took pains to go through the drafts with me. Thanks also to David Ronfeldt, whose original idea on tribes, institutions, markets, and networks was central to my thesis on transitions.

Thirdly, I have had the benefit of the friendship of some of the greatest leaders in finance across several continents over the years. Dick Kovacevich, Sir George Mathewson, Zhang Jianqing, Liu Ming Kang, Ma Weihua, Peter Seah Lim Huat, Piyush Gupta, K.V Kamath, Aditya Puri, Cesar Virata, Chartsiri Sophonpanich, Banthoon Lamsam, Yvonne Chia, Justo "Tito" Ortiz, the late Sir Brian Pitman, and the late Bill Seidman were all paragons of leadership in their respective institutions, countries, and spheres of influence. Tang Ning, Dusan Stojanovic and Patrick Ngabonziza are true pioneers in frontier technologies in their respective areas today. My friendships with each of them gave me a front seat view of their achievements and the visions that guided their respective journeys.

My special thanks to former congressman Barney Frank, co-author of the Dodd-Frank Act, with whom I have a deep and personal friendship that includes long arguments to test my ideas. Also, Richard Sandor, the philosopher-king who created the institutions that have become cornerstones of the US and global financial markets today. The forewords they each wrote are unadulterated statements of their assessments of me that I humbly accept.

I am missing many more names for sure. Dr Beverly Goh Pi Lee kept kicking my butt to get the book published. Suprimi and Uli Antoni gave me free food and lodging in the final phase of getting this book out. I completed this book in the home of Zachary, Grace, and Larry Pederson in Seattle. Vasuki Shastry, who lives in London, introduced me to Chua Hong Koon who became my publisher, and to my editors Sophie Chew and Geysilla Jean Ortiz. The encyclopedic nature of this book is a reflection of the eclectic cross-section of mentors, colleagues, family, and friends across many continents who have influenced my life personally and professionally.

Emmanuel Daniel

Index

A

Aadhar, 83
ACI Worldwide and Fidelity National
   Information Services, 93
Act One, 105
Act Two, 106
Adams, Douglas, 60
Additional Liquidity Monitoring Metrics
   (ALMM), 129
Adoboli, Kweku, 113
Advanced Internal Rating-based Approach
   (AIRB), 178
agents of change, 69–97
algorithmic authority, 117
algorithms, 58, 86, 111, 116, 118, 174, 180
Alibaba, 7, 9, 144, 155
AliCloud, 62
Ali, Muneeb, 23
Alipay, 9
Alternative Reference Rates Committee
   (ARRC), 173
Amazon, 7, 10, 155
Amazon Partner Network, 62
Amazon Web Services (AWS), 59, 155
American Civil War, 80
American Research and Development
   Corporation, 91
anatomy of innovation, 99–118
Anchor, 88
Android, 99
Android operating systems, 7
Anglo-Saxon banks, 122
Anglo-Saxon countries, 80
Ant Group, 94–95
application programming interfaces
   (APIs), 35, 58, 61–65–66, 133
Arab Spring, 99
Archipelago, 164

Ark Fintech, 94
artificial intelligence (AI), 23, 109, 168
Asia-Pacific region, 172
assets under management (AUM), 6, 93,
   141
Assyria, 148
Atkins, Paul, 165
autonomous community organization, 168
Axie Infinity, 33

B

Baidu, 7
balance sheet, 121–125
Ballmer, Steve, 56
Bank for International Settlements (BIS),
   79, 89, 129, 160, 175, 178
Banking Commission Report, 125
Bank of England, 170, 173
bank-owned EDI consortiums, 115
Basel regime, 176–177
Baton System, 68
B2C2, 88
Benkler, Yochai, 56–57, 61
Bent, Bruce, 101
Big Bang, 103
Big Six, 123
Binance, 96
biometrics, 22
Bitcoin, 41, 80, 87, 100
Bits, Bytes and Balance Sheets, 121
black box approach, 132
Black Friday, 10
Black, Gavin, 171
BlockApps, 115
blockchain, 23–24, 33–34, 58, 112–115,
   133
Bogle, John, 102
Brazil, Russia, India, and China (BRIC), 4

Bretton Woods agreement, 80–81, 100
Bronze Age, 119
Brown, Henry, 101
browser technology, 7
Brynjolfsson, Erik, 2
Buterin, Vitalik, 27
buy-now-pay-later (BNPL), 5–6, 46, 104–105

C
cancelable biometrics, 22
capital adequacy, 100, 177
Capital Adequacy Ratio (CAR), 175
capitalism, 163
Cash Management Account (CMA), 102
Cathy Wood's Ark Fintech Innovation ETF, 93
Celente, Gerald, 179
central bank, 81
central bank culture, 81
central bank digital currencies (CBDCs), 77, 79, 84, 86–87, 183
certificates of deposits (CDs), 101
Charles Schwab, 6
Chase Manhattan, 123
Chicago Board Options Exchange's (CBOE) Volatility Index, 172
Chicago Mercantile Exchange, 38
China, 3–5, 8–11, 60, 70, 72, 78, 104, 139, 153, 160
China Banking Regulatory Commission (CBRC), 154
China UnionPay, 5, 8
chlorofluorocarbons (CFCs), 20–21
Christianity, 67
Church, George, 30
Citibank, 123, 150, 178
civil society, 166
cloud-based systems, 59
Coase, Ronald, 120
collateralized debt obligation (CDO), 101, 104
Commodity Futures Modernization Act of 2000 (CFMA), 177
Connolly, Matthew, 171
Consensys, 115

contract for difference (CFD), 42
core banking systems, 183–184
corporations, 40
Coscia, Michael J., 116
Covid-19 pandemic, 160
credit, 149
credit bureau models, 150
credit default swaps (CDS), 104, 177
Creditex, 111
cross-body lead movement, 181
cross-sell-ratios, 3
crowdfunding industry, 152
crowd-lending/crowd-investing, 184
crypto assets, 96
crypto-based assets, 66
cryptocurrency, 11, 89
CryptoKitties, 32
Cryptomorrow, 23
Cultural Revolution, 4
customer relationship management (CRM), 184
customer satisfaction, 155
Cyber Monday, 10
cybersecurity, 17

D
Dama, Caroline, 29–30
Dapper Labs, 32
dark web, 24
debt-to-GDP ratio, 78
decentralized applications (dApps), 27
decentralized autonomous organization (DAO), 28, 58, 180
decentralized finance (DeFi), 25, 59, 88, 185
deception, symmetry of, 116–118
deposit account, 141–148
Depository Trust Corporation, 41
Deutsche Bank, 121–124, 178
developing countries, 70
device-independent, 11–12, 140, 185
Diamond, Jared, 45
Diem project, 85
Digital Equipment Corporation (DEC), 92
digital-only bank, 128
digital platforms, 1–2, 133

digital rights management (DRM), 138
Dimon, Jaime, 145
disintermediation, 188
disruptor, 185
distribution channels, 17
Dizon, Gabby, 33
Dodd-Frank Act, 55, 70, 124, 185
Dogecoin, 96
Drucker, Peter, 168
dysfunctional state, 75–80

E
eBay, 61
economic change, 70
Elastic Compute Cloud, 59
electronic data interchange (EDI), 115
El Salvador, 80
emotional web, 12
energy, 28
enterprise software, 59
Epstein, Jeffrey, 28
ERC-1155, 89
errubatum, 148
esports industry, 32
Ethereum, 27, 88, 96, 180
Eurodollar, 75–76
European Union (EU), 23
Eurozone, 31
externalized data, 76, 78, 86, 186

F
Facebook, 7, 11, 23, 77, 84, 99
Fair Isaac, 93
Fargo, Wells, 3
fear of missing out (FOMO), 83
Federal Bureau of Investigation (FBI), 116
Federal Deposit Insurance Corporation (FDIC), 85, 136
Federal Reserve, 76, 85, 146, 173
Feldstein, Martin, 48
fifth estate, 80–87
Filecoin, 27
finance, 3–7, 19–36, 55–61
finance industry, 1–2, 139
financial crisis, 174–182, 186
financial institutions, 19

financialization, 37–51, 186
financialized corporation, 39–43
financial liquidity, 128
financial platforms, 16
Financial Services Regulatory Relief Act, 145
Financial Times, 78
fintech, 107–108, 151, 186–187
flash loans, 148
Flat World Business, 12
float, 187
foreign exchange (FX), 42
Foroohar, Rana, 40
Fournier, Wayne, 29
FTB, 88
Fundera, 153
FundStrat, 140
Futures Trading Practices Act of 1992, 55
FX market, 133

G
4G, 70
5G, 44, 46, 157
Gangnam Style, 51
Garlinghouse, Brad, 132
Gates, Bill, 120
geek army, 87–91
Geithner, Timothy, 170
General Data Protection Regulation (GDPR), 25
General Electric (GE), 43
General Purpose Technologies, 109
GitHub, 99
Glass-Steagall Act, 3, 71
Global Games Market Report, 31
Goldman Sachs, 121
Goltra, Colin, 33
Google, 23
Gorman, James, 119
Grameen Bank model, 73
Gramm-Leach-Bliley Act, 123
Grassroots Economics, 29
Great Leap Forward, 4
Greenspan, Alan, 19
gross domestic product (GDP), 39, 47, 76
Gutenberg Bible, 35

H
Hadoop, 99
Harvard University, 41, 91
Haskel, Jonathan, 48
Havens Hallmark, 57
Hayes, Tom, 171–172
HeartBleed, 91
high-frequency trading (HFT), 110–111
Holmström, Bengt Robert, 130
home mortgages, 103
Hoskinson, Charles, 65
Houzz, 65
HTTP protocol, 25
hyper-personalization of APIs, 61–65

I
IBM, 56, 107, 114, 121
identity, 21–25
Immelt, Jeff, 44
individualism, 1, 161
industrialization of finance, 3–7
industrialization of information, 38
Industrial Revolution, 120
information on identity, 22–23
initial coin offerings (ICOs), 38, 96
innovation, 71–72, 99–118
institution crumbles, 119–136
Intercontinental Exchange (ICE), 43, 173
intermediation, 188
International Monetary Fund (IMF), 39,
    80, 101
International Organization for
    Standardization (ISO), 174
International Organization of Securities
    Commissions (IOSCO), 168
internet, 16
internet of blockchains, 65
Internet of Things, 32
iOS, 99
iPhone iOS, 7

J
Jassy, Andy, 59
Java C++ programming, 106
JD, 94
Jiko, 145

Joichi, Ito, 28–29
Jovanovic, Boyan, 109
J.P. Morgan, 68, 124

K
Käärmann, Kristo, 131
Kakao Bank, 128
Kaminska, Isabella, 110
Kardashian, Kim, 51
Kaufman, Henry, 103
KBW Nasdaq Financial Technology Index
    (KFTX), 93
Kerviel, Jérôme, 113
key performance indicators (KPIs), 81
King, Mervyn, 170
Klarna Bank, 6
know-your-customer (KYC), 95
Kodak, 137
Kovacevich, Dick, 3, 71

L
layer zero protocol, 66
Leadbeater, Charles, 56
Lee Kai Fu, 7
Lee, Tom, 140
legacy, 187
Lending Club, 133, 145
leverage, 129–130
Libra cryptocurrency, 78
Linux, 56
liquidity, 128–133, 188
Liu Ming Kang, 72
Lloyd, Edward, 164
Lloyd's Act, 164
Lo, Andrew, 95
London Interbank Offered Rate (LIBOR),
    169–171, 187
London Stock Exchange Group (LSEG),
    42–43
London Whale incident, 124
Lumen, 96
Luna, 67, 86
Luna DNA, 30
Luther, Martin, 67
Lyft, 116
Lynch, Merrill, 102

M
Macarena, 51
Ma, Jack, 72
market infrastructure, 54
Markit, 111
Maroutian, Emily, 26
Massachusetts Institute of Technology (MIT), 87
mass amateurization of finance, 55–61
MasterCard, 5, 9, 41, 49, 93–94, 112, 139
McAfee, Andrew, 2
Mercadolibre, 94
Merrill Lynch, 102
Mesopotamia, 27
Metakovan, 90
metaverse, 12
Microsoft, 11, 56, 120–121
Microstrategy, 49
Middle Ages, 119
MintHealth, 31
MIT Lincoln Laboratories, 92
MITRE, 92
mixed martial arts (MMA), 46
Monetary Authority of Singapore (MAS), 63–64
monolithic enterprise infrastructure, 64
Morgan Stanley, 47, 78
Morningstar, 43
Musk, Elon, 44, 51

N
National Basketball Association (NBA) games, 32–33
Negroponte, Nicholas, 12
neo-banks, 126
net asset value (NAV), 93
Netscape moment, 65
Net Stable Funding Ratios (NSFR), 129
network, 179
new-age exchanges, 166
New York Stock Exchange (NYSE), 164
Nike, 33
non-fungible tokens (NFT), 30, 38
non-performing loans (NPLs), 150

O
old-school commercial banks, 126
Onyx, 68
Open Banking Guidelines, 25
Open Banking legislation, 64
Open Banking Working Group, 139
open-ended culture, 62
open-platform approach, 56
operating system, 2
Oracle, 68
Oracle problem, 15
over-the-counter (OTC), 39, 166

P
Parlour, 11
Partior, 68
Payment Services Directive (PSD), 64
Payments Services Directive 2 (PSD2), 25
PayPal, 9, 41, 49
peer-to-peer (P2P), 134, 152–157, 189
peer-to-peer data exchange, 14
People's Bank of China (PBOC), 81–83
perception, 48–51
personalization, 1–17, 19–36, 181–182, 189
platforms, 149, 189
play-to-earn elements, 33
policymaker, 181
political change, 70
post-Bretton Woods creations, 100–105
price-earnings (P/E) ratio of Tesla, 49
private equity-driven funds, 74
product map, 142–143
products-per-customer, 3
proof of concepts (POC), 35
protocols, 190
Provenance and Anchor, 149

Q
Quantemplate, 6
quantitative easing (QE), 39
Quantlab, 111

R
Radius Bank, 133
Radomski, Witek, 89

Raghuram, Rajan, 131
Ramble, 11
Ramp Defi, 89
Randal Quarles, 85
RAND Corporation, 92, 162
Raymond, Eric, 56
Reddit revolution, 54, 132
Regulation Q, 101–102
relational database management system
    (RDBMS), 84
return on investments (ROI), 129
Rifkin, Jeremy, 30, 108, 168
ring-fencing, 125–128, 135, 190
Ripple, 68
Robinhood, 46, 139
robo-advisors, 125
Robomed, 31
robust retail, 147
Ronaldo, Cristiano, 49
Ronfeldt, David, 162–168, 171–172, 178
Rousseau, Peter, 109
Ruddick, Will, 29–30
Russia, 159

S
Salesforce, 61
Sandor, Richard, 71
Sarafu Credit, 29–30
Sarafu Network, 31
Sarao, Navinder Singh, 54–55
Schiff, Peter, 179
Schwab, Klaus, 2
Secured Overnight Financing Rate
    (SOFR), 173
Securities and Exchange Commission
    (SEC), 53, 100, 163
Self-Sovereign Identity (SSI), 23
Serious Fraud Office (SFO), 171
shadow banking, 104
Shanghai Lujiazui International Financial
    Asset Exchange, 154
shareholder value, 50, 105
Sharma, Ruchir, 78
Shirky, Clay, 56, 117
Silicon Valley, 92
Singles' Day, 9–10
Smith, Adam, 120

Smith, Vernon, 179
social credit, 157
Society for Worldwide Interbank Financial
    Telecommunications (SWIFT), 77, 84,
    115, 160
Socios, 33
SoFi, 133
software development kits (SDKs), 62
Southwest Research Institute, 92
sovereign assets, 160
special purpose acquisition companies
    (SPACs), 96
spoofing, 116
Square, 93, 133
Stablecoins, 85–86, 141
Star Trek, 25
Sterling Overnight Index Average
    (SONIA), 173
Stockholm Stock Exchange (SEC),
    164–165
Stripe, 139
Suber, 154
SwapClear, 43
symmetry of deception, 116–118

T
TABB Group, 111
Tapscott, Don, 57
TARGET Instant Payment Settlement
    (TIPS), 82
technology, 17, 120, 157
telecommunication, 8
Tencent, 8
Tenino Dollar, 29
Tesla, 44
test-and-learn approach, 150
Tether (USDT), 34, 86
TikTok, 7, 11
TIMN framework, 162–168
Tirole, Jean, 130
Torvalds, Linus, 55
total value locked (TVL), 88
transition, 12–15, 159–182, 190
TransUnion, 93
triumph of capital over labor, 105–108
tulip bubble of 1637, 175
Twitter, 99

U
Uber, 116
Ukraine, 159, 169
UK's Open Banking Working Group, 64
unbridled capitalism, 26
Unique Identification Authority of India, 83
Unisys, 56
Unity powered software, 62
Uruguay, 81
US Army Quartermaster Corps, 91
US Bureau of Economic Analysis (BEA), 47
US Commodity Futures Modernization Act of 2000, 55
USD Coin (USDC), 34
user experience (UX), 135
US Treasury, 75

V
variable interest entities (VIEs), 42
Venmo, 63
venture capital (VC), 91–97
version control system, 58
Vickers, Sir John, 125
virtual reality gaming industry, 62
Visa, 5, 9, 49, 93–94, 112, 139
Volcker, Paul, 71
Volcker Rule, 124

W
Web 3.0, 2, 13
WeBank, 133
web-based protocols, 88

WeChat, 7, 11
Weimar Republic, 86
WeLab, 156
Wesley, John, 67
Western Union, 93
Westlake, Stian, 48
Whaley, Robert, 172
WiFi moment, 65–68
Wikipedia, 57, 65
Wirecard, 111–112
World Trade Organization (WTO), 4, 106
World War Two, 1, 91
World Wide Web, 13
Wriston, Walter, 22, 71, 121

X
Xiaomi, 151
XW Bank, 151

Y
Yassin, Nuseir, 90
Yasuo Hamanaka of Sumitomo Corporation, 113
Yue Er Bao, 144–145
Yunus, Muhammad, 73

Z
ZenInterest, 59
zero marginal cost, 108–112
Zero Marginal Cost Society, 108
Zhou Xiaochuan, 72
Zopa, 134
Zuckerberg, Mark, 74

Printed in the United States
by Baker & Taylor Publisher Services